3/1/00

Happy Birthday, Chris,

Bon Appétit!

With love,
Mom

CLAMBAKES & FISH FRIES

CLAMBAKES & FISH FRIES

by Susan Herrmann Loomis

ILLUSTRATIONS BY DIANE BOROWSKI

WORKMAN PUBLISHING, NEW YORK

Loomis, Susan Herrmann.
Clambakes & fish fries / by Susan Herrmann Loomis.
p. cm.
ISBN 1-56305-671-2—ISBN 1-56305-295-4 (pbk.)
1. Cookery (Seafood) 2. Cookery, American. 3. Clambakes—United States. I. Title. II. Title:
Clambakes and fish fries.
TX747.L69 1994
641.6'92—dc20
94-2420
CIP

Cover, die cut, and book design: Kathleen Herlihy-Paoli
Cover illustration: Diane Borowski

Workman books are available at special discounts when purchased in bulk
for premiums and sales promotions as well as for fund raising or educational use.
Special editions or book excerpts can also be created to specification.
For details, contact the Special Sales Director at the address below.

Workman Publishing Company, Inc.
708 Broadway
New York, NY 10003
Manufactured in the United States of America

First printing July 1994
10 9 8 7 6 5 4 3 2 1

In memory of Al McClane, dear friend

ACKNOWLEDGMENTS

As I finish writing this book, I am once again astounded at the generosity and good-hearted willingness of so many who became a part of the project. You will meet many of the most important personalities in this book, those who invited us to join them in their seafood celebrations. A huge and heartfelt thank-you to them all, not only for the celebrations but also for the help and friendship offered along the way.

Michael Loomis, forbearing companion, photographer, reader, father, and husband extraordinaire, deserves more thanks than anyone. Our son, Joseph, merits a healthy dose, too. He is a delight, and proved a willing traveler, constant source of joy and laughter, and balm for those long days at the computer and the stove. Father and son are both gifted with patience, and I couldn't live without them.

So many others helped in every way, from telling me about celebrations to aiding me, against amazing odds, obtain the seafood I needed for testing the recipes. Thanks to Steve Lahaie and Craig Hudson for their hospitality, and for being the finest of smelt companions; to Paul McIlhenny and Eugenie Vasser for get-

There are rare people in life endowed with a balanced mixture of careful work habits, good taste, sweet disposition, and humor that sheds light on situations that might otherwise be tense, difficult, or tedious. Barbara Leopold is such a person, and she was invaluable, as the final recipe tester, in the preparation of **Clambakes & Fish Fries.** *She cooked each recipe carefully, tweaking, commenting, suggesting along the way. I count myself lucky to work with such a professional.*

V

ting right into the spirit of this book; to my friends Harry Yoshimura, Des Fitzgerald, and Chick and Vickie Fuller for their generosity and their fish.

Thank-you to Peter Workman, who knew this was a book I wanted to do; and thanks to Suzanne Rafer for her attentiveness and careful editing. Thanks to everyone at Workman, especially Andrea Glickson, for their support and help when needed.

To Susan Lescher I give thanks for many things, not the least among them a long, close look at the Atlantic Ocean. Thanks to Nach Waxman for his suggestions and willing counsel. And to Lila Gault for the same.

Though newcomers to the small town of Belfast on the coast of Maine, we were lucky enough to find friends and compatriots who eased the writing of this book:

Thank-you to Melissa Tonachel, who brightened the office with her efficiency and willingness to do whatever it took to get the book done.

Thank-you Des Fitzgerald and Lucinda Zeising for being wonderful friends; to Martha and Jason Campbell for being willing to eat everything and laugh along with us; to Lib and Herb McClure for their enthusiasm; to Judy and Billy Kao; and to Terra and Don Warner for their love of jambalaya and all things warm. Thank-you all, too, for not thinking me crazy when all I talked about was seafood.

Thanks to Karin Spitfire for her warmth and sense of humor.

Thanks to Ron, the UPS deliveryman, who was always prompt, pleasant, and never complained, no matter the size of the package.

Thanks to everyone at Belfast Area Children's Center for taking such good care of Joe, and for being willing tasters, too.

Thanks to Lisa Maddison for being Joe's best friend.

Thanks to Vicki Mastromarino for proofreading every page of the manuscript.

Thanks to Tangie and Marny at The Good Table for being willing to help however they could, and to everyone at the Belfast Co-op, who made grocery shopping a pleasure and who could obtain the most amazing things.

Our travels took us back to several places we'd been before, and to see dear friends. Thank-you to Ruth Anne and Frank Shuman for one of the most relaxing weeks of our lives; to Miles and Lillian Cahn for comfort along the way; To Julia Child for her interest in and help with this project; to Andy and Marie Keech for their keen friendship.

There are people who by their friendship alone, help projects get done. Among these are Patricia and Walter Wells, Edith and Bernard Leroy and all the family.

Thanks to my parents, Joseph and Doris Bain Herrmann, and to my brothers, sisters, wonderful niece Cynara and nephew Alecko, and Auntie Lu-Lu.

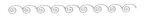

Contents

Buon Natale

ITALIAN CHRISTMAS CELEBRATIONS • 175

WINTER SOLSTICE FISHING CELEBRATION • 194

Northwest Surf 'n Turf

FROM MAUNY KASEBURG—
"THE RADIO GOURMET" • 196

Shad Planking in Virginia

A MEETING OF FOOD AND POLITICS • 205

Port Washington Smelt Fry

A FESTIVAL OF GOODWILL AND SMELT RITES • 211

The Squid Marinara Show

STAR ATTRACTION AT MONTEREY FESTIVAL • 219

John ("J") Mayer, Master of the Fish Boil

COOKING WITH HOOPLA • 226

INTRODUCTION: HOW IT BEGAN

The idea for this book was born several years ago with the taste of boiled whitefish, potatoes, and onions. Sounds inauspicious? Far from it. For that was no ordinary boiled fish and vegetables but a Wisconsin fish boil, held outside at sunset on a clear, warm summer evening in Door County.

I didn't know it then, but that fish boil, which I wrote about and savored both in the kitchen and in my memory, was the first of many seafood celebrations.

Some celebrations I had heard about, like the Port Washington smelt fry that my friend Steve Lahaie, of Shaw's Crab House in Chicago, couldn't stop talking about. There was the oyster gala that William Taylor had urged me to attend many times during our acquaintance, and the North Carolina flounder fries put on each summer by relatives of mine.

Other celebrations I'd experienced firsthand, like the informal tuna roast at Thor and Pam Plancich's and, on a farm in

Maine, the Schartner family's Fourth of July salmon with peas.

Each time I heard about or remembered a seafood celebration, I tucked it away for future use. What fun it would be to write a book about these festivities.

As the research got under way, I became less interested in public seafood festivals and more curious about what people did at home to celebrate local seafoods. I already knew about clambakes and salmon roasts, about smelt fries and fish boils, about po' boys and jambalaya. But what else was out there?

DIGGING DEEPER

I got on the phone. I called people I've worked with and told them what I was doing. I read books, I asked questions, I combed old notes. The book began to take shape.

I'd met Vickie Fuller when I'd ordered some fish through her mail-order seafood business, Simply Shrimp, in Fort Lauderdale. The fish was so gorgeous, and the service she rendered so crisp and professional, I had to talk to her about this book. Her response? "Every year we do a big stone-crab-claw feed for our friends—you've got to come."

My cousins in North Carolina begged us to come to one of their family flounder-

fries; William Taylor immediately signed us up for his oyster gala. Mark Staggs, whom I'd never met but had talked with, explained his squid marinara and then said, "Why don't you come on out and I'll do one for you?"

I got the same response again and again, but none was more excited and enthusiastic than that of Eugenie Vasser, former owner of Flagon's Wine Bar and Bistro in New Orleans: "Oh, y'all have to come down. You've gotta meet my Cajun friends in Houma, then we'll spend a few days in New Orleans, then I'll take ya' home to my mama's in Natchez so you can have a real Mississippi catfish fry. That'll be fun!"

ON THE ROAD

I traveled about 15,000 miles researching seafood celebrations. Some of the traveling I did alone, some I did with my family. Our most memorable trip took place in the fall of 1992, when we packed our station wagon full (mostly of toys and snacks for our almost-two-year-old son, Joe) and headed off on a monthlong odyssey. Unlike our other trips, which went from dawn to dusk, mile after mile, visit after visit, this trip incorporated plenty of time to stop.

We started in Belfast, Maine, on a sunny morning. Most days we drove for about five hours and then spent long afternoons in parks, at beaches, wherever we spied a likely play area.

We saw old friends and made new ones, and we tasted some of the best meals of our lives, most of them simple and simply delicious. We ate dozens of oysters in Klahanie, Maryland, prepared at the hands of

William Taylor. We had unforgettable crab balls and clam fritters at the Harborside Restaurant on Smith Island. We ate sweet, tender flounder, luscious striped bass, incomparable shrimp. The Bahamian chowder at Chick and Vickie Fuller's goes down in history as one of the most delicious things we've ever eaten, though we could say that about many preparations in this book. Every dish we ate during a celebration at Flagon's, prepared by Steve Calderera, a talented chef and native of New Orleans, was truly better than the last.

We had our tongues gently seared by boiled crab in Cypremort Point, Louisiana, prepared by Paul McIlhenny and company with a secret ingredient. We ate shrimp until we almost popped on Bayou Petit Caillou south of Houma, where they were teamed with a variety of vegetables, and poolside in Joanne Clevenger's New Orleans backyard, where her brother Bruce set up an impromptu shrimp boil accompanied by lots of Turbo Dog Abita beer. Then there were mountains of smelt, luscious salmon with peas, and succulent bluefish.

JOIN THE CELEBRATION

With this book you will share in memorable seafood celebrations, enjoyed with several of my favorite people. You may recognize a few of them, those who've played a part in my previous books; some I've known for many years yet never had the opportunity to write about. Others are new friends who shared their seafood, their secrets, their homes, their friends. They did it for the love of seafood and the pure enjoyment of a great time.

I've learned that a celebration can happen anytime, under any circumstances. In the case of these recipes, all you need is the seafood. Celebrations and people to enjoy them just seem to follow.

You will find seafood celebrations in here for two and for twenty. I hope you will revel in them and in the happy times that surround them.

Buying and Cooking Seafood

All of the seafood called for in this book is readily available, whether it be squid caught off the coast of California or trout farmed in Idaho. In the past ten years the quality of seafood in this country has improved dramatically, which makes buying and eating it a pleasure whether you live by the shore or not.

The jump in quality is owed in large part to fishermen, who realized that the quality of what they harvest is as important as the quantity. It can also be attributed to a more discerning public, who no longer accepts less than high-quality seafood.

Freezing and attendant transportation techniques today are geared to capturing and preserving the quality of seafood. The technique of flash freezing immediately after harvest (so there is little or no cell damage to the fish) has dramatically expanded the variety and quality available to the public. When such carefully frozen fish is thawed slowly at a cool temperature, it looks and tastes as if it had just jumped from the water.

Aquaculture, too, has made a tremendous contribution toward quality seafood. Salmon farmed in Maine is delicious, and farmed catfish is a good performer in the frying pan. Farmed seafood, including shrimp, may not be quite as tasty as its wild cousins, but it is available daily, year-round, at reasonable prices.

KNOW YOUR SEAFOOD

No one and nothing can guarantee perfection all of the time, and it is still important to be a knowledgeable consumer. This isn't difficult. You need only two tools for buying seafood: your nose and your eyes. Of those, the nose is the more important.

Seafood lets us know when it isn't fresh. It begins to smell, and the smell is not pleasant. When you go to a supermarket or fish market, the first thing to do when you walk in the door is to inhale. If you smell a fishy aroma, beware. Then look at the fish. Good-quality fish is bright, firm, glistening; it looks appetizing. Shellfish has a lively look to it, too.

Nothing, neither steaks nor fillets, should be sitting in a pool of liquid. Cut fish should be in a metal tray set on ice, or on a vegetable leaf or something that will protect it from direct contact with the ice. A whole fish, however, can rest right on the ice. Its

belly should be stuffed with ice, and the ice should be piled well up and around the fish.

Shellfish should be kept cool and moist. It should be misted regularly, and should be placed in a container that will drain, so fresh water doesn't collect around it. If the shells of live shellfish are open, they should close when you tap them, an indication that they are alive. If they stay open, they are dead and unfit to eat. The only exception to this is pink scallops, also called singing scallops, harvested in Puget Sound, Washington, which always stay open.

Shucked shellfish, such as oysters or clams, should smell sweet, should look plump and fresh, and should be packed in clear liquid. Occasionally clams or oysters are in a slightly milky liquid, but it shouldn't be viscous or unpleasant-looking or -smelling.

Live lobster and crabs should be kept in saltwater tanks, and they should look animated when pulled from the water. A lobster will instinctively curl and flap its tail—if it does so with vigor, it's a good candidate for the lobster pot. A healthy crab will wave its claws, trying to pinch anything in sight.

Whole squid with its skin on will be grayish to purple with a bright white background. If it's been cleaned and skinned, it should be bright white.

Shrimp in the shell should be firm. Their shells should have no black marks, which indicate spoilage, and their meat should be white.

Scallops should be a pale flesh color, and they should look firm and elastic.

If instead of glistening, lively fish and shellfish you see brown and sagging fillets, gaping shellfish, or bedraggled shrimp, choose pork or chicken over seafood.

Once your eyes have determined what looks good, ask the person behind the counter to let you smell it. Few will refuse to do so, and it is worth the extra few seconds. Get close and sniff. Good-quality fish and shellfish smells fresh, like a sea breeze. Some fish, like salmon, smells like cucumber, suggesting coolness. Cod smells sweet. Shrimp smells clean with an iodine aroma; scallops smell sweet and hint at succulence; and oysters, mussels, and clams smell briny.

Bad fish looks unappealing and smells fishy. Bad shellfish—particularly scallops, shrimp, and squid—smells rotten, like sulfur.

TREAT YOUR SEAFOOD RIGHT

If the seafood you want passes the sight and smell tests, buy it. Ask the person behind the counter to wrap a bag of ice with it. If you're going to be out for an extended period, bring along a cooler so your fish will stay cool and moist. Warm temperatures are anathema to seafood and will cause it to deteriorate rapidly.

Once you get your seafood home, place it on the bottom shelf (the coolest spot) of the refrigerator. Try to use it the evening of the day you buy it, or within 24 hours. If you can't, be sure it stays cool. I rinse fish with cold water, cover it in fresh wrapping, and set it atop a metal baking pan filled with crushed ice. Put shellfish in

Educated Consumption

Be an educated consumer. Increasingly, the seafood industry is educating its members in order to provide consumers with better-quality seafood and more information. In addition, the seafood industry has introduced strict inspection regulations, which are followed by a growing number of fishermen and processors. Ask your fishmonger where your fish and shellfish come from.

PHOSPHATE AND SULFITE WARNING

Be aware that farmed catfish is soaked in phosphates to extend its shelf life. This practice also causes the fish to absorb water and gives it a slippery feel. Other kinds of fish, including monkfish, are treated this way as well.

Most shrimp are rinsed in a mild sulfite solution to prevent deterioration.

Note, however, that the FDA has determined that neither of these practices is generally harmful. On the other hand, neither improves the quality of the product.

a colander, cover it with a damp kitchen towel, and set the colander on a plate to catch any liquids that drain.

Freezing fish in a home freezer won't improve its quality. Nonetheless, if you've got a mess of freshly caught fish and can't eat or give any more of it away, carefully follow these simple instructions for the best possible home-frozen fish.

To freeze 4 pounds of large, whole fish, fillets, or steaks: Combine ¼ cup bottled lemon juice and 1¾ cups water in a small saucepan. Measure out ½ cup of the mixture and reserve. Bring the remaining lemon juice mixture to a boil. Dissolve 1 package unflavored gelatin in the reserved liquid. Whisk the gelatin mixture into the boiling lemon juice mixture. Remove from the heat

DON'T WORRY ABOUT SHELLFISH!

Adverse publicity has plagued shellfish, but there's no real reason to stay away from it. The danger of contamination has been exaggerated. On a weekly, sometimes daily, basis inspectors sample waters where shellfish is harvested. If any contamination is found the problem is publicized and the area is closed for harvesting until the water tests clean again.

In fact, most contamination of shellfish occurs at the point of sale—in restaurant kitchens or behind seafood counters. To avoid problems, buy shellfish from reputable sources. Resist buying shellfish from harvesters or merchants you do not know.

HEAVY METALS

PCBs, DDT, and dioxin can accumulate in the fatty tissue of fish—particularly in some freshwater fish, in fish that swims close to shore, and occasionally in deep-water predator fish such as swordfish. To guard against contamination, water quality in this country is monitored for heavy metals, major trouble spots are spotlighted, and commercial fishing is generally prohibited from any areas deemed excessively polluted. Fish from other countries is not as carefully monitored. It pays to ask where the fish comes from.

and let cool to room temperature. Dip the fish into the glaze to cover completely. Wrap in waxed paper and aluminum foil, and freeze as quickly as possible.

To freeze small, whole fish: Thoroughly clean a milk carton with soap and rinse well with water. Cut the carton down, if necessary, place the fish in it, then fill it with cold water to within 1 inch of the top,

allowing for expansion. Wrap the carton in aluminum foil, and freeze.

Whole fish, steaks, or fillets can also

be wrapped in polyvinylidene chloride or polyvinyl chloride plastic wrap, and frozen.

To thaw frozen fish, place it on a plate in the refrigerator and thaw it slowly, allowing at least overnight for small fish, steaks, or fillets, and up to 48 hours for large whole fish.

When cooking seafood, less time is better. An undercooked piece of fish can always be put back on the heat. An overcooked piece of fish is done, ruined. To cook fish properly, in general use moderate heat so it cooks evenly (there are exceptions, for instance the

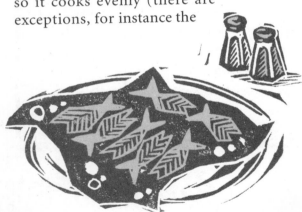

seared tuna recipe in this book). Cook just until it is opaque through. If you check it and it is not quite but almost cooked through, remove it from the heat; the residual heat will continue to cook it, so that by the time you get it to the table it will be perfectly cooked.

Cook shellfish until the shells open, then another minute so the meats are fully cooked.

CELEBRATING WITH SEAFOOD

Seafood can be transformed into very complex dishes or just grilled or baked for a quick, simple meal. You'll find that the celebrations here are mostly of the quick and simple variety. The recipes reflect the tastes and traditions of people around the country. Follow them closely if you like, or let them serve as inspiration. Never consider a recipe a hard-and-fast rule. Read it, use what you like, change it to suit your taste.

Good fishing, good eating, good celebrating!

The Coastal Maine Clambake

A CLASSIC NORTHEASTERN TRADITION

When I lived in Belfast, Maine, where the rocky shore is lined with quaint homes and cottages, I felt ideally positioned to experience one of the ultimate seafood celebrations—a New England clambake. As summer and, with it, the clambake season approached, I began to search for one that was authentic, where you dig a pit on the beach, gather rocks, and cover everything with seaweed.

I was amazed at how difficult it was. Even old-timers found it too much trouble and instead boiled everything together in a pot. Still, I persisted. Finally a clambake presented itself.

Friends were urging me to join the Bayside Yacht Club, a grand-sounding title for a friendly group who get together to sail, have picnics, and enjoy the brief Maine summer. The clincher came when Terra Warner, a friend and an avid member, said, "They have this great old-fashioned clambake on the Fourth of July, and it's just wonderful." I joined immediately.

I got the name of the "bakemaster," Ned Lightner, and called him. An enthusiastic and generous fellow, he immediately fell in with my idea to help with and document his clambake.

After many conversations and much planning, July third dawned; this was the day we were to collect the stones and dig the pit. It was a typical Maine early summer day, rainy and cold. As luck would have it, I was as sick as the day was gloomy. On the Fourth, the best I could muster was a weak appearance, apologies, and, later, a good cry. Now where would I find a real clambake?

Ned, whose heart is big and generous, assured me he always had two each summer and that he would invite me to the second. But as the summer drew to a close, he was finding it tough to coordinate schedules. He finally said to me in exasperation one day, after a group of friends once more wouldn't cooperate, "I'm a man who wants to do a clambake. All I need is a crowd."

SECOND-CHANCE CLAMBAKE

The timing was propitious. My birthday falls at the end of August, and my husband had already invited our friends to a party. We simply alerted them to a change of location, and we had a group ready for a time-honored clambake.

We borrowed a beach from our friends Jerry and Gail Savitz, assembled all the ingredients, and got up early on a foggy August morning to meet Ned at the shore. The weather report was grim, but we were determined.

Ned was an exacting taskmaster. He'd learned the art of the clambake from an elderly man some years ago, and he didn't veer from tradition. He assessed the shore where we'd chosen to do the bake— and decided it wouldn't do. "High tide is early today, and it'll wash everything away," he said. Instead of digging a pit, he and my husband, Michael, hefted pounds and pounds of sand up to a grassy shelf and built a six-inch-high rectangular dike that we lined with rocks to simulate a sand pit.

Ned instructed us to look for dry igneous rocks (which wouldn't explode in the fire). I took our son, Joe, who was eighteen months old at the time, and together we ranged the shore gathering rocks— which took us a good part of the morning because Joe had to make frequent stops to throw pebbles into the bay.

Then Michael and I piled what felt like tons of seaweed into a little rowboat and pulled it along the shore to our spot, where we covered it with a tarp so it would stay wet. Next Ned sent me on a special errand: to hunt for a "cooking stone."

"It's a rock with an unbroken white band around it, and superstition has it that the cooking stone does all the cooking," he said. I found one and set it carefully aside.

Ned didn't want to collect driftwood since he feared it wouldn't burn hot enough, so we pilfered hardwood from our winter supply and carried it to the beach. We put a huge piece of canvas and an old piece of felt into the water to soak.

Following Ned's instructions, we laid out a fire with kindling, then built up the wood around and atop it, log-cabin-style, strategically placing rocks as we went. We had to be careful because we wanted them to fall into the middle of the fire as the wood burned away. When it was four feet high, we topped it off with the almost mythical cooking stone.

Drizzling a small amount of kerosene—his "secret fire starter"—over the pile, Ned checked our handiwork once more; then he threw in a match and flames began to build. The fire would burn for three hours to heat up the rocks, so I settled down nearby to keep an eye on it. The fog had burned away to reveal a glorious summer day. The sun was warm but not hot, the air clear and clean, the water dazzling. I basked in it, relaxing after the morning's endeavors.

I was equipped with a long-handled shovel with which I was supposed to corral any errant rocks or shift the pyre should it start to list. Now twenty minutes into it, a sharp explosion interrupted my leisure. A wet rock had burst and sent pieces flying out of the fire. I moved way back to continue my vigil.

Ned took over halfway through, and I went to collect the ingredients. The first stop was a farm where I'd reserved corn and potatoes, the next the lobster pound for lobsters, clams, and mussels. Then home for the onions, the butter, and the baby.

Three hours and several explosions later, we were all assembled back at the fire.

After carefully pulling out any logs that hadn't burned, what we had was a pile of red-hot rocks, embers, and coals, which we spread out. They were so hot that we could hardly approach them, and we quickly spread a ten-inch layer of damp seaweed on top.

It was exciting to see the clambake come together as we arranged clams and mussels on one of Ned's wire mesh racks and set it on the seaweed. We covered it with more seaweed and then set down a rack of lobsters, which we covered with another fine layer of seaweed. The third rack held the vegetables, because they take the longest to cook.

We obscured it all with seaweed, topped with the wet canvas, then felt, and plugged the holes with more seaweed so no steam or smoke escaped. I felt that something magic was happening, something ancient and fundamental. I looked at Ned. He looked worried.

"I'm going to go take a walk along the shore," he said mysteriously. "I just can't take this part of it. I'm always so nervous that either the food won't cook or it will be burned to a crisp."

Friends began to gather. Many were native Mainers, but few had been to a traditional clambake. We were all riveted by the steaming mound before us.

ENJOYING THE FRUITS

After an hour Ned returned, popped open a beer, and gingerly began to uncover the bake. Steam clouded out of the mound and a heavenly aroma filled the air as vegetables, lobsters, and shellfish came to light. We loaded up trays with food and found places to sit on the grass and the rocks. We'd picked wildflowers for a bouquet, set out baskets of bread and bowls of salad, and positioned a big pot of melted butter on a log to one side. No one used it—it wasn't necessary.

For a moment the only sound was the cracking of shells as everyone dug into a lobster.

The lobster was unlike any I'd ever tasted. Clearly some alchemy had occurred under that magic pile of seaweed. The meat was sweet, smoky and buttery, and I slowly savored each morsel. The clams and mussels were plump and smoky, too, the vegetables soft and delicious.

Joe Mastromarino and his wife, Vicki, both groaned with pleasure. "This is what I was telling you about last summer," Joe said. "This incredible smoked lobster happens when you do a real clambake."

Sated, we watched the children play on the sand as we sat on that grassy shelf above the shore. Two little girls were digging up an old lobster trap buried under sand and rocks, others were hunting hen clams down by the shoreline, Joe was climbing on the rocks, visiting us now and then for a bite of lobster. Martha and Jason Campbell, both native Mainers, donned bathing suits and plunged into the chilly water.

Michael suddenly emerged from behind a little shack on the shore, trailed by a couple of children. In his hands was a large platter that held a sky-high cake he'd somehow found time to make. Instead of candles he had sparklers to hand out to all the guests, and we lit them to the sound of "Happy Birthday to You."

On that crystalline summer day it was easy to believe we were re-enacting an ancient ritual. We'd harvested the local bounty, taken time to fashion an outdoor oven, and waited most of a day for our food, which we shared with friends. It was elemental, elegant, magical. It was truly a Maine clambake.

A Clambake at Home

Lobster prepared according to the traditional clambake method emerges tender and gently smoked. Few of us have a beach we can run to for a traditional feast, but anyone can achieve the same results in a barbecue grill. All it takes is a rousing bed of coals, some moist wood chips, and a quick half hour. Everything but the corn must be parboiled; then it all gets tossed on the grill together.

2 pounds clams, preferably steamers, or 1 pound clams and 1 pound mussels, in the shell, scrubbed
Sea salt
¼ cup cornmeal
4 large or 8 small ears corn, unhusked

4 medium waxy potatoes, such as Yukon Gold or Yellow Finn
4 medium onions, skins left on
4 small (1¼-pound) lobsters
4 tablespoons (½ stick) lightly salted butter, melted (optional)

1. Purge the clams: Place the clams in a large bowl or bucket of salted water (about 3 tablespoons sea salt to 1 gallon water), and stir in the cornmeal. Leave the clams in a cool place for 2 hours. Drain the clams and then rinse them.

If you are also using mussels, rinse and scrub the shells, and remove the beards—the tangle of threads hanging from their shells—by sharply pulling on them, with either pliers or your fingers. Don't do this more than a couple of hours in advance, or the mussels will die.

2. Prepare the corn: Gently pull back the husks so that they remain attached at the stem end, and remove the corn silk. Bring the husks back up around the corn, so the kernels are completely covered. (If you are using husked corn, wrap it up in parchment paper or aluminum foil.)

3. Fill a large kettle with water, add salt, and bring it to a boil over high heat. Add the potatoes and the onions, and cook until the potatoes are tender but still have some crispness in the center, about 15 minutes. Drain the vegetables.

4. Meanwhile, build a large fire in a barbecue grill. Soak 2 cups of wood chips in water to cover.

5. Parboil the lobsters: Fill a large kettle with 3 inches of water, and bring it to a boil over high heat. Remove the rubber bands from the lobster claws, and add as many lobsters to the pot as will easily fit. Cover and cook until the lobsters have turned bright red, about 3 minutes. Remove them from the water and repeat with any remaining lobsters.

6. When the barbecue fire has burned down to red-hot coals with some flames still licking at them, drain the wood chips, squeezing out as much water as possible, and spread them over the coals. Immediately place the rack on the grill, and arrange the lobsters as close together as you can on the rack. Place the corn on top of the lobsters, and arrange the remaining ingredients around and on top of the corn. Cover, leaving the grill vents open, and cook until everything is cooked through and the clams and mussels are open, 25 to 30 minutes. Remove from the grill and serve immediately, with the melted butter alongside.

4 SERVINGS

The Party's Over

The meal was finished and neat piles of lobster shells decorated the shore, alongside clamshells, corncobs and onion skins. The fire from the clambake burned down low as people clustered near for its remaining warmth. Everything was carefully removed from the beach, the warm rocks and logs would wash out to sea as the tide came in, and the following day there would be little sign that twenty people enjoyed a true Maine clambake here. I packed things away in the back of the car, including the leftover potatoes and onions, a small bucket of clams and—surprisingly—a couple of lobsters. It had been a long day, and I didn't think much about the remaining food except to get it into the refrigerator before I collapsed for a good night's sleep.

The following evening I surveyed the shriveled potatoes and onions, which gave off a gentle whiff of smokiness. We were hungry but in no mood for anything elaborate. I popped the interiors of the onions from their skins, peeled the potatoes, removed the lobster meat and the clams from their shells. A little puréeing, chopping, and slicing, and it wasn't long before I served steaming bowls of lightly smoked chowder, a post-clambake sensation. We loved it so much we thought it almost worthwhile to do another clambake just for the leftovers!

Post-Clambake Chowder

This chowder is fabulous made from clambake leftovers because of the tenderness of the lobster and the subtle smokiness that has pervaded all the ingredients. However, if you can't go to the trouble of doing a clambake, make it from scratch in your kitchen. I think you'll be equally pleased.

2 large onions, peeled, cooked, puréed in a food
    processor
5 medium waxy potatoes, peeled, cooked, cut into
    ¼-inch dice
½ cup heavy (or whipping) cream
2 cups milk

Meat from two cooked 1¼-pound lobsters,
    cut into bite-size pieces
½ cup cooked clam meat (about 2 pounds in shell)
Salt to taste
3 tablespoons unsalted butter
Cayenne pepper, for garnish

1. Place the puréed onions in a heavy saucepan over medium heat. Add the potatoes, cover, and bring to a simmer. When the potatoes are hot through, about 5 minutes, add the cream and the milk and heat through, 5 minutes more. Add the lobster meat and the clams, and continue heating until the lobster is hot through, 3 to 5 minutes. Do not boil. Season with salt.

2. Ladle the soup into four warmed soup bowls, garnish each with a dab of butter and a sprinkling of cayenne pepper, and serve immediately.

4 GENEROUS SERVINGS

Note: To make this from scratch, steam the onions and the potatoes separately until they are tender through (20 minutes for the onions, 15 for the potatoes). Steam the lobsters until they are nearly cooked, about 12 minutes for a 1¼-pound lobster. Steam the clams until they open. Remove the meats from the shells. Strain and set aside the clam cooking liquid. Proceed with the recipe, adding the clam cooking liquid to the potatoes and onions as they simmer.

Black and White Cake

At my birthday clambake my husband, Michael, presented me with one of the tallest cakes I'd ever seen. Once I had blown out all the candles I cut into it to discover four alternating layers of black and white, the chocolate flavored with coffee, the white with orange zest. The sight and the flavor were unforgettable.

The recipe comes from Cathy Burgett, a friend of ours and one of the finest pastry chefs in the country, who currently lives in California. We always call her when we have a question, need a tip, or are looking for a recipe for something extra-special, and she unfailingly comes through. I trust her recipes without exception because her hand is deft and light, her palate unimpeachable.

This cake is rich and buttery, yet light. Her secrets, which she is adamant about, are having the ingredients at room temperature and beating the eggs and sugar until they are almost white, which takes about five minutes in an electric mixer. It is also a good idea to make the cake a day in advance so the flavors have a chance to mellow.

I don't suggest that you reserve this cake for your next clambake, however. Make it now, immediately, and then tomorrow invite the neighborhood over for a taste!

FROSTING
2 cups heavy (or whipping) cream
16 ounces bittersweet chocolate, preferably Lindt or Tobler

CAKE
8 ounces bittersweet chocolate, preferably Lindt or Tobler
¼ cup very strong, hot brewed coffee
4⅔ cups cake flour

4 teaspoons baking powder
½ teaspoon salt
1½ cups (3 sticks) unsalted butter, at room temperature
3 cups sugar
2 teaspoons vanilla extract
8 large eggs, at room temperature
1½ cups milk
Grated zest of 2 oranges

1. Preheat the oven to 325°F. Heavily butter four 9-inch round cake pans.

2. Prepare the frosting: Combine the cream and the chocolate in a large saucepan over medium heat. Watch the mixture closely, and as soon as the chocolate has melted, remove the pan from the heat and whisk well. Set the pan aside until the frosting is cool and somewhat hardened, about 20 minutes.

3. For the cake: Melt the chocolate in the top of a double boiler over simmering water. Then add the hot coffee and whisk until com-

bined. Remove the pan from the heat and allow the mixture to cool.

4. Sift the cake flour, baking powder, and salt together onto a sheet of waxed paper.

5. Cream the butter and the sugar together in a large bowl, or in the bowl of a heavy-duty electric mixer using the paddle attachment, until the mixture is fluffy and white. This will take at least 5 minutes in an electric mixer. Stir in the vanilla extract.

6. Add the eggs one at a time, mixing well after each addition. Don't overmix or the mixture will curdle.

7. By hand, fold the dry ingredients into the butter mixture in thirds, alternating with the milk and beginning and ending with the dry ingredients.

8. Divide the batter between two bowls. Fold the orange zest into one bowl of batter. Fold the chocolate-coffee mixture into the other.

9. Pour half of each bowl of batter into each cake pan, sharply rapping the pan on the counter to release any air. You should have 2 chocolate layers and 2 white layers. Place the pans in the center of the oven and bake the white cakes until they are golden and spring back when pressed, about 30 minutes. The chocolate cakes will take slightly longer; bake until they spring back, about 35 minutes. Remove the cakes from the oven and let them cool on wire racks for 10 minutes. Then run a knife around the edge of the cake pans, flip them over, and remove the cakes from the pans. Let the cakes cool on wire racks.

10. To frost the cake, first trim the mounded top from 1 of the chocolate layers, so it is flat. (If necessary, trim the tops from the white layers to make them flat, too.) Then place a white layer on a cake plate or platter, and frost it with about ⅓ cup of the frosting. Top with the trimmed chocolate layer and frost it. Repeat with the remaining layers. Once layered, make sure the cake is covered with frosting on all sides and has a thick layer on the top. (If the frosting isn't firm enough to spread, chill it just until it is.) Ideally, this cake should sit overnight before it is served.

ONE 9-INCH CAKE; 10 TO 15 SERVINGS

New England Clam Chowder Supper

How I Found the Chowder, and All About It

I've been writing about seafood for ten years, and for nearly as long I've turned to the New England Fisheries Development Foundation, in Boston, with questions. Everyone there is helpful, but the person I rely on most, and the one I've gotten to know best over the years, is George Nardi.

Our acquaintance is based on my quest for information. George is extremely knowledgeable about East Coast seafood species. He is patient, too, answering every call and query and pointing me in the right direction if he doesn't know the answer himself.

When I told George about my new book, he offered this story about his own family seafood celebration, and recipes.

In the Nardi family, summer means clamming on the beach at Cape Cod. As the temperatures warm, the entire family rolls up their pants legs and walks, clam rakes in hand, down to the flats in front of the house. There Sally Nardi is the expert, digging, according to her brother George, "more clams with her feet than anyone could dig with a rake."

The Nardis, who now number nineteen, have gone to Cape Cod for forty years and still gather there during the summer. "We try to go in June and July when friends and family can get together, and we go even more often now than when we were growing up," George said. "There are lots of nephews and nieces, and my sisters love to go clamming. It's become kind of a teaching thing for the kids. They learn all about the clams and the beach, and we continue a great tradition."

The family plays and digs into the afternoon, filling their buckets of seawater with softshells, littlenecks, and big quahaugs. At home the clams become a feast. They eat the littlenecks on the half shell, steam the softshells to dip in butter, and make a huge pot of chowder out of the quahaugs.

A NO-RUSH AFFAIR

Preparing the chowder includes sitting around as a group and shucking the quahaugs. Anyone who has ever done that understands the time it takes. "The idea is that we're making this together and there isn't any hurry, so we eat clams and shuck and spend a lot of time at it," said George.

Though the Nardi chowder is always a group effort, its ingredients have varied depending on who was in charge. George, the fourth of five brothers and sisters, is now the chief chowder maker, and he decides what goes in and what stays out.

"I like lots of onions and not too many potatoes, and I usually add a dollop of bacon fat, too, though there's family dissension on that," he said. Still, the chowder chief's word goes.

Like any good New England chowder, George's takes time to make. He cooks the broth long and slowly so the flavors blend, then adds a few ingredients that aren't traditional, like sherry and celery, but that add depth and complexity without disturbing the pure clam flavor. When he decides the flavors have blended properly, he adds the family's catch of the day.

"I always love it when there's variety," George said. "But you never know, so the recipe depends on what we've dug or caught that day."

When the seafood is just about cooked, George pours in just enough milk or cream to make the chowder satiny smooth. "And whether I use milk or cream depends on how guilty everyone is feeling that day!" he said.

When all the ingredients are in the pot, the family sits down to . . . a big pizza dinner. Why not chowder? Because the secret to its goodness is held in a time-honored New England practice. "Let it sit overnight at least," George said. "That's what my mother always did."

The Nardis eat the chowder for lunch the day after it is made. "The flavors are rich, the potatoes have kind of thickened it, and it's smooth and wonderful," George said. And nothing goes to waste. What's left-over is warmed and served as an appetizer for the evening meal.

"We all love this tradition," George said. "It's a way to celebrate the season and the family."

The Nardi Family Chowder

Here is the celebrated Nardi chowder, which is still served in summer to family and friends. But don't wait for warm weather to enjoy it.

When making it, George prefers to shuck the clams live, rather than steam them open. "You're not supposed to make this chowder in a hurry—you're supposed to take your time and sit around shucking clams with the family before you cook it," he says.

He does allow that if you're not in a beach house on Cape Cod and you still want to make the chowder, it is all right to steam open the clams. Be sure to reserve the cooking broth for the soup, along with the meats.

This is a thin chowder with plenty of broth and lots of fish. George says that his chowder usually gives about three clams per bowl; in this one you will find a few more. If you have a tough time finding good clams, try mussels instead.

Also, George occasionally uses bacon fat for flavor. This recipe calls for bacon, which is an optional garnish.

Purging is important because it rids clams of any sand that might have collected in their bellies. Some clams are purged before they're sold, however, so ask your fish merchant when you buy them.

For the full taste of a traditional Nardi family seafood supper, serve toasted garlic bread and a green salad alongside this chowder—and plenty of chilled beer.

CLAMS

4 pounds steamer or Manila clams, or 7 pounds
    cherrystones, in the shell, scrubbed

Sea salt

⅓ cup cornmeal

CHOWDER

2 tablespoons unsalted butter

2 large (7-ounce) onions, diced

2 ribs celery, strings removed, cut into ⅛-inch-
    thick slices

1 pound waxy potatoes, peeled and cut into
    ½-inch cubes

10 cups fish stock (page 119, through Step 2)

¼ cup water

2 ounces (2 slices) slab bacon, rind removed,
    diced (optional)

2 pounds whitefish fillets, such as hake, cusk,
    haddock, lingcod, or petrale sole

1 cup milk

1 cup heavy (or whipping) cream

2 tablespoons dry sherry

Salt and freshly ground black pepper to taste

Cayenne pepper to taste (optional)

½ cup (loosely packed) Italian (flat-leaf) parsley
    leaves, for garnish

Unsalted butter, for garnish

Paprika, for garnish

1. Purge the clams: Place the clams in a large bowl or bucket of salted water (about 4 tablespoons sea salt to 1½ gallons water). Stir in the cornmeal. Leave in a cool place for 2 hours.

2. When you are ready to cook the chowder, melt the butter in a large, heavy kettle over medium-low heat. Add the onions and sauté until they are translucent, about 5 min-utes. Then add the celery and cook 5 minutes more. Add the potatoes, stir, and then add the fish stock. Increase the heat to medium-high and bring the stock to a boil. Reduce the heat to medium-low, and simmer until the potatoes are not quite cooked through, about 10 minutes.

3. While the potatoes are cooking, steam the clams (see Note). Remove them from the salt water and rinse them thoroughly. Place them, with the ¼ cup water, in a large saucepan and bring to a boil over medium-high heat. Cover and cook just until they open, which shouldn't take longer than 3 to 4 minutes. As soon as the clams open, remove them from the pan. Continue cooking until all the clams are open (discard any that don't open). Remove the pan from the heat.

4. Remove the clam meats from the shells. If the clams are large, such as cherrystones, dice them with a sharp knife. If they are small, such as Manilas, keep them whole. If you are using steamers (softshell clams), which make excellent chowder, remove the skins from the clams' siphons before adding them to the chowder. Discard the shells, and strain the cooking liquid into a large bowl through two thicknesses of dampened cheesecloth. Place the clams in their cooking liquid and set them aside.

5. If you are using the bacon, cook it in a large skillet over medium heat until it has just rendered its fat and is beginning to turn golden but is still tender. Remove the bacon from the pan, reserving it and discarding the fat it rendered. Cover and refrigerate until you're ready to serve the chowder.

6. Add the whole fish fillets to the potatoes, and cook just until opaque and beginning to fall apart, 8 to 10 minutes. Stir in the clams with their cooking liquid, and then add the milk and cream. Heat the chowder gently. Add the sherry, and season with salt and pepper. Remove the chowder from the heat and let it cool to room temperature. Then cover and refrigerate for at least 8 hours or overnight.

7. When you are ready to serve the chowder, carefully bring it to a simmer. Season with cayenne pepper, if you like.

8. Mince the parsley leaves. Slowly reheat the bacon until warmed through.

9. To serve, ladle the chowder into warmed shallow bowls, garnish with butter as desired, and sprinkle with the minced parsley and either cayenne or paprika. Serve the bacon alongside for sprinkling on top of the chowder.

12 TO 14 SERVINGS

Note: If you prefer to shuck the clams raw, use an oyster knife. Insert the knife just to the side of the hinge of the clamshell. When the knife blade enters, twist it slightly to further open the shell, and then run the blade of the knife around the interior of the shell to sever the muscle. Remove the top shell, and run the knife blade under the clam, severing the other muscle. Place the clam in a bowl, and pour the clam liquid into another bowl. When all the clams are shucked, strain the clam liquid through 2 thicknesses of cheesecloth and reserve both meats and liquid. Raw clams will take the same amount of cooking time as steamed ones in Step 6.

Crisp Salad Greens

This simple green salad is excellent as a part of any seafood celebration. Use whatever mixture of greens you prefer, but be certain they are lively and fresh. I like to prepare the dressing about an hour in advance so the pungent tastes of the shallots and garlic mellow, and all the flavors meld.

2 tablespoons balsamic vinegar
1 teaspoon Dijon mustard
6 tablespoons extra-virgin olive oil
2 shallots, sliced paper-thin
1 clove garlic, minced
Salt and freshly ground black
    pepper to taste
10 cups torn mixed salad greens,
    such as escarole, arugula, red
    leaf lettuce, and mâche

1. In a large bowl whisk together the vinegar and the mustard; then slowly whisk in the olive oil in a thin stream. Add the shallots and garlic, stir, and season with salt and pepper. Set aside for 1 hour.

2. Quickly whisk the dressing if it has separated, adjust the seasoning, and add the greens. Toss thoroughly, until the greens are coated with the dressing, and serve immediately.

8 SERVINGS

Fragrant Garlic Bread

This is a fresh, aromatic garlic bread that goes well with any feast, but particularly with clam chowder. I like to use the Po' Boy Bread (see Index) for this, although any good-quality French-type loaf will do. Adjust the amount of butter and garlic to the size of the loaf—you want it to be well soaked. For a little change, sprinkle the bread with dried red pepper flakes as well.

1 long loaf French bread
6 tablespoons (¾ stick) lightly salted butter
3 large cloves garlic, minced
¼ teaspoon dried red pepper flakes (optional)

1. Preheat the broiler.

2. Cut the bread in half lengthwise. Place both halves on a baking sheet, cut side up.

3. Melt the butter in a small pan over medium heat. Add the garlic, and cook until it begins to turn golden in the butter, about 5 minutes. Remove from the heat.

4. Drizzle the butter over the cut sides of the bread, making sure you scrape all the garlic pieces onto the bread. (If you prefer, use a pastry brush to brush the butter and garlic on the bread.) Sprinkle the bread with the red pepper flakes, if desired. Broil until the bread and the garlic have turned golden, about 3 minutes. Serve immediately.

8 SERVINGS

Chocolate, Chocolate, Chocolate Cake

This cake was inspired by a frosting recipe sent to me by my friend Nancy Lord. Nancy is a native of Maine and lives in Hope, not far from Camden and the coast. She's a wonderful cook, and the dishes she presents are classic New England foods that to her seem prosaic, but to me seem wonderfully rich and full of tradition. Each time I ask her for a recipe she smiles modestly and says, "Oh, but my family really never did anything special." Yet she takes great pride in sharing her recipes and the stories that accompany them say something different.

I was asking her one day about chowders and desserts, and she immediately mentioned Rocky Road Frosting. She sent me the recipe a few days later, with the following note attached:

"You could use baby marshmallows, but it doesn't seem the same! Also, sometimes the nuts were pecans or black walnuts if the family and I had just come home from the South.

"As for the cake, it varied, depending on the cook—Nana, Maggie, who worked for us, or my aunt Lee. But it was always a fudge type, not feathery. It *had* to be sturdy to hold up the frosting!"

I borrowed Nancy's frosting recipe and developed a delicious chocolate cake to use it on. Together they are a knockout.

I have to admit to a real failing here, however. I don't care for lumps of marshmallow in my frosting, so I leave them out and add more nuts. I know that's not a true rocky road frosting, but it is the privilege of the cook! On the other hand, if I hear too many grumbles when I'm preparing the cake, I generally give in.

CAKE

2 cups unbleached all-purpose flour
2 teaspoons baking powder
2 teaspoons ground cinnamon
½ teaspoon freshly grated nutmeg
6 tablespoons unsweetened cocoa powder
½ teaspoon salt
12 tablespoons (1½ sticks) unsalted butter, at
    room temperature
1¾ cups sugar
2 large eggs, separated
1 cup warm mashed potatoes (from 1 large russet
    potato)
½ cup milk
Pinch of salt

FROSTING

8 tablespoons (1 stick) unsalted butter
8 ounces bittersweet chocolate, preferably Lindt
    or Tobler
½ cup heavy (or whipping) cream
4 cups confectioners' sugar, sifted
2 teaspoons vanilla extract
2 cups marshmallows, chopped (optional)
2 cups walnuts, lightly toasted (see Note) and
    coarsely chopped

1. Preheat the oven to 350°F. Heavily oil two 9-inch round cake pans.

2. Sift together the flour, baking powder, cinnamon, nutmeg, cocoa powder, and ½ teaspoon salt onto a piece of waxed paper.

3. In a large bowl or the bowl of an electric mixer, cream the butter with the sugar until the mixture is fluffy and pale yellow, almost white. This will take about 5 minutes in an electric mixer. Add the egg yolks one at a time, mixing well after each addition. Then add the warm mashed potato and mix well.

4. By hand, fold in the dry ingredients in thirds, alternating with the milk and beginning and ending with the dry ingredients.

5. Add the pinch of salt to the egg whites, and whip until they are stiff but not dry. Fold them into the batter. Divide the batter between the prepared cake pans, smoothing it out on top. Bake in the center of the oven until the cakes are puffed and spring back when touched, 30 to 35 minutes. Remove them from the oven and allow to cool in the pans for 10 minutes. Then remove them from the pans and let them cool to room temperature on wire racks.

6. Prepare the frosting: Heat the butter, chocolate, and cream in a double boiler over simmering water. When the chocolate has melted, remove the pan from the heat and whisk in the confectioners' sugar until smooth. Then whisk in the vanilla, and set the mixture aside to cool slightly.

7. Stir in the marshmallows and the walnuts, and mix well. The marshmallows will melt slightly, which is fine. If you make the frosting in advance and it hardens too much to spread, place it back over hot water just until it softens.

8. To assemble the cake, place one layer on a cake plate or platter. Top it with one third of the frosting, spreading it all over the cake, including the sides. Add the second layer and the remaining frosting, spreading the frosting all over any exposed cake. Cover the cake and let it sit overnight to mellow before serving.

ONE 9-INCH CAKE; 8 SERVINGS

Note: To lightly toast walnuts, bake them in a 350°F oven until lightly golden, about 8 minutes.

Cypremort Point Crab Boil

A LOUISIANA BAYOU GET-TOGETHER

It was a warm, mosquito-rich night on Cypremort Point, about an hour outside New Iberia, Louisiana. As guests of Paul and Judy McIlhenny, we were visiting Sue and Roland Sylvester's fish camp—a bayouside weekend home—along with their friends Joseph and Carolyn Sorci.

The three couples are old friends who assemble often at the fish camp for fishing, cooking, and eating. We were there on a specific mission, however. Paul, who is the president of Tabasco, Inc., a company his great-grandfather started more than a hundred years ago, had promised to show us a real south Louisiana crab boil (or cra'bowl, as natives pronounce it). He thought Cypremort Point, known locally for its beauty and good fishing, was the ideal spot, his friends the perfect company.

Paul provided the ingredients for the crab boil. The men jealously guarded the right and privilege of cooking the crabs, and the women happily let them.

FORAY INTO THE BAYOU

Before any preparations began, Roland offered to take us on a swift tour of the bayou and the shore of Hammock Lake in the waning light of the day. With Paul acting as co-pilot, Roland navigated his motorboat slowly through a leg of the bayou and out into open water. Once clear, he opened up the throttle and we flew, dipping and skimming along the contours of the shore.

The lake is lined with fish camps, but as Roland explained, they are the fancy version, large and multi-roomed like regular homes. Some still showed evidence of Hurricane Andrew, which had swept through just two months before, leaving random destruction in its wake.

As we returned to the bayou, Roland cut the motor way back and the boat sank onto the surface of the water. Away from the open lake, the air was warm and close. Mosquitoes whined, and bird squawks punctuated the air. I wanted to dangle my fingers in the water but felt sure there were alligators nearby, just out of sight.

Along the bayou we saw another side of fish camp culture, which Roland said was more "real." Tucked away on every curve were tiny little places, almost shacks though neat and tidily arranged. They had screened windows and a porch, a small dock, sometimes a yard. And always there was a gas burner, with a crab boiling pot and barbecue stowed somewhere.

"These camps aren't supposed to be fancy," shouted Roland above the motor. "Ya' come, ya' fish, ya' cook, and ya' eat."

It was midweek and election night, and there were few people around. We scared up a huge American White Pelican that galumphed its way off the water, and in the distance saw a Great Blue Heron. Closer were Gray Ducks, paddling at the edge of the marsh in search, no doubt, of dinner.

A patch of late wildflowers bloomed at the edge of the bayou, and Roland nosed the bow among them so I could pick a centerpiece for the table.

With the vestiges of daylight disappearing and our stomachs beginning to rumble, we roared home. Judy and Sue came running down the steps to greet and help us from the boat, to offer drinks, and to fight over who got to carry our son, Joe, up to the house to play.

Sue took me into the house, which was raised high enough to include a screened-in daylight basement. The living area was up a flight of outdoor stairs. "This camp is really simple," she said, indicating

the two large upstairs rooms, which were wonderfully homey and comfortable. "You know, I've tried to change the furniture—spruce it up, make it a little fancier—but Roland, he's adamant, he just won't hear of it."

She laughed. "I've really given up, and I just love it out here anyway. We all get together with the kids and everybody has a great time." She and Roland both spend most of their time at the camp fishing; then they come home and cook whatever they've caught.

We followed their example and enjoyed ourselves, too. The boiling of the crab was a rousing affair carried on downstairs, in the daylight basement. All three men were masters, with my husband, Michael, apprenticing alongside.

ARGUABLY LOUISIANA'S BEST BOIL

The men argued passionately over seasoning, and Paul finally gave in. Then he pulled me aside. "Ya' know, I'd add an espresso cup full of that mash, but they're afraid to because they think it'll be too hot," he confided.

Paul was referring to pepper mash, a special ingredient he gets from the big factory on nearby Avery Island, where Tabasco is made. Mash is left over after the Tabasco peppers have soaked in vinegar and then been squeezed of their tart and fiery juice, which is what Tabasco sauce consists of. The mash is full of fire and Tabasco pepper flavor.

Crabmeat—It's Better to Lump It

Lump crabmeat is a term used primarily for large nuggets of body meat from the blue crab (Callinectes sapidus). For her salad, Judy McIlhenny uses lump crabmeat, which she has no trouble getting because blue crabs swim in Louisiana waters.

Whether from the blue crab, the Dungeness (Cancer magister), or the Rock Crab (Cancer irroratus, also known as the Maine crab), the larger the pieces of meat, the better for this salad. If you live on the East Coast, where crabs are small and industries have arisen around picking the meat carefully and quickly from the shell, you can buy fresh crabmeat in season in 4- to 6-ounce tubs. If you live in the West, where crabs are large and easy to handle, you are better off picking your own. Avoid canned or frozen crabmeat. Both are of marginal quality.

The other two men heard him and hooted, but they didn't relent. They added several packets of seafood boiling spices and a bit of mash and let that boil for a while, then added the vegetables and cooked them almost through. Paul hefted a huge cooler full of the fattest blue crabs I'd ever seen and deftly poured them into the pot.

There was more arguing as they determined timing, and there Paul prevailed. The water returned to a boil, and fifteen minutes later those crabs were drained and dumped into an insulated container to stay warm.

Roland and Joe sprinkled them liberally with spices and toted them up the stairs. Paul and Michael followed with a container of vegetables, and they poured it all onto a newspaper-covered table in the kitchen.

"Don't you just love our linens?" Judy laughed as she set a roll of paper towels on the table.

We loved everything about the evening, from the companionship, to the laughter, to the delicious food. We all had juice streaming down our arms and tears streaming from our eyes as we laughed and ate. There was little left by the time dessert was served.

We drove away late that night, guided back down the winding bayou roads by the glimmer of Roland and Sue's taillights. Paul had given me a big jar of pepper mash "to remember the flavor."

As if we'd ever forget it, or the time we had at Cypremort Point.

Judy's Crabmeat Salad

While we were gone on a whirlwind tour of the lake and the bayou, Judy McIlhenny had begun to assemble this simple, delicious salad. When we returned she put the bowl on the table with some crackers. Roland, Joe, Paul, and Michael went to light the burner and prepare for the crab boil downstairs in the daylight basement, and we stayed upstairs to indulge.

Though this salad has several ingredients, the essence of the sweet crab prevails. Judy makes it often and insists the secret is plenty of freshly squeezed lemon juice.

2 tablespoons best-quality mayonnaise
1 teaspoon coarse-grained mustard
2 tablespoons freshly squeezed lemon juice
3 drops Tabasco sauce, or to taste
¼ cup curly parsley leaves

1 cup very finely diced celery (about 3 ribs)
3 small scallions, trimmed and cut into thin rounds
Salt and freshly ground black pepper to taste
1 pound lump crabmeat, carefully picked over

1. In a large bowl whisk together the mayonnaise, mustard, and lemon juice. Add the Tabasco, and taste for seasoning.

2. Mince the parsley and add it to the dressing, along with all the remaining ingredients except the crabmeat. Toss well. Then add the crabmeat, toss gently but thoroughly, and taste for seasoning. Serve immediately. (You may make this salad up to 4 hours in advance. Remove it from the refrigerator 15 minutes before serving, and toss gently.)

8 APPETIZER SERVINGS

Paul's Crab Boil

Paul McIlhenny takes enormous pride and enjoyment in cooking. He loves a party centered around the table, and a good old-fashioned Louisiana crab boil is one of his favorite meals for a celebration.

When Paul masterminds the cooking, pepper mash—the pulverized peppers left over from the production of Tabasco sauce—is an essential ingredient. It is not easy to obtain, so I use Tabasco sauce instead, a generous amount right in boiling water.

If you don't have a pot large enough to hold all the crabs and vegetables, use two smaller ones and divide the ingredients between them.

¼ cup Tabasco sauce
⅔ cup kosher (coarse) salt
1 teaspoon cayenne pepper
2 bags (1½ cups) Zatarain's Crab and Shrimp
   Boil seasoning, or other quality brand
8 medium onions, peeled

2 pounds small new potatoes, scrubbed
18 good-size live blue or Maine crabs
8 ears corn, husked
2 tablespoons Old Bay Seasoning
1 teaspoon salt

---

1. Fill a large kettle half full with water, and add the Tabasco, coarse salt, cayenne, and Boil seasoning. Cover, bring to a boil over medium-high heat, and boil for 15 minutes.

2. Add the onions and potatoes. Cook, partially covered, until the potatoes are nearly cooked through, about 18 minutes.

3. Add the crabs, pushing them down into the water as much as possible. Cover the pot and cook the crabs until they are bright red, 8 to 10 minutes. Add the corn, laying it over the crabs, and cook, covered, until it is tender and hot through, about 5 minutes.

4. In a small bowl, mix together the Old Bay Seasoning and the salt. Transfer the mixture to a small serving dish, and set it aside.

5. Drain the crabs and vegetables, and arrange them on large serving platters. Serve immediately, and pass the seasoning mixture for sprinkling.

8 SERVINGS

Cypremort Fruit Pie

Carolyn Sorci brought a fruit pie for dessert the night of the Cypremort Point crab boil. She pulled it from the refrigerator, and sated as we were from the crab, everyone had a large piece. Fresh and simple, it was the ideal finale to the meal.

This is an adaptation of Carolyn's recipe. Something wonderful occurs between the pineapple and the warm pastry cream. It is as though they exchange molecules—the pineapple takes on a gentle sweetness while the pastry cream absorbs a little zing. (Make sure you have the pineapple slices ready so the cream is still warm when you arrange them.)

I love fresh raspberries, but I really like to use frozen berries here because they are just beginning to soften by the time the pie gets to the table, and they offer a cool counterpoint.

CRUST
1 individual package of graham crackers, finely crushed (1½ cups crumbs)
2 tablespoons sugar
¼ teaspoon ground cinnamon
6 tablespoons (¾ stick) unsalted butter, melted

PASTRY CREAM
2 cups milk
1 vanilla bean, split
4 large egg yolks
½ cup sugar
6 tablespoons unbleached all-purpose flour
Pinch of salt

TOPPING
½ fresh pineapple (halved lengthwise), peel and core removed
1 banana, sliced into paper-thin rounds
1 cup raspberries, fresh or frozen
1 cup heavy (or whipping) cream
2 tablespoons confectioners' sugar
1 teaspoon vanilla extract
1 cup pecans, lightly toasted (see Note, page 148) and finely chopped

1. Preheat the oven to 350°F. Chill a medium-size bowl and a whisk, or the whisk attachment or rotary blades of an electric mixer, for whipping the cream.

2. Make the crust: Combine the graham cracker crumbs, sugar, cinnamon, and melted butter in a large bowl and stir until combined. Press evenly into a 9-inch pie plate. Bake the crust until golden, about 10 minutes. Remove from the oven and cool on a wire rack.

3. Make the pastry cream: Place the milk and the vanilla bean in a medium-size saucepan over medium-high heat. When bubbles form around the edge of the pan, remove it from the heat, cover, and set aside for 10 minutes. Then remove the vanilla bean, and either discard it or rinse and dry it to use in vanilla sugar (see Note).

4. In a large bowl whisk the egg yolks with the sugar until the mixture is thick and pale yellow. Quickly but thoroughly whisk in the flour and the salt. Then add the hot milk, whisking it into the egg yolk mixture until combined. Return the mixture to the saucepan and bring it to a gentle boil over medium heat, whisking fre-quently until it bubbles. Continue cooking, stirring frequently, until the pastry cream thickens and then becomes slightly thinner (which shows the flour is cooked), at least 2 minutes. Remove it from the heat and pour it into the cooled graham cracker crust.

5. Cut the pineapple half in half lengthwise. Slice each wedge into ⅛-inch-thick slices. Arrange the pineapple slices over the warm pastry cream in a single layer, overlapping slightly. Top with the banana slices and the raspberries.

6. Whip the cream with the confectioners' sugar and the vanilla until it forms stiff peaks. Spread it over the pie, top with the chopped pecans, and serve immediately.

6 TO 8 SERVINGS

Note: To make vanilla sugar, nestle 1 or 2 dry vanilla beans in a jar holding 4 cups sugar. Seal the jar and let sit for at least 2 weeks. Use in place of regular sugar in any dessert recipe.

The Schartners of Thorndyke, Maine

AN INDEPENDENCE DAY DINNER WITH CANADIAN FLAVOR

Phyllis Schartner, a Canadian-American who has lived on a farm in Thorndyke, Maine, for almost a decade, remembers her mother preparing stuffed salmon each year for the Fourth of July. She always served it with peas, following a time-honored New England custom.

After emigrating from Canada, "my parents were so proud to be American citizens that they observed all the American holidays and customs," she explained. "But my mother always used good old Canadian recipes."

During the years when her seven children were growing up and they were living in Massachusetts, Phyllis always made her mother's salmon and peas on the Fourth of July. These days, however, the Fourth dawns in the middle of strawberry season, which is one of the busiest times of the year at the Schartner farm. They invite people in to gather strawberries, and from earliest light their fields are full of pickers piling their baskets high. Nonetheless, if any of Phyllis's children are home, she makes salmon and peas for supper.

THE FARMING LIFE

Phyllis has uncommon energy and a fiery spirit. She and her husband, Herb, work alone at their farm, tilling the soil, planting and picking the crops, supervising the strawberry pickers, and harvesting the precious raspberries they're famous for.

Phyllis sells most of their produce at a nearby farmers' market, which entails rising at 3 A.M. most days to finish harvesting, then loading a converted U-Haul truck from floor to ceiling with fruit, vegetables, jams, jellies, chutneys, and a huge tent. She drives to the town of Brewer, half an hour away, and spends an hour and a half setting up. Two days a week, Herb takes a pickup truck full of produce to a smaller market in nearby Belfast.

Farm life is tough in the best of circumstances, and the life the Schartners have chosen may be tougher than most. Maine's short growing season and extreme climate really don't encourage the varieties of fruit they produce, yet neither Phyllis nor Herb lets that stop them. Farmers all their lives, they thrive, they produce beautiful fruit organically, and they sell every last piece. Come the Fourth of July, they celebrate.

KID-GLOVE TREATMENT

Phyllis likes to serve wild salmon, so she calls upon her Canadian relatives, who have a decent chance of finding one. She'll make the trip north to get it or have someone bring it down. She caresses the big fish as though it were a puppy.

"Isn't he gorgeous?" she exclaims. "Takes me back to being a kid and the huge fish we had then. They aren't getting any easier to find."

She rinses the fish inside and out, managing it as best she can as it slithers around the kitchen sink. Her counters are full of paraphernalia—the ingredients for the pickle stuffing on one side of the sink, clean dishes on the other, stacks of papers on the nearby kitchen table.

"Where'll I put this fellow?" she asks, hugging the fish with one arm and sweeping a counter clean with the other. "There," she says, and checks out the fish from head to tail, salts and peppers the belly, and sets it on a rack in a pan.

"Canadians insist on cooking salmon with milk, because they say it takes away the fishy smell," Phyllis says, pouring milk under the fish and adding some onion. "I don't know as that's true, but I'm not going to change a winning combination."

Pickles are another Canadian secret, according to Phyllis. "The tartness, it's the tartness," she says as she mixes the bread, onions, pickles, and butter and pats it inside the fish, then sews it up with a needle and thread. "No one argues with my technique, right?" she asks, laughing at herself as she takes huge stitches and manages to close the belly flaps around the stuffing.

She checks her work, gives a satisfied cluck, and puts it in the oven. "How about a drink," she says, moving into the den where a fire burns though it's midsummer. The skies are dark, the air cool, the berries struggling to ripeness. None of this dampens Phyllis's spirit as she prepares the feast which, this year, will be for only a tiny part of her large family. Herb is off helping one of their children and the rest are due to arrive soon.

She strides back into the kitchen to check on the fish and to start cooking the rice. The phone rings a half dozen times and she discusses apples, pears, the state of the coddling moth in Maine, walking around the kitchen with the phone cradled between shoulder and ear.

The timer rings, and Phyllis hangs up the phone and runs to the oven with a large spoon in her hand to baste the salmon, pouring in extra milk to be sure there's enough.

"It's looking good," she says, rubbing her hands together. "If we lived in a different climate, I'd serve potatoes with the fish. But we don't have any from the garden—in fact we barely have peas."

We retire back to the den and talk about the many things the Schartners are involved with in the course of a season. We talk about tradition, about catching wild salmon, about waiting with held breath to see if the peas will be ripe for the Fourth.

Four more bastings and the salmon is ready to serve. Phyllis hefts it onto a huge

platter and shows her handiwork to all present. She fluffs the rice into a bowl, shapes it into a cone, and pours the peas on top so they cascade down like pebbles. She always bakes extra stuffing, which emerges from the oven with a golden crisp top.

By mealtime the family has arrived with much ado and quickly helped set the table. Phyllis says a brief blessing as we sit, mouths watering from the aroma of the stuffing blending with the salmon.

"You know," she says, looking around the table at the children who have managed to make it for the feast, "everyone is so busy now with their lives and their families that it gets harder and harder to get us all together. If you all didn't come, I wouldn't cook salmon and peas. Thanks for coming."

Phyllis's Whole Stuffed Salmon

Phyllis Schartner loves to cook when she has the time, and despite her busy schedule she tries to make time on the Fourth of July. "What would it be without salmon and peas?" she asks rhetorically.

In Maine, contests are held in towns all over the state for the year's first ripe peas, which usually mature sometime in late June or early July. And long ago when wild salmon filled the rivers, it was a simple matter to fish one out to cook alongside. Now the fish comes from farms, though Phyllis tries to get wild salmon from a relative in Canada. She always has peas in the big garden behind the barn, and these she gently steams and serves over rice.

"We don't have potatoes in the garden at that time of year, so traditionally we have rice," she said.

Phyllis doesn't measure when she cooks, and how she finds anything in the happy clutter of her farm kitchen is a mystery. However, she wastes no time looking for things. She makes a meal so fast, it's hard to believe it when it comes time to sit down. "That's the only way I can do it, because I just don't have much time," she explained.

She chopped pickles for the stuffing and laughed. "It's kind of different to put pickles in the stuffing, but that's another Canadian thing. My aunts always said you had to have something tart with salmon, so they always put a pickle in the stuffing."

Those Canadians have the secret because her salmon emerged perfectly cooked, succulent, and full of flavor. The stuffing became an instant favorite, too, because of its tart counterpoint. Having seen how simply it came together, I thought it could easily become a tradition at our house.

You may find that very little of the stuffing fits inside the salmon. Place what you can there, then put what remains in an ovenproof dish. Cover and cook it for the final 30 minutes the salmon is in the oven.

Serve Basmati Rice with Scallions and Peas (see opposite) alongside, and either sliced fresh tomatoes or a big green salad.

1 whole salmon (5 to 7 pounds), cleaned, head and tail on

STUFFING
6 tablespoons (¾ stick) unsalted butter, melted
½ cup heavy (or whipping) cream
2 large eggs
½ cup diced dill pickles (about 2 large pickles)
1 medium onion, finely chopped
1 cup Italian (flat-leaf) parsley leaves
8 cups cubed bread (about 14 slices), toasted

Salt and freshly ground black pepper to taste

SALMON
Freshly ground black pepper to taste
¾ cup hot water
2 tablespoons unsalted butter
1 cup milk

GARNISH
2 lemons, cut into 12 wedges
Italian (flat-leaf) parsley sprigs

1. Rinse the salmon inside and out with cold water, and pat it dry. Refrigerate loosely wrapped in waxed paper until ready to cook.

2. Prepare the stuffing: In a small bowl whisk together the melted butter, cream, and eggs. In a medium-size bowl toss together the pickles, onion, and parsley leaves. Add the cubed bread, toss, then add the butter mixture. Season with salt and pepper, and set aside.

3. Preheat the oven to 400°F.

4. Season the belly of the salmon with pepper. Stuff it firmly but gently with as much stuffing as it will hold, and either sew it closed using string and a large needle or hold it closed with skewers. Place the remaining stuffing in an ovenproof dish; cover and set aside.

5. Bring the water to a boil over medium-high heat, and add the butter. Stir until melted, and keep warm.

6. Place the salmon on a rack in a roasting pan. Pour the milk around the salmon (it will make a pool underneath it), and cover the pan. Bake the salmon in the center of the oven, basting it every 15 minutes with the milk in the bottom of the pan and the butter and water mixture, until the flesh is opaque through, 45 minutes to 1 hour. Thirty minutes before the salmon is ready, place the remaining stuffing, uncovered, in the oven.

7. To check the salmon for doneness, make a slit at the base of the head along the backbone and look into the meat. If it is nearly opaque, with just a slight translucence right near the bone, it is done. Remove the salmon from the oven and let it sit for 10 minutes, covered, before serving.

8. Remove the strings or skewers from the belly flap, and transfer the salmon to a large heated platter. Garnish with the lemon wedges and parsley sprigs, and serve. Pass the extra stuffing separately.

8 TO 10 SERVINGS

Note: If you can't find a whole salmon, or don't want to cook that much, use a good-size fillet (2½ pounds) and bake it for about 40 minutes, basting regularly. Adjust the amounts of the other ingredients according to the amount of salmon.

Basmati Rice with Scallions and Peas

Phyllis served us Rice and Peas with her Fourth of July salmon, but there's no reason to limit it to special celebrations. I like to serve this any time I can get either fresh peas or top-quality frozen ones, such as Cascade brand organic peas.

RICE
2 cups basmati rice or other long-grain white rice
4 cups water
½ teaspoon salt
2 tablespoons unsalted butter

PEAS
2 tablespoons unsalted butter
1 bunch scallions, trimmed and cut into thin
    rounds
4 cups fresh or frozen (unthawed) green peas
⅓ cup water
Salt and freshly ground black pepper to taste

43

1. Place the rice, water, and salt in a large heavy saucepan over high heat, and bring to a boil. Boil until the rice has absorbed most of the water and there are bubble holes on the surface, about 10 minutes.

2. Cover the rice and reduce the heat to medium. Cook for 10 minutes.

3. Turn off the heat under the rice, but leave it covered. Let it sit for 10 minutes.

4. While the rice is resting, cook the peas: Melt the butter in a medium-size heavy skillet over medium heat. Add the scallions and cook, stirring, until they soften and begin to turn golden on the edges, about 8 minutes.

5. Add the peas, water, and salt and pepper, cover, and bring to a boil. Reduce the heat to low and simmer until the peas are bright green and tender, about 5 minutes for fresh peas, about 9 minutes for frozen peas.

6. To serve, cut the remaining 2 tablespoons butter into several small pieces. Place the rice on a warmed serving platter and scatter the butter over it. Then pour the peas over the rice, and serve immediately.

8 TO 10 SERVINGS

Cottage Pudding with Nutmeg Syrup

This is the dessert Phyllis Schartner's family has always enjoyed on the Fourth of July after their feast of salmon and peas. It's not really a pudding—it's a cake adorned with a pungent nutmeg syrup.

"My aunts told me you have to serve nutmeg after salmon, because the flavor cleanses the fish from your palate," Phyllis said. Phyllis adheres to the tradition, whether or not she's convinced it's true.

The last thing I want to do is to erase the flavor of fresh salmon from my palate, but I like this unusual dessert. It's full of flavor yet light and satisfying after a good meal. That's grounds enough to try it.

Be sure to serve the syrup warm and the cake at room temperature. Should you have any leftover syrup, try it over vanilla ice cream or on pancakes in the morning.

CAKE

1½ cups sifted cake flour
1 teaspoon baking powder
¼ teaspoon salt
½ cup milk
1 teaspoon vanilla extract
5 tablespoons unsalted butter, at room
    temperature
¾ cup sugar
2 large eggs
Minced zest of 1 orange

NUTMEG SYRUP

½ cup sugar
1½ teaspoons unbleached all-purpose flour
Pinch of salt
1 cup boiling water
1 tablespoon unsalted butter
2 teaspoons freshly grated
    nutmeg

1. Preheat the oven to 350°F. Generously butter a 9-inch round cake pan.

2. Make the cake: Sift the dry ingredients together onto a piece of waxed paper. In a small bowl, mix together the milk and the vanilla.

3. In a large bowl or the bowl of an electric mixer, cream the butter until it is pale yellow and light. Add the sugar, and cream until the mixture is light and fluffy.

4. Add the eggs one at a time, mixing well after each addition. Then add the orange zest and mix well. Add the dry ingredients alternately with the milk mixture, beginning and ending with dry ingredients. Pour the batter into the prepared pan, and bake in the center of the oven until the cake is puffed and golden and springs back when touched, about 25 minutes.

5. Remove the cake from the oven and let it cool in the pan for 15 minutes. Then turn it out onto a wire rack and let it cool completely.

6. To make the nutmeg syrup, mix together the sugar, flour, and salt in a medium-size saucepan. Whisk in the boiling water; then place the pan over medium heat and bring to a

boil. Reduce the heat to medium and cook, stirring constantly, until the dry ingredients have dissolved and the syrup is slightly thick, 8 to 10 minutes. Whisk in the butter and cook until it has melted; then whisk in the nutmeg. Turn the heat to low and keep the sauce warm, stirring it occasionally. (You can make the sauce in advance, cool it, and reheat it just before serving.)

7. To serve the cake, cut it into wedges, and poke the top of each wedge in several places with a skewer. Pour warm syrup over each piece, and serve immediately. Pass any remaining syrup separately.

ONE 9-INCH CAKE AND 1 CUP SYRUP;
8 SERVINGS

A Celebration to Come

SEAFOOD FETE ON A NORTHWESTERN ISLAND

The first weekend we ever spent with Chris and Randy Shuman was an adventure in oysters. Randy is an oyster farmer and we were staying at their house near his oyster beds on Willapa Bay, in southwest Washington State. We harvested, hefted, and cleaned oysters alongside Randy and Chris, and though I know we helped a great deal I'm not sure we were economically feasible. Like raspberry pickers among the canes, we ate as many oysters as we let go, so enraptured were we with their clean and briny flavor.

That was our first gastronomic adventure with the Shumans, but far from our last. When we lived in Seattle we all got together frequently, usually over meals we prepared together. Often the talk would turn to cooking, the outdoors, and Balaclava Island. A 110-acre piece of paradise off the coast of British Columbia, the island is a destination for Randy and Chris each summer, when they go there to relax, fish, and cook what they've brought from the sea.

They've invited us to Balaclava every year since we've known them, and we've never been able to go. But we've heard and talked so much about it that each July our blood quickens as we try to work out how we can join them. Sometime we will, and we know this celebration-to-come will be a wonderful one.

ANTICIPATING ISLAND FLAVOR

The Shumans and the Lazaras, Chris's family, own a big chunk of the island, and it has become a family tradition to go there as a group. When all the heads are counted, including friends invited along, there are at least ten and sometimes fifteen making the trip.

A trip to Balaclava is not for the faint of heart. The journey from Seattle takes twelve hours by car, ferry, and boat or plane. Once there, the living is rustic. Over the years the family has built tent platforms and a modest shelter, but it's still a vacation among the elements.

The reason Balaclava comes up in conversation so much, though, often has little to do with its pristine beauty and remoteness, the exciting fishing trips that Randy and Mike Lazara, Chris's father, get involved in, or the mysterious little nooks and crannies of the island. Instead, we talk about it because of the meals that are prepared and eaten there, all of which are sumptuous.

They depend for their main courses on whatever is hauled from the sea or pried off rocks. On Balaclava that might be anything from lingcod to salmon to fat-bodied rockfish.

Whatever fish or shellfish is the centerpiece, each meal is a celebration that has been carefully and thoughtfully planned for months. Carol, Chris's mother, is a natural organizer and spearheads the planning by assigning meals to each family. Chris has two sisters, Nancy and Kathy, and they have all learned over the years that a meal includes everything from appetizers and wine to after-dinner coffee. Balaclava may be out in the middle of nowhere, Carol reasons, but that doesn't mean they can't eat well there.

Variety is the norm. They all have their favorite dishes that appear year after year, like Chris's gingerbread, but they try to surprise one another, too.

Chris, for one, takes her meal-planning duties very seriously. As soon as she gets the calendar from her mother, she turns to a folder of tried-and-true Balaclava recipes. Then she goes to another filled with recipes she's collected over the past year. While they plan, the phone lines buzz with meal conferences, as no one wants to duplicate dishes. Friendly competition among the women guarantees plenty of new dishes each summer.

There is a small obstacle to cooking on Balaclava, though the Shumans and Lazaras have never allowed it to hamper them. The cook surface is a three-burner propane stove, and there is no oven. "It just means we have to be creative," Chris said with a laugh.

BALACLAVA CUSTOMS

They usually arrive at Balaclava midmorning, tired from the trip and ready to relax. The air is briny and moist, filled with a cacophony of birdsong and surf.

Each family claims a spot to pitch their tent. They unpack, settle in, and then head off to their favorite spots. Randy goes straight to the "reading rocks," a huge field of glacial boulders rounded over time so that they look like overstuffed armchairs. "It's a great place to hide," Randy says. "I look up from my book once in a while at the mountain range and the water."

Chris has a favorite fishing hole that is accessible only in fine weather because of murderous rocks that stick above the water, and she will often go there to hunt for rockfish. Last year she impressed everyone and fulfilled a lifelong dream by pulling in a long, fat lingcod, a fish prized in the Northwest for its sweet white meat.

Some days they go out exploring on the island, and on others they get in the Zodiac and race across the channel to another island, where they've found remains of Native American villages.

"The island across from Balaclava was important to the Native Americans for trade," said Chris, who has a strong interest in Native American history and art. "Stories are told about the chief there who was so wealthy that he threw trade beads into the water as traders paddled away, just to impress them."

Last year while they were poking around their own woods and beaches, Chris found three trade beads. "I couldn't believe it," she said. "That means Balaclava was important too."

By late afternoon everyone assembles back at the main camp. Someone is dispatched to clean fish, others begin chopping, someone else opens a bottle of wine, and before long the call for hors d'oeuvres goes out. If the weather is fine, cocktail hour takes place on the beach, with everyone sitting around a fire where a salmon bakes in foil or a lingcod simmers in marinade. If it's warm the children will still be scrambling over rocks or swimming in the shallow water. Summer daylight on Balaclava lasts until 10:30 P.M., so there is plenty of time to play.

If guests are invited from either the lighthouse on the point or one of the other camping spots on the island, they arrive dressed warmly for the evening, because once the sun dips it's cool on Balaclava.

Not long into the evening, everyone ambles up to the "dining room," where the table is set with bright checked cloths, can-dles, and open bottles of wine.

It's a simple setting where good friends become better friends. On Balaclava the food is fresh from the sea and the meals are better than they could be anywhere else.

Grilled Salmon with Yogurt-Dill Sauce

This is the way Chris prepares salmon on Balaclava. Serve both the Yogurt-Dill Sauce and the Pineapple Chutney with the fish. These accompaniments are an inspired combination of tart and sweet, yin and yang, which balance the rich salmon.

SALMON
1 whole salmon (4 to 5 pounds), cleaned, head and tail on
Salt and freshly ground black pepper to taste
1 large handful fresh dill sprigs
1 lemon, thinly sliced
1 small bunch fresh herbs, such as thyme, tarragon, rosemary, oregano, or dill
Handful of edible flowers, such as pansies, geraniums, roses

YOGURT-DILL SAUCE
¾ cup (loosely packed) fresh dill fronds
2 cups plain yogurt
Salt and freshly ground black pepper to taste

Pineapple Chutney (recipe follows)

1. Build a good-size fire in a barbecue grill. You do not need to oil the grill rack.

2. Rinse the salmon inside and out with cold water, and pat it dry. Refrigerate loosely wrapped in waxed paper until ready to cook.

3. Prepare the yogurt-dill sauce: Mince the dill and stir it into the yogurt. Season with salt and pepper, and set aside. (If making the sauce more than an hour before eating, cover and refrigerate.)

4. When the coals have burned red and are dusted with ash, place the rack over the fire. Place the salmon on a piece of aluminum foil large enough to fold up around it. Season the belly cavity with salt and pepper, and then lay the dill sprigs inside the belly. Tuck the lemon slices inside the belly as well.

5. Bring the aluminum foil up and around the salmon, crimping it closed near the head and the tail, and leaving it open over the body of the fish. Place it on the grill rack, cover the grill, and cook until the salmon is opaque through, which will take 25 to 30 minutes. To test the salmon, insert the blade of a sharp knife into the meat right behind the head and pull back. If the flesh is still very translucent, continue cooking. If it is nearly opaque through, remove it from the grill.

6. Transfer the whole fish to a warmed serving platter, or remove the fillets and place them whole on the platter, or cut the fillets into serving pieces and arrange them on the platter. Remove the skin if you wish. Garnish the platter with the herbs and flowers, and serve the sauce and the chutney alongside.

8 TO 10 SERVINGS

Pineapple Chutney

This is an unconventional accompaniment to freshly grilled salmon, which Chris always takes along to Balaclava.

2 cups diced fresh pineapple
1¼ cups sugar
½ cup golden raisins
½ cup distilled white vinegar
¼ cup crystallized ginger, coarsely chopped
2 tablespoons minced onion

2 tablespoons freshly squeezed lime juice
Grated zest of 1 lime
1 clove garlic, finely chopped
¼ teaspoon ground cinnamon
⅛ teaspoon cayenne pepper

1. Place all the ingredients in a large heavy saucepan, and bring to a boil over medium-high heat. Reduce the heat and simmer until the mixture has thickened slightly, about 25 minutes.

2. Allow the chutney to cool. Refrigerate (the chutney will keep for at least 3 weeks in the refrigerator), or ladle into sterilized canning jars and process according to the manufacturer's instructions.

3. To serve, reheat the chutney gently until warmed through.

1⅔ CUPS

Scallion Fry Bread

A standby appetizer at the Shuman-Lazara camp on Balaclava Island, this fry bread is "perfect for making on top of the stove, and we all love it," Chris said. "Plus it gives a little Asian flair to a meal."

It's quick and easy, and ideal for those off-island days when the oven is full or when you just don't want to turn it on.

I like to vary the flavor by adding dried red pepper flakes and kosher salt, and you may think of other things to add.

From start to finish, including making the bread dough, it takes an hour and a quarter. I like to roll it out while people look on and serve it hot from the stove. If you can't do that, keep the bread warm in a low oven until all the batches are cooked.

1 cup lukewarm water
1 envelope (2½ teaspoons) active dry yeast
2½ cups unbleached all-purpose flour
1½ teaspoons salt
1 cup thinly sliced scallions

2 teaspoons Japanese sesame oil
2 teaspoons peanut oil
1 teaspoon dried red pepper flakes (optional)
1 teaspoon kosher (coarse) salt (optional)

1. To make the bread, place the water and the yeast in a large bowl, or in the bowl of an electric mixer, and mix well. Add 1 cup of the flour, mix well, and then add the salt. Continue

adding the flour, ½ cup at a time, mixing well after each addition, until the dough becomes stiff. If you are using an electric mixer, change to the dough hook and knead the dough until it is elastic and no longer sticks to the sides of the bowl. Or knead it by hand on a lightly floured work surface until the dough is elastic and no longer sticks to your hands, 6 to 8 minutes. Cover the dough with a kitchen towel and let it rise at room temperature until it has doubled in bulk, about 1 hour. (The dough can be made ahead to this point. Place it in a bowl, cover with foil, and refrigerate overnight. Bring the dough to room temperature before proceeding.)

2. Punch down the dough, and gradually knead the scallions into it. Keep working the dough until the scallions are thoroughly combined—they will have a tendency to pop out of the dough, but just gently work them back in. Divide the dough into 4 pieces, and let them rest for about 15 minutes.

3. Heat ½ teaspoon of each of the oils in a heavy 10-inch skillet (preferably cast-iron) over medium-high heat.

4. Roll out 1 piece of the dough on a lightly floured surface until it is about ⅛ inch thick and about the circumference of the skillet. Transfer it to the hot skillet, sprinkle the top lightly with ⅛ teaspoon of the dried red pepper flakes and ⅛ teaspoon of the kosher salt, if desired. Cover, and cook until the top puffs and begins to look baked, about 5 minutes. Flip the bread, repeat with ⅛ teaspoon each of the red pepper flakes and the salt, and continue cooking until it is baked through, 4 to 5 minutes. Remove the bread, cut it into quarters, and serve immediately. Repeat with the remaining dough and seasonings.

12 TO 14 SERVINGS

Balaclava Tomato Salad

This salad is a perfect example of Chris's creative flair. It has a spicy twist that accentuates the sweetness of just-ripe tomatoes. I love it alongside her grilled salmon or served as an appetizer beforehand.

Whether made on an island or right at home, the salad requires tomatoes just before they hit their peak of ripeness—when flavorful but still slightly firm.

2 tablespoons extra-virgin olive oil
2 teaspoons freshly squeezed lemon juice
Salt and freshly ground black pepper to taste
⅛ teaspoon ground turmeric or curry powder
½ teaspoon ground cumin
1½ pounds medium tomatoes, cored and cut into eighths
1 shallot, sliced paper-thin

1. In a large bowl, whisk together the olive oil and lemon juice. Add the salt and pepper, turmeric, and cumin, and mix well.

2. Add the tomatoes and the shallot, and toss until they are thoroughly coated with the dressing. Adjust the seasoning, and let sit for 1 hour before serving.

8 SERVINGS

Stovetop Gingerbread with Pineapple Sauce

Finding the right kind of recipe for Balaclava is a challenge, but Chris triumphs, as this gingerbread demonstrates.

Her family likes it so much they request it each year, and Chris likes it so much she doesn't just reserve it for Balaclava. She makes it at home in Seattle, too. "We love it, and it's so easy," she said. "You cook it on top of the stove, so the oven can be free for other things."

This gingerbread is delicious, and the light yet dense texture is perfect. I've served it many times and always get rave reviews. One friend who tried it at our house said, "I've got to have the recipe now—I can't wait for the book." That's a vote of confidence!

For the recipe to work, you will need a very heavy 3-quart flameproof casserole with a lid such as Le Creuset makes. When you turn out the bread (which is really much more like a cake) after it has baked, some of the topping may stick to the buttered aluminum foil. Just scrape it off and spread it on the cake.

I sometimes serve this with lightly sweetened whipped cream. If the cake needs a face-lift, spread the cream on top. Otherwise, serve it alongside.

PINEAPPLE SAUCE

2 tablespoons freshly squeezed lemon juice
¼ cup (lightly packed) dark brown sugar
1 teaspoon arrowroot powder
2 cans (8 ounces each) crushed pineapple
¼ cup raisins

CAKE

2½ cups unbleached all-purpose flour
1 teaspoon ground cinnamon
1 teaspoon ground ginger
¼ teaspoon ground cloves
½ teaspoon salt

12 tablespoons (1½ sticks) unsalted butter, at room temperature
¾ cup (lightly packed) dark brown sugar
2 large eggs
¾ cup molasses
2 teaspoons baking soda
1 cup orange juice, or 2 tablespoons freshly squeezed lemon juice plus water to make 1 cup

GARNISH (OPTIONAL)

1 cup heavy (or whipping) cream, chilled
2 tablespoons confectioners' sugar

1. Line a lidded 3-quart flameproof casserole with aluminum foil, and butter the foil.

2. Make the sauce: In a medium-size heavy saucepan, whisk together the lemon juice, brown sugar, and arrowroot powder. Then add the pineapple and raisins, and mix well. Bring to a simmer over medium heat and cook, stirring occasionally, until the mixture has thickened

slightly, about 5 minutes. Remove from the heat and pour into the prepared casserole.

3. Make the cake batter: Sift the flour, cinnamon, ginger, cloves, and salt together onto a sheet of waxed paper, and set aside. In a large bowl, or in the bowl of an electric mixer, cream the butter until it is pale yellow and light. Add the brown sugar and beat until the mixture is fluffy. Add the eggs one at a time, mixing well after each addition, then add the molasses and mix until thoroughly combined. Fold in the flour mixture.

4. In a small bowl, combine the baking soda and the orange juice. It will foam dramatically, but don't be concerned. Mix to combine, then stir into the batter and mix well.

5. Pour the batter over the sauce in the prepared casserole. Cover, and cook over the lowest heat possible until the cake has puffed up and springs back when touched with a finger, 35 to 40 minutes. (The cake may take longer to cook on an electric burner. Keep the heat low and check the cake frequently.)

6. If you are using the garnish, whip the cream with the sugar in a large bowl until it forms stiff peaks.

7. To serve, turn the cake upside down onto a large serving platter. Peel off the foil carefully. The topping may stick slightly in the center; if it does, scrape it carefully with a knife. Top the cake with the whipped cream, if you like, or serve it separately.

8 SERVINGS

Bainbridge Island Halibut

SUPPER HOT OFF THE GRILL

Jerry Erickson, who lives on Bainbridge Island, Washington, grew up in the great outdoors. As a boy he was as comfortable sleeping in a tent and cooking over a wood fire during hunting and fishing trips, as he was negotiating around the family kitchen at home.

Jerry had good role models for the cooking he now enjoys with gusto. His mother cooked for a school and his father cooked for a restaurant during the Depression. As Jerry got older, he cooked for the family too, and he still does. He actually considered a career in cooking and took a year off to work in a restaurant not far from the island. He loved it, he learned a lot, and he was glad to get back to his own kitchen once it was over.

Both the freedom of the outdoors and the discipline of cooking for a crowd each night have given Jerry real ease in the kitchen. He loves to entertain, and when he does he talks as much as he cooks. A tall counter just in front of the stove is a natural spot for friends to rest and watch as Jerry swings from sink to cutting board to stove.

NO ORDINARY GRILL

In the summer Jerry spends a good deal of his leisure time outside over a gigantic grill that he made out of a boiler drum. It stands on three legs in the center of the patio alongside a blowsy herb garden that sends creepers of rosemary over the walkway. The grill is ideally positioned because Jerry, apron on, grill tongs in hand, can reach over and pluck herbs to sprinkle over the food or to throw directly on the fire.

The grill is so large that it easily accommodates food for fifty. Each summer Jerry and his wife, Patti, have a large party when the grill is filled to maximum. People wander the sloping grounds of the small farm, talking to the three goats in the highest pasture, picking Yellow Transparent apples from the little orchard in the corner, and checking out the sprawling vegetable garden. Patti plans and minds the garden, and it's the kind of place you want to land in

with both feet, amidst the perfumes and the large, textured plants and flowers.

WHAT'S FOR DINNER?

Jerry prepared halibut the night I visited. It was a cool summer evening, the scent of brine from Elliott Bay mingling with the aroma of bronze fennel in the garden and smoke from the charcoal. The goats are natural hams, and they cavorted like circus animals, keeping us all entertained when we weren't mesmerized by the magic on the grill.

There Jerry had a field's worth of new potatoes browning next to the halibut. He covered the fish with a large lid so it would bake gently over the coals and left the potatoes to crisp in the open. Now and then he'd touch a fillet to see if it was cooked.

Jerry loves the flavor of halibut so much that he will often grill it and simply drizzle it with butter and lemon juice. That night he teamed it with sweet peppers and shrimp because the small Hood Canal shrimp were in season and he wanted me to taste the inspired combination.

The recipe here is a version of Jerry's, one that is easy to re-create in any kitchen. For a simple summer supper cooked quickly outdoors, you will be surprised at the elegant outcome.

Halibut is often sold in fillets, or *fletches*. Buy a piece at least 2 inches thick, with the skin on, or buy a thick (2- to 4-inch) steak. If you buy a steak, cut the meat from the bone and cook the halibut with the skin side down.

The secret to cooking halibut so it doesn't dry out is to build a good-size fire and let it burn past its hottest point, until the coals are bright red and covered with a substantial amount of ash. Cover the fish, watch it, and within about 20 minutes the halibut will be cooked and succulent. As Jerry did, I brush the fish with butter, oil, and a touch of cayenne, which sets off its delicate flavor and protects it from the heat of the fire.

As we sat down to dinner with great decorum, lovely classical music played in the background. Patti is the doyenne of music in the household, and by dessert she was getting restless. She jumped up, put different music on the stereo, and the room was suddenly alive with the sound of the Pixies, a Seattle band that plays its own version of grunge rock. She cranked the music up as high as it would go, intent on making sure I had a true Northwest experience.

Laughing through dessert, a delectable Apple-Rhubarb Crunch (see Index), I had to admit that I liked it all, from halibut, to crunch, to grunge rock—an unforgettable evening.

Grilled Halibut Inspired by Jerry Erickson

Despite being cooked outdoors, this is an elegant dish. I serve it whenever I can get good-quality halibut because I love the flavors and colors and the simplicity of its preparation. Sometimes I set the dining-room table with linens and silver; other times I serve it informally on the porch, where the summer breeze catches the napkins. However you decide to serve the halibut, be sure to have a light Washington white wine alongside, such as Arbor Crest Sauvignon Blanc.

4 pounds halibut fillet, with skin on
2 pounds small shrimp, in the shell
4 small red bell peppers
4 tablespoons plus 4 teaspoons unsalted butter
½ teaspoon dried red pepper flakes
4 tablespoons freshly squeezed lemon juice
4 shallots, minced

½ cup dry white wine, such as Sauvignon Blanc
2 cups heavy (or whipping) cream
Salt and freshly ground white pepper to taste
2 teaspoons extra-virgin olive oil
¼ teaspoon cayenne pepper
1 large bunch chives
½ cup Italian (flat-leaf) parsley leaves

1. Rinse the halibut and the shrimp with cold water, and pat dry. Refrigerate loosely wrapped in waxed paper until ready to cook.

2. Roast the peppers by holding them on a long-handled fork over the flame of a gas burner until the skin is black all over. (If you have an electric stove, preheat the broiler, place the peppers on a baking sheet, and broil, turning the peppers occasionally, until the skin is black all over, about 15 minutes.) Place the peppers in a paper bag, seal it, and let them steam for 15 minutes. When the peppers are cool enough to handle, remove the skin, the core, and the seeds. Rinse the peppers if necessary, and pat dry. Place the peppers in a food processor and purée. Set the purée aside.

3. Melt 2 tablespoons of the butter in a large skillet over medium-high heat. Add the shrimp and the red pepper flakes, and sauté until the shrimp are curled and nearly pink, about 7 minutes. Add the lemon juice and continue cooking until the shrimp are evenly pink, an additional 2 to 3 minutes. Remove from the heat, and when the shrimp are cool enough to handle, peel them. Discard the peels.

4. Build a medium-size fire in a barbecue grill, and let it burn until the coals are bright red and have burned down. Thoroughly oil the grill rack using paper towels dipped in vegetable oil. Set the rack aside.

5. Meanwhile, make the sauce: Melt 2 tablespoons of the butter in a medium-size saucepan over medium heat. Add the shallots, stir, and cook until they are translucent, about 8 minutes. Stir in the wine, and bring it to a boil. Boil until the liquid is reduced by one half,

about 6 minutes. Then stir in the cream and the pepper purée. Bring the sauce to a gentle boil and reduce by one third, about 8 minutes. Season with salt and pepper and set aside.

6. Heat the olive oil with the remaining 4 teaspoons of butter, and brush over the halibut. Sprinkle the halibut on all sides with the cayenne pepper. Place the oiled grill rack 3 inches above the coals, set the halibut skin side down on the rack, and cover the halibut. Cook until the fish is nearly opaque through, which should take 18 to 20 minutes for a piece that is about 2 inches thick. To check, insert the blade of a sharp knife into the fish and gently pull back. If the flesh is nearly opaque, it can be taken from the grill; it will continue to cook with the residual heat. Let the fish sit uncovered for 5 minutes before serving.

7. Add the shrimp, with any juices, to the sauce. Place it over medium heat and heat just until the shrimp are hot through. Adjust the seasoning.

8. Mince the chives and parsley leaves together. Divide the halibut among four warmed dinner plates. Drizzle some of the sauce over part of the halibut on each plate, and make a pool of the sauce around the fish. Garnish with the herbs, and serve immediately.

8 SERVINGS

Grilled Potatoes

These are the grilled potatoes Jerry Erickson served the night I visited him and his wife, Patti, for an unforgettable halibut meal. The secret to great grilled potatoes, as I learned watching Jerry, is to precook and marinate them, then set them at the edge of the fire where they gently turn golden. I like to toss mine quickly in the remaining marinade just before serving, while they're still hot from the grill.

¼ cup fresh rosemary leaves, or 1½ tablespoons
   dried
¼ cup olive oil
2 cloves garlic, diced

Salt and freshly ground black pepper to taste
3 cups water
2 pounds new potatoes, scrubbed

1. Mince the fresh rosemary (if you are using dried rosemary crush it in your fingers). In a large bowl whisk together the oil, garlic, rosemary, and a generous amount of salt and pepper. Set aside.

2. Bring the water to a boil in a vegetable steamer, and steam the potatoes until they are just cooked through, 15 minutes. Remove from the heat, and when they are cool enough to handle, cut them in half and add them to the marinade. Toss gently, and set aside for at least 1 hour. Toss them occasionally so they marinate evenly. (The potatoes may be prepared up to this point the night before serving.) Cover and set them in a cool spot. It isn't necessary to refrigerate them.

3. Place the potatoes around the edge of the oiled grill, cut side down, and cook until they are golden and hot through, 5 to 10 minutes depending on the heat of the fire. Watch them carefully if the fire is hot, because they burn quickly.

8 SERVINGS

Summer Apple-Rhubarb Crunch

The Ericksons have a Yellow Transparent apple tree in their yard which yields fragile, tart, crisp, and juicy fruit in July. The apples are wonderful for cooking, and they give this crunch a real summer tang. In the Northwest's mild maritime climate, rhubarb is still abundant in midsummer, and it makes a wonderful combination with the apples. If you don't have rhubarb, try any berry, or just use a variety of apples.

½ cup rolled oats
½ cup plus 2 tablespoons sifted unbleached all-purpose flour
1 cup (lightly packed) dark brown sugar
½ teaspoon freshly grated nutmeg
8 tablespoons (1 stick) unsalted butter, chilled and cut into 8 pieces
¼ cup granulated sugar

½ teaspoon ground cinnamon
2 cups diced rhubarb
2 pounds tart apples, such as Pippins, Winesaps, Yellow Transparents, or Granny Smiths, peeled, cored, and cut into eighths (about 5 cups)

1. Preheat the oven to 350°F.

2. Place the oats, ½ cup of the flour, the brown sugar, and the nutmeg in a food processor, and process briefly to blend the mixture. Add the butter and process with short pulses until the ingredients are mixed. Be careful not to overmix—you want to maintain the texture of the oats. The mixture will be somewhat dusty looking.

3. In a small bowl, mix the remaining 2 tablespoons flour with the granulated sugar and the cinnamon. Place all the fruit in a large bowl, add the flour mixture, and toss until well mixed.

4. Place the fruit mixture in a non-reactive (glass or earthenware) 12½ × 8½-inch baking dish. Cover it evenly with the oat topping, patting it gently into place. Bake in the center of the oven until the topping is golden and crisp and the fruit is bubbling, about 1 hour.

5. Remove the dish from the oven and let it cool to room temperature before serving.

8 SERVINGS

North Carolina Flounder Fry

A LOCAL CUSTOM EASY TO ADOPT

Every fall and winter, gorgeous fat flounder are pulled from the inlets and sounds of North Carolina, and as fast as they're brought in, they're snapped up by hungry fans eager for a "flounder fry."

"Flounder fries are as common as goin' to church around here," said my cousin, Pat Reid, a native Northwesterner who has lived in North Carolina for forty-five years and has adapted to its ways.

"We always did 'em, Pete and I," she said, referring to her husband, who is a successful hog farmer in Elizabeth City. "We'd do 'em for our family once a week, and it seemed like every church in the neighborhood was puttin' one on, too."

The churches, the schools, and everyone else gets into the flounder fry act to raise money, yet as common as they are, each is a big success. "We just love fried flounder around here," Pat said with a shrug. "It's in the genes I guess."

The Reids still get together over fried flounder, but now Pam Sanders and her husband, J.D.—Pat and Pete's daughter and son-in-law—do the cooking.

PASSING THE BATON

Pam begins preparing the salads and dessert the night before, under the watchful eyes of her mother. She usually takes all the ingredients up to her mother and dad's house, which is just a few miles from her own, and makes everything there so that if she has a question along the way, her mother can quickly answer it. It also gives Pat and Pam a chance to spend some time together, a rarity now that Pam and J.D. are in the process of taking over the hog farm.

It was late fall when we visited, and a wicked wind was whipping around the house. Pam and J.D. were putting on a fish fry for Pam's extended family, which included nine people of all ages. She had potatoes, hush puppies, cole slaw, and fresh flounder at the ready, as well as a pound of shrimp she and J.D. had caught and frozen earlier in the year.

J.D. built his own fish fryer, a heavy-duty rectangular steel box heated with propane, and he hauls it around to friends and neighbors when they need to borrow it, or to borrow his services as a cook. J.D. has developed a finely honed sense of when the fish is done to perfection.

On this blustery afternoon, J.D. had set up the fryer in the shelter of the garage, and we all migrated there, drawn by the aroma. First J.D. fried the shrimp, which we ate like popcorn. Then he slid the flounder fillets into the oil, which let off a low, rumbling sound. Lost in conversation, we didn't look up until he cried, "The first one's ready!" and transferred a steaming crisp fillet to several thicknesses of waiting brown paper bags. I had the honor of tasting it, and indeed it was luscious, to the point that it disappeared as everyone took a sample.

Finally we sat down to the salads, the tomatoes, the hush puppies, and mounds of fried flounder. The iced tea flowed freely, the talk swirled around our family memories and my grandmother's recipes, and the sun sank low in the sky. It was a fish fry to remember, even for northerners with no southern "flounder love" in their genes.

J.D.'s Fried North Carolina Flounder

These thick, mild, succulent flounder fillets emerge crisp and savory from the hot oil. J.D.'s secrets are to buy firm, high-quality flounder, to use a crisp cornmeal batter, to keep the oil at a constant 375°F, and to drain the fish on an unprinted brown paper bag after frying, so it doesn't steam the way it would if drained on paper towels.

Though J.D. is king of the fryer, Pam is queen of everything else, down to dredging the fillets. Her trick for making the batter stick is to dip each fillet in water, then in the cornmeal batter. It works like a charm, so put a big bowl of cold water next to your cornmeal and follow her example. If you can't get good, meaty flounder, try any good-quality white fillet, such as haddock, petrale sole, or lingcod, and adjust the cooking time according to the thickness of the fillet.

A note here: Cornmeal in the South is finer than that in other parts of the country and gives a slightly different result. With what I call "northern" yellow cornmeal, the result is a crunchy, nutty batter that contrasts with the fish. Lighter, finer southern cornmeal gives a crisper, more delicate coating. Both are delicious.

4 pounds flounder fillets, cut into 4-ounce pieces
Mild vegetable oil, such as safflower, for deep-
    frying
3 cups yellow cornmeal
¾ teaspoon cayenne pepper

Salt and freshly ground black pepper
    to taste

1. Rinse the fillets with cold water, and pat them dry. Refrigerate loosely wrapped in waxed paper until ready to cook.

2. Fill a large heavy-duty saucepan, Dutch oven, or deep-fryer with 4 inches of vegetable oil, and heat the oil to 375°F over medium-high heat.

3. On a large piece of waxed paper, combine the cornmeal, cayenne, and a generous amount of salt and pepper.

4. Fill a large bowl with cold water. Dip each fillet first into the water, let it drain briefly over the bowl, and then dredge it in the cornmeal. Gently pat the cornmeal onto the fillet on both sides. Place the fillets on a plate or a metal rack and let them sit for at least 10 minutes. Then dredge them a second time with the cornmeal. Refrigerate the fish loosely covered with waxed paper until the oil is ready to cook it.

5. Fry up to 3 pieces of fish at a time, until they are golden and cooked through. The time will vary greatly depending on the thickness of the fillet. If it is under ½ inch, it will take 3 to 4 minutes. If it is ½ inch thick, it will take about 6 minutes. To test for doneness, remove the fillet and using a sharp-bladed knife, look into the center of the flesh. If it breaks apart easily and is opaque through, the fish is cooked. If it is still very elastic and translucent, it needs additional frying.

6. Using tongs, remove the fish from the oil and hold it briefly over the pan so that any excess oil drips off. To drain the fish further, place the pieces on a baking sheet lined with unprinted brown paper bags. This will absorb the oil without steaming the fish, leaving it very crisp. Serve immediately.

8 SERVINGS

Seashell Macaroni Salad

When Pat organized and prepared the family flounder fries, she nearly always made this salad to go alongside. When I tasted it I stopped short, because there was something very familiar about it. I tasted again, looked at Pat, and asked where she'd gotten the recipe. Sure enough, it was from my grandmother's collection.

I remember my grandmother making this salad when we would visit her in Oregon during the summer. She loaded it with tiny Oregon shrimp, and even then I loved the herbs and the toothsome pasta (we called them noodles in those days). I'm usually not wild about pasta salads, but I still think there's nothing quite like this one for its combination of colors and its bright, refreshing flavor. It gets better with age, too, so make it the night before you plan to serve it.

Instead of mixing in the scallions, you may want to shower them over the salad as a garnish. And instead of using tiny Oregon shrimp the way my grandmother did, I use the best medium-size shrimp I can find and poach them in a lightly seasoned broth. They are delicious.

SHRIMP
12 ounces medium shrimp, in the shell
2 cups water
1 small onion, cut into ¼-inch-thick rounds
1 rib celery, cut into 1-inch pieces
1 small carrot, cut into 1-inch pieces
1 bay leaf
5 peppercorns

SALAD
2 tablespoons best-quality red wine vinegar
1 clove garlic, minced

Salt and freshly ground black pepper to taste
⅓ cup extra-virgin olive oil
2 tablespoons water
1½ teaspoons dry mustard
¾ cup best-quality mayonnaise
1 pound seashell pasta
1 cup Italian (flat-leaf) parsley leaves
2 cups diced celery (about 6 ribs)
1 cup thinly sliced scallions (about 5 medium scallions)
¼ cup drained capers
⅓ cup pimiento-stuffed green olives, sliced

1. Rinse the shrimp in cold water, and pat them dry. Refrigerate loosely wrapped in waxed paper until ready to cook.

2. Combine the water, vegetables, bay leaf, and peppercorns in a medium-size saucepan. Cover and bring to a boil over medium-high heat, and cook until the onion softens, about 20 minutes. Reduce the heat to medium-low, add the shrimp, and simmer, uncovered, just until the shrimp begin to turn pink, about 5 minutes. Remove the pan from the heat and let the shrimp infuse, still covered, for an additional 10 minutes. Drain, discarding the vegetables and herbs. Peel the shrimp, and cut them into ½-inch pieces. Cover and refrigerate.

3. Prepare the salad: In a large bowl, whisk together the vinegar, garlic, and salt and

pepper; then whisk in the olive oil as you add it in a fine stream. In a small bowl, whisk the water into the dry mustard until smooth; then whisk in the mayonnaise. Set aside the vinaigrette and the mayonnaise mixture.

4. Cook the pasta in a large kettle of salted water (about 1 tablespoon salt to 1 gallon water) until it is al dente (tender but still firm to the bite). Drain the pasta thoroughly and add it to the vinaigrette. Toss until the shells are well coated with dressing, and let cool to room temperature.

5. Mince the parsley. Add it, along with the remaining ingredients and the shrimp, to the pasta. Toss well. Pour the mayonnaise mixture over the salad, and toss until all the ingredients are thoroughly combined. Cover and refrigerate overnight.

6. Remove the salad from the refrigerator at least 30 minutes before serving. Adjust the seasoning, and serve.

1O TO 12 SERVINGS

Tomato Bread Pudding

This tomato pudding is a recent addition to the Reid family fish fry. With its sweet and tart spiciness it acts like a chutney, balancing the rest of the meal.

The pudding can be cooked the night before and then be served at room temperature. It is also delicious eaten hot the day it is made, after it has had a chance to cool a bit. Nothing is hotter than tomatoes straight from the oven—the sizzling juices will scald tender mouths—so beware before digging in.

1 can (28 ounces) plum tomatoes, with juices
1 cup chicken stock, fish stock (page 119, through
   Step 2), or water
½ cup (packed) dark brown sugar
¾ teaspoon ground cinnamon
1 teaspoon dry mustard

¼ teaspoon ground allspice
Salt and freshly ground black pepper to taste
2 tablespoons unsalted butter, melted
6 slices best-quality white bread, cut into
   ½-inch cubes

1. Preheat the oven to 375°F.

2. In a medium-size saucepan combine the tomatoes with their juices, crushing them with your fingers as you place them in the pan, with the stock, brown sugar, cinnamon, mustard, allspice, and salt and pepper. Bring to a boil over medium-high heat. Then reduce the heat to medium and cook until the mixture has thickened and the sugar has dissolved, 10 to 15 minutes. Adjust the seasoning.

3. Brush the inside of an 11 × 7-inch baking dish with some of the melted butter. Arrange the bread cubes in the dish in an even layer, and drizzle with the remaining butter.

4. Pour the tomato mixture over the bread, and gently stir it so the tomato evenly permeates the bread. Place the dish in the center of the oven and bake until the pudding is golden and firm, about 1 hour.

5. Remove the baking dish from the oven. Let the pudding cool for about 10 minutes and then serve, or let it cool completely and refrigerate it, covered, overnight (Bring it to room temperature before serving.)

8 SERVINGS

Pat's Lemon Bars

This is an ideal dessert after any fish meal, but Pat especially likes to serve these after a flounder fry. They are light and luscious and very lemony, and taste best the day they are made.

PASTRY

8 tablespoons (1 stick) unsalted butter,
    at room temperature
¼ cup confectioners' sugar
1 cup unbleached all-purpose flour
Pinch of salt

FILLING

¼ cup unbleached all-purpose flour
½ teaspoon baking powder
Pinch of salt
4 large eggs
1½ cups granulated sugar
Minced zest of 2 lemons
6 tablespoons freshly squeezed lemon juice

1. Preheat the oven to 350°F.

2. Prepare the pastry: In a food processor, combine the butter and confectioners' sugar and mix until smooth. Add the flour and the salt, and process until combined. The mixture will be crumbly.

3. Evenly press the dough into the bottom of a 9-inch square baking pan, and bake it in the center of the oven until the edges are golden and the center has puffed slightly, 15 minutes. Remove from the oven and let cool on a wire rack.

4. Meanwhile, prepare the filling: Sift the flour, baking powder, and salt together onto a piece of waxed paper. In a large mixing bowl, whisk the eggs and the sugar until pale yellow and foamy. Add the zest and the lemon juice, then add the flour mixture, and continue whisking until all the ingredients are thoroughly combined.

5. Pour the lemon mixture onto the pastry, and bake in the center of the oven until golden and puffed, 25 minutes. Remove the pan from the oven and let it cool thoroughly on a wire rack. Cut into 1½ × 3-inch bars.

18 BARS

The Tylers of Smith Island

HARBORSIDE
FAMILY REUNION

Every August, when the heat lays like a blanket over Smith Island, in Maryland, Eloise Tyler takes a break from cooking in her restaurant, the Harborside. Instead of hanging up her apron, however, she keeps it on to cook up a huge feast for her family. August is a banner month for Eloise, a lively, robust woman in her fifties, for Maude Whitelock, her eightysomething-year-old mother, and for the rest of the Tyler clan. It's one of two times a year that they get to see each other. And when the Tylers assemble, they celebrate in the finest of ways, with a huge meal.

At a Tyler family reunion you won't find hamburgers and hot dogs. Instead, Eloise prepares a spread that includes clam fritters, crab balls, and sautéed soft-shell crab. Marilyn, Eloise's daughter, makes pies—fruit pies, meringue pies, custard pies—and Maude chips in to prepare vegetable dishes, like slow-cooked greens and stewed tomatoes.

Tables are set up outside under shade trees and laden with dishes. The meal is the centerpiece on the day when the Tylers strengthen their family ties through the enjoyment of familiar foods and faces.

LIKE REUNION, LIKE RESTAURANT

Many of the dishes served at Tyler family reunions, family favorites all, are served at the Harborside, too. And like the reunions, they come to the table family-style so each guest can have his or her fill.

Though Eloise cooks for up to one hundred diners a day, seven days a week most of the year, she never tires of the cooking or the food. She somehow avoids panic and stress—her attention is focused, her attitude gentle and sunny.

The boxy, light restaurant kitchen looks like a large home kitchen. Part of its atmosphere comes from three comfy, old, over-stuffed armchairs strategically placed outside the traffic pattern where Eloise, Maude, or Marilyn sink if they need a break. The rest of it comes from the banter in the kitchen, the easy way the three women work together, the friendliness between them and the waitstaff who charge in and out from the dining room.

With her gently curled hair, careful make-up, and leggings and t-shirt ensemble, Eloise looks more like she should be going out to lunch than cooking it. The day we visited she talked as she worked about how she became proprietor of this thriving enterprise.

It was an accident, really. With her two sons and daughter grown, she went to work for a friend who had opened a restaurant on the north side of the island. She enjoyed it and moved around to different

kitchens, including that of Frances Kitching, former doyenne of Smith Island cooking.

"Mrs. Kitching taught me a lot about cooking," Eloise said as she prepared crab balls. "And I use my mother's and grandmother's recipes, too. We're all real proud of our cooking here, and we share a lot."

After she spent several years in restaurant kitchens, her children convinced Eloise to open one of her own. "We owned this land, and they said 'Why not just build a restaurant,'" she reminisced, shaking her head. "We built this little place, and my son operates the *Island Princess* that brings tourists to the island, so it works out pretty good."

Smith Islanders make their living from the sea, and Eloise is proud to use what they harvest. "They're all watermen out here," Eloise says. "And I get the best crab that anyone has ever seen. You can't get it better anywhere else."

She's equally proud of the local clams, which she uses in tender little fritters, and the Smith Island oysters. "They've gotten too expensive to serve at my restaurant," she said, "but I just made an oyster pie this week at home, and we'll have another one for Christmas."

Dessert pies are another specialty at the Harborside, and they're all made by Marilyn. "She makes all kinds of pies, like coconut and apple crunch and pumpkin, and they're all just great," her mother said.

Marilyn was whisking the egg whites for the pumpkin meringue pie as we spoke. "You can tell it's the end of the season," Eloise remarked. "We don't mess with meringue during the summer because it's too tedious. We wait till things slow down."

CELEBRATING CHRISTMAS

When the restaurant closes for the winter, Eloise takes a break, cleans her house, and gets into a winter routine of community service and island administration. She finds plenty of time to cook, too.

"I love to have people come over and eat," she said. "And I never have done the same menu."

Eloise and Maude begin planning the family's Christmas feast, another Tyler family get-together, in late October. "My mother cooks Christmas dinner for all twenty-one of us," Eloise explained. It's usually turkey or roast beef with stuffing and all the fixings.

"Of course, I make the crab balls and the clam fritters. I don't think we'd really believe it was a meal if we didn't have those," Eloise said. "But mother makes just about everything else, including the oyster pie, which we all do love."

Eloise opens the Harborside in May of each year, right around Mother's Day. If you're in the vicinity, don't miss a visit. The boat leaves Crisfield, Maryland, around noon and again around 4 P.M. There is lodging on the island, or you can make it a day trip, with time for lunch and a stroll around the island.

Eloise's Clam Fritters

These are the lightest, most intensely clam-flavored fritters I've ever eaten, and the secret is the fresh, briny clams.

Eloise Tyler makes these up each day for her restaurant, and she is very particular about their preparation. The batter goes together quickly and it shouldn't be overworked, so the fritters will stay light and tender.

"You've got to have the frying oil hot so the fritters stay light," Eloise said. "And the other thing about these: don't add the baking powder and soda until right before you make them, or it will turn bitter."

Eloise uses fresh cherrystone clams to make her fritters. Shucking them is easy if you use my system, which involves steaming them in either water or white wine *just* until they open and not one second more. Done this way, they aren't cooked and are still full of juice. If you can't find cherrystones, use any clam in the shell. What you are after is 1 full cup of clam meat.

I like to make these just about any time, but they do make a wonderful appetizer before dinner. And they are delicious for breakfast as well.

3 pounds (10 large) cherrystone clams, in the shell, (to yield about 1 cup drained clam meat), scrubbed
Sea salt
⅓ cup cornmeal
½ cup water or dry white wine
Freshly ground black pepper to taste

¾ cup unbleached all-purpose flour
½ teaspoon salt
¼ teaspoon baking soda
¾ teaspoon baking powder
1 large egg
¼ cup mild vegetable oil, such as safflower

1. Purge the clams: Place the clams in a large bowl or bucket of salted water (about 3½ tablespoons sea salt to 1½ gallons water) and stir in the cornmeal. Leave the clams in a cool place for 1 hour. Drain and rinse. Refrigerate until just before using.

2. Place the clams in a large heavy saucepan, add the water, and grind a generous amount of black pepper over them. Cover the pan and bring the water to a boil over medium-high heat. Steam the clams, removing them as they open so they don't cook. Drain the clams, reserving the cooking liquid. Strain the cooking liquid through a cheesecloth lined mesh strainer and set it aside. Remove the clams from their shells, and discard the shells. Coarsely chop the clams.

3. Sift the dry ingredients together onto a piece of waxed paper.

4. In a large bowl, whisk together the egg and ¾ cup of the reserved clam cooking liquid until thoroughly combined. Add the dry ingredients, and whisk just until they are moistened; do not overwork the mixture. Fold in the clams.

5. Heat the oil in a large heavy skillet over medium-high heat. When a wisp of smoke comes off the oil, spoon the batter into the pan, using a medium-size serving spoon. The fritters will run slightly, so leave room between them. Cook until small bubbles appear on the tops of the fritters and the bottoms are golden, about 2 minutes. Quickly flip them, and cook until the other side is golden, 1 minute. Transfer the fritters to a baking sheet lined with unprinted brown paper bags, and drain briefly before serving.

16 FRITTERS; 8 APPETIZER SERVINGS

Harborside Crab Balls

These are Eloise Tyler's famous and fabulous crab balls. What makes them special is, of course, the freshest, sweetest crabmeat you can find. Beyond that it's a matter of quickly combining the ingredients using a light hand so you don't over-mix them. Although you can buy cracker crumbs, I prefer to make my own out of saltines.

2 quarts mild vegetable oil, such as safflower
1 large egg
2 tablespoons best-quality mayonnaise
2 teaspoons Dijon mustard
¼ teaspoon cayenne pepper, or to taste

Salt and freshly ground black pepper to taste
    (optional)
1 pound lump crabmeat, carefully picked over
1 tablespoon diced onion
⅓ cup fine cracker crumbs (about 16 unsalted
    saltines)

1. Fill a heavy saucepan, deep-fat fryer, or Dutch oven with at least 4 inches of the vegetable oil. Preheat the oil to 375°F. Line a baking sheet with unprinted brown paper bags.

2. In a large bowl, whisk together the egg, mayonnaise, mustard, cayenne, and salt and pepper, if desired. Using a wooden spoon, gently mix in the crabmeat and the onion until they are thoroughly coated with the egg mixture. Add the cracker crumbs, and mix lightly until they are incorporated. Taste for seasoning.

3. Use your hands to form slightly heaping tablespoons of the crab mixture into balls. Gently slide them into the hot oil, about 6 at a time, and cook, turning them occasionally, until they are deep gold on the outside, which will take about 4 minutes. Remove them from the oil with a slotted spoon, and place them on the lined baking sheet. Repeat with the remaining crab balls, keeping them warm in the oven until they are all cooked. Serve immediately.

24 CRAB BALLS; 8 APPETIZER SERVINGS

Maude's Oyster Pie

Maude Whitelock, mother of Eloise Tyler and grandmother of Marilyn, acts as the family food consultant and historian. Most of the recipes used at the Harborside Restaurant come from Maude, who in turn got them from her mother.

Maude also prepares meals at home, including the Christmas feast for twenty-plus family members, when the main course is always oyster pie with plenty of side dishes. "She's already got her greens and some of her vegetables done," said Eloise when I spoke with her a couple of weeks before Christmas. "She likes to get them done and freeze them so she isn't rushed at the end. That's what gets her bothered."

Eloise prepares the crab balls and clam fritters, but the oyster pie is all her mother's. "We get the oysters from one of the men around here and shuck 'em, and they're just so good," Eloise declared.

The pastry Maude uses is a cross between pie pastry and biscuit dough. She rolls it out, prebakes it, then fills and covers it. "The oyster and milk soak into the bottom, and it makes it real good," Eloise said. "It's like oyster stew in pastry."

It's gorgeous, too, emerging from the oven steaming, golden, and puffed. You may want to serve it in shallow bowls, or at least in a plate with a rim, because, although the pastry does absorb some of the liquid, the filling is still runny. The oysters cook to tender plumpness in this irresistible pie.

PASTRY
1 cup cake flour
1 cup unbleached all-purpose flour
1 teaspoon salt
2 teaspoons baking powder
8 tablespoons (1 stick) unsalted butter, chilled, cut into 8 pieces
⅔ cup milk

EGG WASH
1 large egg
2 teaspoons water

FILLING
36 medium-size shucked oysters, with their liquor, carefully picked over
1 cup milk
Salt and freshly ground black pepper to taste
2 tablespoons unsalted butter, melted

1. Preheat the oven to 425°F.

2. Prepare the pastry: Sift the dry ingredients together into the bowl of a food processor. Add the butter pieces, and process using short pulses until the mixture resembles coarse cornmeal. Transfer the mixture to a mixing bowl and slowly add the milk, stirring with a fork just until the mixture holds together. Handle the dough very little as you don't want it to get tough.

3. Divide the dough in half, and press each half out to form a disk. Loosely cover one disk with a kitchen towel. Roll out the other disk to fit a 10-inch pie plate. Transfer the dough to the pie plate, leaving the edges hanging over the rim. Line the pie shell with parchment paper or aluminum foil, and fill it with pastry weights or dried beans. Place it on a baking sheet and bake it in the center of the oven until the edges begin to turn golden, about 10 minutes. Using a sharp knife, cut off the hanging edges of the pastry, letting them fall to the baking sheet. Remove the scraps of pastry from the sheet and the paper and weights from the pastry, and continue baking until the pastry is golden, another 10 minutes. Remove the pie shell from the oven.

4. Roll out the second disk so it will cover the pie plate.

5. Make the egg wash by whisking together the egg and the water in a small bowl.

6. In a large bowl combine the oysters and the milk, and season with a bit of salt and a generous amount of pepper. Pour the mixture into the baked pie shell, and drizzle the butter over the filling. Paint the edges of the pastry with the egg wash. Lay the dough top over the filling, pressing it gently onto the bottom pastry. Fold any edges back and roll them over, crimping them so they look attractive. Paint the dough top with egg wash, cut 8 slits in it, and place it on a baking sheet. Bake in the center of the oven until the pastry is golden and puffed and steam is coming from the vents, about 40 minutes. Remove from the oven and serve.

8 SERVINGS

South-East Green Beans

This dish combines the recipe for the beans I tasted at the Harborside Restaurant with the one for the beans I was served in Natchez, Mississippi, as part of a southern catfish fry (see Index). Though from completely different parts of the country, the methods are remarkably similar. Both are flavored lightly with pork, both are well salted and seasoned with pepper, and both are fresh and flavorful. Elizabeth Wilson, in Natchez, contributed the brilliant idea of adding the potatoes.

You'll discover a whole new taste in beans when you try this. For the authentic flavor, be sure to season them generously with salt and pepper.

2 *pounds green beans, trimmed and cut into*
   2-inch lengths
2 *ounces salt pork, cut into 2 pieces*
1⅓ *cups water*
Salt and freshly ground black pepper to taste
1½ *pounds waxy potatoes, such as Yukon Gold or*
   Yellow Finn, peeled and cut into eighths

1. Place the beans, salt pork, and water in a large heavy saucepan. Sprinkle with salt and a generous amount of black pepper, cover, and bring to a boil over medium-high heat. Reduce the heat to medium-low and cook until the beans are olive green, about 40 minutes.

2. Stir the potatoes into the beans, sprinkle with additional salt and pepper, and cook, covered, until the potatoes are tender, about 20 minutes. Serve immediately.

8 SERVINGS

Marilyn's Pumpkin Meringue Pie

Eloise Tyler's daughter, Marilyn, makes all the pies served at the Harborside Restaurant. Her repertoire includes at least a dozen varieties, from cherry crumb to apple, so Marilyn makes her choice according to what's fresh at the market.

Just from looking at it, I knew I'd love this pie, with its light combination of spiced squash and delicately flavored meringue. I adapted the recipe slightly when I returned home, but it is true to the fat slices we dug into at the Harborside.

CUSTARD
1 can (16 ounces) pumpkin purée
4 large eggs, separated
¾ cup plus 1 tablespoon sugar
Salt
¾ teaspoon vanilla extract
2 tablespoons unbleached all-purpose flour
½ teaspoon ground cinnamon
½ teaspoon ground ginger

¾ teaspoon freshly grated nutmeg
Minced zest of 1 orange

MERINGUE
1 egg white, at room temperature
Pinch of salt
2 tablespoons sugar
½ teaspoon vanilla extract

1 prebaked 9-inch pie shell (page 125)

1. Preheat the oven to 350°F.

2. In a medium-size bowl, whisk together the pumpkin and the egg yolks until combined. Whisk in the sugar, a pinch of salt, and the vanilla. Then add the flour, the spices, and the orange zest, and whisk until smooth.

3. In another bowl, whisk 2 of the egg whites with a pinch of salt until they form stiff peaks. (Reserve the other egg whites, at room temperature, for the meringue.) Fold the whites into the pumpkin mixture, and then pour the mixture into the prepared pastry shell. Bake until the pumpkin is solid and is just beginning to crack on top, 35 to 40 minutes. Remove from the oven and let cool to room temperature.

4. Prepare the meringue: Combine the 3 egg whites (2 remaining from the custard, plus the 1 additional) and a pinch of salt in a large bowl, and whisk with a mixer until they are white and foamy. Continuing to whisk, add the sugar and the vanilla. Whisk until the egg whites are glossy and form stiff peaks.

5. Preheat the broiler.

6. Spread the meringue over the cooled pie, making sure it reaches the edge of the pastry. Either smooth it out or, using a flexible knife blade, make little peaks all over the top.

7. Place the pie 3 inches below the broiler, and broil just until the meringue is golden, 3 to 5 minutes. Serve warm.

8 SERVINGS

Uncanny Tuna on the Grill

AN ALFRESCO SPREAD
WITH FRIENDS

Coals were heating in the grill when I arrived at Pam and Thor Plancich's house in the lush, tree-filled suburb of Seattle where Thor has just finished construction on their huge, two-story house. He spent years on its planning, and it is custom built from top to bottom. One thing he was sure to include was a wrap-around deck that looks into a wooded glen. Since he spends a lot of time grilling, and they eat outside when possible, Thor wanted to be sure they had both a good view and plenty of privacy.

Thor was on the deck building a fire in the grill, and I walked out to join him. He fishes for tuna from his boat, the Scorpio, in summer and fall, and freezes his catch to enjoy year-round. He was going to grill some tuna for a summertime barbecue and he was preparing the fire carefully, knowing from experience just how large to make it. He wanted it to burn slowly so the fire would be powerful, and so he could easily catch it before it burned past the perfect temperature.

Sitting nearby was a pan-load of tuna chunks marinating in an aromatic mixture of herbs and oil. It was cool enough to keep them outside and Thor had been nursing them most of the afternoon, turning the chunks so they'd evenly absorb the marinade. There was at least an entire fish worth of meat. "I want everyone to eat their fill," Thor said, then added with a grin, "Besides, we make tuna salad with the leftovers so I'm kind of hoping there'll be some. This is nothing like the fish from the can. You wouldn't believe how good it is."

I would believe it. I've enjoyed many seafood meals with Thor and Pam, and the seafood has always been incredible. It is either caught by them or obtained fresh from other fishermen. Once they served a feast of shrimp that Thor had bought right off the boat of an old friend, an Alaska shrimper. Cooked Thor's favorite way, with olive oil and garlic, they were scrumptious.

SEAFOOD AND SLIDE SHOW

There's nothing quite like a Plancich celebration. The guests are varied and include fishermen, Thor's carpentry colleagues, and neighbors. The conversation revolves around fishing tales, which both Thor and Pam tell with style. Pam is an amateur photographer, and a Plancich celebration also includes a short, stunning slide show with her narration. Through her slides, we've visited dozens of bays and shorelines along the West Coast. We've come up against glaciers in Alaska, seen the sun set from Newport, Oregon, and watched Thor wrestle fish onto the boat.

No story they tell is ever the same, and they manage to make fishing seem exciting and relaxing, glossing over the hard work and difficulty, with one exception. Thor loves to tell about the time his engine froze up in port and he had to put off fishing until he had hauled it out of the boat, disassembled it—piece by tiny, oily piece—and finally solved the problem. He makes it sound like one of the more fascinating things he's ever done.

While Thor and Pam prepare for the meal, they welcome any help that comes along. That means rolling out pastry dough, putting the finishing touches on the table, turning the tuna. Today, Thor and Pam gave a tour of their house, a work of art from the graceful, sweeping, handcrafted, staircase that Thor designed and built, to the bathroom with a tub that looked large enough to hold several tuna.

Back out on the deck, with everything but the fish prepared, Pam silently signaled Thor. The fire was right for the fish and with a flourish he placed it on the grill.

Not ten minutes later Thor paraded through the kitchen and into the dining room, heaped platter held high. Everyone cheered, and the tuna feast began.

The Chase

For more than twenty years, Thor and Pam Plancich have fished together during the summers, when the tuna come to swim in warm Northwest waters. Pam, a schoolteacher, exchanges her skirts and blouses for jeans and t-shirts to become first mate. Thor lays down the hammer and saw he wields in winter to take the helm of his converted salmon trawler, the Scorpio.

They range the Pacific Coast, going as far north as Alaska and as far south as southern Oregon, on the hunt for fish. Over the years they've fished for just about everything, but lately they focus on tuna.

They love it because the tuna tests the fisherman's skill, patience, wiliness. The tuna loves to travel at high speed, and it gives no sign of its presence, even when it bites. It grabs the hook so quickly that Pam says she's never seen one do it.

Thor and Pam use tuna jigs, which are double-pronged hooks without barbs that attach to lines running out from the sides of the boat in a V-shape. Each hook is hidden in a rubber, squid-shaped jig that wiggles in the water like a fish in current.

Thor and Pam usually fish twelve lines at once, which range from 12 to 20 fathoms (a fathom is 6 feet) long. Once out, Thor keeps the boat moving about 5 knots an hour, and the lines drag from 6 to 10 fathoms deep.

Thor keeps a keen eye on sonar, radar, and temperature readings. "Ya' try to stay where the water's warm," Thor said. "If ya' see a sudden rise, say from 58 to 60 degrees, you'll usually find fish there."

He tries to outsmart the tuna, and often succeeds, by turning or changing speeds. "They're usually following us," Pam said. "Once you make a change, they'll bite."

They know a fish is hooked because a line becomes taut. "Their first impulse is to dive," Thor said, shaking his head. "They'll give ya' a fight. But that's what's fun."

CAREFUL HANDLING

Once they've wrestled a fish from its plunge, they bring it up by hand or with a winch, and land it carefully in a chute on the side of the boat, so the skin isn't scratched. Thor cuts the gill and the still-pumping heart rids the fish of blood, which ensures high-quality meat. He frees it from the hook and it slides gently down to the deck.

Thor and Pam have respect for the tuna, and for the people who will eventually sit down to eat it. "We try to be real careful when we're handling them so they don't get bruised," Pam said. "Sometimes they're so wild they'll bite each other, but other than that, because of the chute system, they aren't damaged."

The Scorpio is designed so that sea water

constantly washes over the deck, keeping it and the fish clean, and helping cool down the fish.

Once the fish is cool Pam places it in the hold. "Tuna are warm blooded so we can't just put them on ice or they'd melt a hole around themselves," she said.

Within three hours of being taken from the water, though, the tuna are iced inside and out and they stay that way until the Scorpio docks, a once-a-week event.

Unlike many fishermen who don't eat what they catch, Thor and Pam revel in it. Their meals aboard Scorpio are legendary—they bake tuna, and other fish that may come up on their lines, in their tiny oven, and they always have fresh vegetables, thanks to a friend with a garden who meets them when they dock.

Pam brings along bunches of herbs, which she hangs in the galley, and Thor, a self-proclaimed garlic addict, makes sure there is enough on hand for the summer. Though they are a crew of two, that doesn't prevent them from enjoying their catch, or taking the time and trouble to prepare it their favorite ways.

Thor's Favorite Snack

Whether he's fishing or hammering nails, Thor Plancich snacks on one thing. Not peanuts, not candy, not popcorn, but crusty bread doused with red wine vinegar and garlic. He carries a bottle of his own garlic vinegar—bottled red wine vinegar that he stuffs with smashed garlic cloves—wherever he goes, whether it's in his pickup truck or on his boat. "My favorite lunch is bread with vinegar and garlic on it," he says, laughing. "I don't smell too good, maybe, but I don't care because I love it."

Thor figures he picked up his taste for garlic from his Croatian forebears. Wherever it came from he continues it, adding garlic to everything he cooks.

I keep this version of Thor's sauce on hand to serve as an appetizer with fresh warm bread. You can vary it with different types of vinegars, such as balsamic, with different oils, or by adding herbs. Tightly covered, it will keep indefinitely in the refrigerator. Just take it out at least 30 minutes before you plan to serve it, so the oil comes to room temperature. Pour it into a bowl.

5 *large cloves garlic*
1 *teaspoon salt*
¼ *cup olive oil*
½ *cup plus 2 tablespoons best-quality*
    red wine vinegar

Mince the garlic with the salt until it is almost a paste. Transfer it to a medium-size bowl. Whisk in the olive oil, then the vinegar, until they are combined. Serve immediately, or refrigerate until ready to serve.

1 CUP

Grilled Marinated Tuna

*T*hor Plancich, whose background is a blend of Croatian and Norwegian, is an inveterate fisherman and fish cook. As down-to-earth as anyone you'd ever want to meet, he loves nothing more than sharing fishing tales and fish meals with his friends.

When Thor and his wife, Pam, return from a summer on the water, they bring with them several fish for the freezer. Though at one time they fished for a variety of species, they now concentrate on tuna. We look forward to calls from Thor, because we know that if it's an invitation for dinner, tuna will be on the menu. Thor often prepares it this way to feed a crowd.

The marinade is necessary for the albacore tuna that Thor catches, which can be slightly dry. But I always use it on tuna, no matter what the species, because it also protects the meat from the fire and keeps it moist. Don't marinate the tuna for longer than two hours because the lemon juice will dry out and "cook" the fish.

Serve with potatoes—either grilled (see Index) or steamed. This recipe can be increased indefinitely.

4 *pounds fresh tuna, cut into 2-inch-thick steaks,*
    with skin on, if possible
1 *cup Italian (flat-leaf) parsley leaves*
½ *cup fresh tarragon leaves*
2 *tablespoons freshly squeezed lemon juice,*
    with pulp

2 *tablespoons olive oil*
Grated zest of 2 lemons
6 *cloves garlic, minced*
Freshly ground black pepper to taste
Fresh tarragon or curly parsley sprigs,
    for garnish

1. Rinse the tuna with cold water, and pat it dry with paper towels. Refrigerate loosely wrapped in waxed paper or aluminum foil until ready to cook.

2. Mince the parsley and tarragon leaves and set aside.

3. In a small bowl, whisk together the lemon juice and the olive oil. Add the lemon zest, garlic, and minced herbs, and mix well. Place the tuna in a nonreactive dish, and spread the mixture on all sides of the fish, patting it onto the flesh. Season the fish generously on all sides with pepper, cover, and refrigerate for up to 2 hours.

4. Prepare a medium-size fire in a barbecue grill. Using paper towels, thoroughly oil the grill rack with mild vegetable oil. When the coals glow red and are thickly covered with ash, place the rack 3 to 4 inches above the coals, and arrange the fish on the rack. Cover the grill, making sure the vents are open, and cook just until the tuna is golden brown on one side, about 5 minutes. Turn, and continue cooking until the fish is nearly opaque through, another 5 minutes. The time may vary, depending on the size of the fire, so check the tuna occasionally to be sure it isn't overcooking. When it is done, the tuna will be somewhat firm but still juicy. Remove it from the grill and let it sit for about 5 minutes before serving, so the juices retreat back into the flesh.

5. Arrange the tuna on a warm serving platter, garnish with the herb sprigs, and serve immediately.

8 SERVINGS

Pam's Broccoli Salad

Pam usually serves this salad alongside Thor's grilled tuna because it goes so well with fish, and because it can serve a crowd.

It's an odd combination of ingredients but surprisingly addictive with its crunch, its play of salty and sweet, its vibrant flavors that blend so well. I like the crisp textures, and I love eating broccoli barely cooked like this, when it has an assertiveness that it loses in further cooking.

Should there be any left over, it will still be delicious the following day. Bring it to room temperature to soften the bacon.

2 large heads broccoli
Ice water
2 cups water
2 tablespoons olive oil
2 teaspoons plus 2 tablespoons best-quality
    red wine vinegar
Salt and freshly ground black pepper to taste

½ cup raisins
½ cup salted roasted peanuts
4 scallions, trimmed and sliced into
    ⅛-inch-thick rounds
5 ounces slab bacon, rind removed,
    cut into bite-size pieces
2 cloves garlic, minced

1. Separate the florets from both heads of broccoli and cut them into bite-size pieces. Reserve the stems for another use. Fill a large bowl with ice water. Bring the 2 cups water to a boil in the bottom of a vegetable steamer. Place the broccoli florets in the steamer basket, cover, and steam until they are bright green and just tender but still somewhat crisp, about 4 minutes. Immediately plunge the florets into the ice water. When they are cool, drain and pat them dry.

2. In a large bowl whisk together the olive oil, 2 teaspoons vinegar, and salt and pepper. Add the broccoli florets, raisins, peanuts, and scallions to the bowl, and toss until evenly coated with the dressing.

3. Cook the bacon in a medium-size skillet over medium-high heat until it is golden and nearly crisp, about 4 minutes. Add the garlic and cook, stirring frequently, until it begins to turn translucent and slightly golden at the edges, about 1 minute. Pour the remaining 2 tablespoons vinegar into the pan.

(This will produce a great deal of steam. Don't be concerned, but stand slightly back.) Stir the bacon, scraping any browned bits from the bottom of the pan, and then pour the sauce over the broccoli salad. Toss until all the ingredients are coated with sauce.

4. Adjust the seasoning, adding a generous amount of pepper, and serve immediately.

8 SERVINGS

Thora's Blackberry Pie

You've already met Thor and Pam Plancich. Now meet Thor's mother, Thora, creator of mouthwatering berry pies. Thor and Pam pick the wild blackberries or raspberries, but it's Thora who does the baking. She always has. Thor brags about her cooking, and it is undoubtedly her influence that has given him his own good hand in the kitchen.

The blackberry bushes are so prolific in their area that Pam always picks plenty to freeze so she can get Thora to make a pie at the drop of a hat.

This is the traditional post grilled-tuna dessert in the Plancich household, and the one we enjoyed with them. You may do as Pam requests of Thora and omit the sugar. Or do as Thora does and make two pies, one for Pam and one for people who want their pie a little sweeter.

If you can't find blackberries, use whatever berries are available. (If they're frozen, don't thaw them.)

Thora's Pastry Dough (recipe follows)
½ cup sugar, or more to taste (optional)
2 tablespoons unbleached all-purpose flour
5 cups blackberries
1 tablespoon milk

1. Preheat the oven to 400°F.

2. Roll out 1 of the pastry dough disks on a lightly floured surface to form an 11-inch round. Ease it into a 9-inch pie plate. Roll out the second disk to form an 11-inch round, and set it aside.

3. Mix the sugar and the flour in a small bowl. Spread a light layer of this mixture over the bottom of the pie shell, and then spoon in half the berries. Sprinkle the remaining sugar-flour mixture over them, and then add the rest of the berries. (If omitting the sugar, sprinkle the berries with the flour.)

4. Use a pastry brush to paint the edges of the bottom dough with some of the milk, and place the dough top over the pie. Trim the edges so they extend about ¼ inch beyond the rim of the plate. Fold the bottom dough up and over the dough top pressing the edges together gently. Crimp the edges, and brush the dough top lightly but thoroughly with the remaining milk. Make at least 8 small slits in the dough top to allow steam to escape.

5. Bake the pie in the bottom third of the oven until the crust is golden and the berries are bubbling up through the slits, about 50 minutes.

6. Remove the pie from the oven, and let it cool slightly before serving.

8 SERVINGS

Thora's Pastry Dough

Thor and Pam Plancich live and die by Thora's pie crust, and I'd heard about it for years before I tried it. I admit to being skeptical—I love butter in my pie pastry, and have always thought nothing else would do. This is made with oil instead, "for health," says Thora, who in her seventies has the energy of a woman half her age. Also, it doesn't need chilling, so it can be rolled out immediately. I was amazed at the flakiness of the pastry. It's perfect if you can't have butter.

2 cups unbleached all-purpose flour
½ teaspoon salt
½ cup mild vegetable oil, such as safflower
¼ cup cold water

1. Place the flour and the salt in a large mixing bowl, and blend well.

2. In a small bowl, whisk the oil and water together until the mixture is frothy. Make a well in the flour and add the oil mixture, blending quickly with a fork. When the dough begins to come together, divide it in half and press each piece out to form a disk about 5 inches across. Either wrap the dough in waxed paper and refrigerate it, or use it immediately.

PASTRY DOUGH FOR ONE
9- OR 10-INCH DOUBLE-CRUST PIE

Give Me Bull
With Those Oysters

MARYLAND BEEF AND OYSTER ROAST

We don't normally associate oysters with politics, but there was a time when oyster scalds were held at all the polling places in Calvert county, Maryland. Citizens would cast their votes and then chase them with a bag of scalded oysters and a draft of cool beer.

"Scalded" means "steamed" in Calvert and St. Mary's counties, and it's still a common way to prepare oysters there. They are put in a net bag, lowered into boiling water, and when they "open their mouths", they're ready to eat, dipped in a little melted butter.

From the polling places, scalded oysters caught on as a public event and local groups elaborated on the custom for fund-raising projects. "We'd have 'em fried, stewed, scalded, grilled, any way we could think of," said Dan Barret, a member of the Solomon's Island Yacht Club. "People still do it all the time."

To attract people from "town," who neither lived in oyster country nor appreciated the fine points of the bivalve, the groups began grilling beef so everyone would have something to eat. The events came to be known as "bull and oyster roasts."

"It really began with the Lion's Club, which started having a bull roast sometime in the sixties," explained Al Kersey, another yacht club member. "They started off cooking sirloin butts in long cinderblock pits. They'd put apples on the grill with it, and baste it with water, vinegar, salt and pepper and dry mustard, and turn the pieces with an old pitchfork. I always hoped that old pitchfork was clean."

Along with the oysters and beef came baked beans, potato salad and fresh tomatoes, tossed salad, and crab soup. "And you can't forget the draft beer, which was spread around pretty loosely," Al said.

Al helped cook at the yacht club and he was an expert with the beef. He didn't like the traditional basting sauce, so he brushed his beef instead with olive oil, salt, pepper, and cayenne. "And the real secret," he says, "is to maintain the meat temperature at about 125°F, a good medium."

"It was always a lot of fun," he said. "People would come and spend all day—it was really that kind of affair."

BULLISH ON OYSTERS

Oysters are still served every way imaginable at county fairs and other public events in Maryland, though the public bull and oyster roast is a thing of the past.

What began as a way to satisfy everyone turns out to be a felicitous combination. Both beef and oysters are gutsy in their own way, and the combination is sublime. A simple way to prepare them, and one that Al counsels, is to put the beef and the oysters on the grill at the same time. "Make sure you've got the cup of the oyster down so that when it opens, the juices don't all run out," he said. "Then you invite all your friends over and have a big party. That's the only way to do Bull and Oysters."

Calvert County Oyster Stew

This simple stew is always served at a bull and oyster roast, and I think it is a must any time there are oysters in the house. I love it as an appetizer, or as a meal. Make it for two or for fifty—it takes about five minutes to put together. And don't be tempted to garnish the stew—it needs nothing else at all.

48 oysters, in the shell, scrubbed, or good-quality
jarred
8 cups milk
12 tablespoons (1½ sticks) unsalted butter,
cut into pieces

1. If the oysters are in the shell, shuck them, reserving their liquor. If they are jarred, do not drain them.

2. Place the milk and the butter in a large heavy saucepan over medium heat, and heat until the milk is steaming, being very careful not to let it boil. Whisk until the butter has melted thoroughly.

3. As the milk heats, place the oysters and their liquor in a small heavy saucepan over medium heat, and cook just until the oysters' edges curl and they and their liquor are hot, 1 to 2 minutes.

4. Pour the oysters and their liquor into the milk mixture, stir, and serve immediately.

8 SERVINGS

Bull and Oysters

Beef and oysters is an inspired combination, and when I eat it I like to drizzle the beef with oyster liquor. Somehow it adds just the right touch atop the peppery seasoning. This is Al Kersey's recipe for the "bull"; it gives the tender meat a little kick.

When I tested this recipe on the outdoor barbecue at home, the thermometer outside read −13°F. It didn't feel so cold as I arranged newspapers, kindling, and charcoal in a pile, then lit it all with a match. When I walked inside, however, the tea towel hanging from my apron, which had been damp when I walked outside, was frozen stiff.

After a few false starts, the fire blazed. When the coals were ready, I took the steaks and oysters outside and set them on the grill, quickly covered them, opened the vents, and ran back in. A couple more trips to check on things, and dinner was ready. I was chilled to the bone by this time, just from running in and out.

When we sat down I immediately ate an oyster hot from the shell, and never has anything tasted so warming, so revivifying. A neighbor stopped by as we were savoring our Bull and Oysters, and he said, "I had the strangest sensation when I passed your grill on the porch. It felt warm."

We just smiled at him until he saw what was on our plates "Are you crazy? It's thirteen below out there!" he thundered.

I just kept smiling and eating my oysters hot from the shell.

---

8 boneless sirloin butt steaks, 6 to 8 ounces each
½ cup extra-virgin olive oil
Heaping ½ teaspoon cayenne pepper, or to taste
1 tablespoon freshly ground black pepper,
    or to taste
2 teaspoons salt, or to taste
48 oysters, in the shell, scrubbed

1. Rinse the steaks and pat them dry. Rub them all over with the olive oil. Mix the peppers and salt in a small bowl, and sprinkle the mixture lightly all over the steaks. Marinate the steaks at room temperature, covered, for at least 2 hours, or refrigerated, covered, for up to 24 hours.

2. Build a good-size fire in a barbecue grill. Thoroughly oil the grill rack, using a paper towel dipped in vegetable oil. When the coals are glowing red and a few flames are still licking at them, place the rack about 4 inches above the coals. Place the steaks on the rack, and arrange the oysters around the edge of the grill, with the cups (rounded parts) of their shells downward.

3. Cover the grill, leaving the vents open, and cook until the oysters open, about 4 minutes. Turn the steaks and cook until they are done to your liking. For medium-rare, this will be approximately 3 more minutes. If you plan to cook the steaks longer, remove the oysters and keep them warm. Transfer the steaks to a large warmed serving platter, surround them with the oysters, and serve.

4. The way to eat Bull and Oysters is to open an oyster, slip it down your throat, and pour the juices over the steak. Chase it with a bite of steak, then another oyster, then a bite of steak . . . until your plate is clean. (First make sure the oysters aren't so hot that they'll scald you.)

8 TO 10 SERVINGS

Real American Potato Salad

Nothing could be simpler than this moist, satisfying potato salad created by William Taylor, who calls himself the "American Dinner Designer" because he caters traditional American dishes in Hollywood, Maryland. William researches historic regional recipes, and this is one he uses all year round. I borrowed it from him to serve along with Bull and Oysters, also a Maryland specialty.

You may think there are too many eggs here, but try it—the results are delicious.

William Taylor is very firm about making this salad the night before you plan to serve it, and he is absolutely right. It improves and mellows with age. Nonetheless, we loved it hot off the press, too.

This is an oniony potato salad. If it is too strong for you, reduce the amount of onion to your taste.

3 pounds waxy potatoes, such as Yukon Gold
1 tablespoon kosher (coarse) salt
12 large eggs, hard-cooked
1 cup best-quality or homemade mayonnaise
1 cup (packed) Italian (flat-leaf) parsley leaves

2 cups finely diced celery (about 3 large ribs)
2 cups finely diced onion
Salt and freshly ground white or black pepper to taste
Cayenne pepper to taste

96

1. Place the potatoes in a large kettle, and add enough water to cover them by 2 inches. Add the kosher salt, cover the kettle, and bring to a boil over high heat. Cook until the potatoes are just done, with no crispness left in the center, about 20 minutes. Drain. When they are cool enough to handle, peel them and cut them into bite-size pieces.

2. Cut the eggs lengthwise into quarters, then cut each quarter crosswise in half.

3. In a large bowl combine the mayonnaise, parsley, celery, and onions. Season liberally with salt, pepper, and cayenne. Add the potatoes, and combine gently using a rubber spatula. Then add the eggs and mix gently. Check for seasoning, and adjust. Keep in mind that the flavor of the cayenne pepper will emerge over time.

4. Cover and refrigerate for at least 8 hours before serving. Then adjust the seasoning, mix gently, transfer to a serving bowl or platter, and serve.

8 TO 10 SERVINGS

Smoky Baked Beans

These are my interpretation of the baked beans traditionally served along with Bull and Oysters. They have a sweet smokiness and a little zip from the cayenne, but overall they're very pure and simple-tasting.

These beans certainly couldn't be easier to prepare, though they merit checking every hour while they bake because beans absorb water at very different rates, depending on their age. If they appear dry on top, give them a stir, and if they still seem dry, add more liquid, 2 cups at a time. Be sure to adjust the seasoning as they cook.

1 pound dried pink or navy beans
1 bay leaf
10 peppercorns
3 ounces slab bacon, rind removed
1 tablespoon unsalted butter

1 tablespoon olive oil
2 medium onions, diced
Salt and freshly ground black pepper to taste
¼ teaspoon cayenne pepper, or to taste
¼ cup (packed) dark brown sugar

1. Place the beans in a large pot, cover them with cold water, and bring to a boil. Remove from the heat and soak for 1 hour. Drain the beans, discarding the liquid.

2. Return the beans to the pot, cover them with fresh cold water, and add the bay leaf and the peppercorns. Cover the pot and bring to a boil. Reduce the heat to medium-low and simmer, partially covered, until the beans are tender but not soft, about 30 minutes. Drain the beans, reserving the cooking liquid.

3. Preheat the oven to 325°F.

4. Cut the bacon into sticks measuring approximately 1 × ¼ × ¼ inch.

5. Heat the butter and oil in a large (3½-quart) heavy flameproof pan or casserole over medium heat. Add the onions and cook, stirring, until they are translucent, about 10 minutes. Add the bacon, and cook just until the fat turns translucent, about 10 minutes. Then add the beans, salt and pepper, cayenne, brown sugar, and 2 cups of the reserved bean cooking liquid. Stir well, cover, and transfer to the oven. Bake until the beans are tender and have absorbed the flavors of the onion, bacon, and brown sugar, about 5 hours; check them every hour to see if they need additional water. If they are dry on top, give them a quick stir and add some water if necessary, and additional seasoning. Cover and continue to cook. The beans are done when they are full of flavor.

8 TO 10 SERVINGS

The Mid-Autumn Bluefish of Des Fitzgerald

A SPUR-OF-THE-MOMENT CELEBRATION

Des Fitzgerald is the owner of Ducktrap River Fish Farm in Belfast, Maine. An inveterate ichthyophile, he charts the seasons by the fish he finds available, reveling especially in anything new or unusual. In the twelve years since he started Ducktrap, Des has smoked just about everything that swims. Some have become well-loved products; some never made it past Ducktrap's own tasting panel.

Smoked bluefish has become a favor-ite, and Des has a standing year-round order for fresh bluefish with wholesalers up and down the East Coast. A stickler for quality, Des wants only the best fish for Ducktrap. The fact that he often brings home a fillet for dinner is a not inconsiderable benefit.

A CALL OUT OF THE BLUE

One chill autumn evening, with nothing before us but a plate of pasta, we got a call. It was Des, inviting us over for a meal of

grilled bluefish. "Let's celebrate," he said. "This fish is beautiful."

We accepted without hesitation, and when we arrived at his home on Megunticook Lake, Lucinda Ziesing, Des's wife, greeted us each with a glass of wine. Lucinda enters into even the smallest events with drama and fancy, and she'd laid the table with a beautiful blue cloth and matching napkins, blue candles in blue-tinged holders, and a most fitting centerpiece. Lying on a silver tray was a bright blue plastic fish, filched from Des's eight-year-old son, Ryan. It lay there regally, surrounded by tiny foil-wrapped chocolate fish.

"It's a bluefish celebration," Lucinda said. "What else could I do?"

Lucinda returned to the kitchen to put the final touches on a huge panful of twice-baked potatoes arranged like soldiers in a row. She turned often to Des for advice, which came in teasing fashion. "I don't know a lot about cooking but I'm a willing student," she said, laughing.

Des ministered to the bluefish, which had been absorbing the flavors of a special marinade for the past 2 hours. "You know I always take the bloodline out of bluefish before I cook it," he said, turning the fillet to show me where the dark strip of meat had been cut out. "I like its flavor, but if there is any heavy-metal concentration in the fish, that's where it will be."

He tasted the marinade, added a jot more wine, and along with my husband, Michael, disappeared out on the deck to prepare a fire in the grill.

Lucinda sprinkled Parmesan cheese on the potatoes, put them back in the oven, and turned to the salad.

"I do know about salad," she said, whipping up an avocado-rich dressing. "Here, you taste it. What do you think—more acid?" She answered her own question as she squeezed more lemon juice into it.

We stepped outside and watched the moonlight bounce off the water. A sharp wind toyed with the fire in the grill, but finally the flames took hold and we all ducked back inside to sit by the fire, nibble on cheese and crackers, and discuss the fine points of fish, grilling, and wood shavings.

IT'S ALL IN THE WOOD SHAVINGS

Des has an endless supply of shavings at his disposal, the snowflake tailings from the wood that is chipped daily at Ducktrap. They give a sweet woodsy flavor to foods, and he's thought of packaging and selling them. "I'll use 'em at home, but what business does a fish smoker have selling wood shavings?" he asked, thinking it over. "Kinda sounds like something that might put me out of business."

Back outside he surveyed the red-hot coals and threw a large handful of the moistened shavings on them, which sent up a roiling column of smoke and steam. He quickly laid the fish on the grill, covered it, opened the vents, and left it to cook for 10 minutes.

When Des brought the grilled fish to the table and set it beneath the flickering candles, it sent up a heavenly aroma. We raised our glasses of lightly chilled Beaujolais to the bluefish, and then enjoyed it as though we'd never seen food before. Des's timing, undoubtedly perfected by years in the smoking business, was impeccable. We ate the fish until it was gone, enthralled by its flavor and tenderness.

Steamed, smoked, and grilled, Des had hit on the ideal method for cooking bluefish. Sitting back, full of food and bathed in moonlight, we planned another bluefish celebration, this one for summertime, when the sleek Maine bluefish run almost literally outside the door.

The Ducktrap Empire

There must have been plenty of talk in Lincolnville, Maine, when flatlander Desmond Fitzgerald started blasting bedrock near the Ducktrap River twelve years ago.

Des was hard at work creating his dream. He had visions of a trout farm, and into the voided bedrock went raceways, which soon ran with pristine water from nearby Pitcher Pond, and fingerling rainbow trout. Within a short time he was selling the trout to local restaurants.

Two years into the farm, which he called Ducktrap River Fish Farm, Des bought a smoker and began to toy with smoking the trout. "I gave them away to friends, and to the restaurants that bought the fresh trout," he said.

He had no way of knowing it then, but those smoked trout were the seeds of a small smoked fish empire. Ducktrap now smokes everything from Maine mussels to Columbia River sturgeon and sells it throughout the country.

Des, whose ruddy freckled skin, blue eyes,
and copper hair are trademark Irish, still seems slightly stunned by his success. "We've just stumbled along," he said slowly, rubbing his eyes. "I sure didn't know anything about business. I've got a degree in biology."

Success didn't come easily. "It was trial and error," he said. "We'd hang the trout by their heads in the smoker, and I can't tell you how many times I opened the kiln and found them in a heap at the bottom because they'd smoked too long and fallen off the line. They were gonzo, shot."

Those heaps of trout, which tasted just fine, led to a smoked trout pâté that is still a steady seller at Ducktrap. "I did learn early that pâté is absolutely necessary if you've got a lot of fish that tastes fine but doesn't look great," Des said.

MASTERING SALMON

Once Des mastered smoked trout, he turned to salmon. In keeping with his general philosophy he chose to smoke the best, troll-caught Alaskan kings.

"I don't even like to think about how many pounds of salmon I destroyed, almost to the point of going out of business," he said. "Then I went to Scotland and visited a bunch of smokehouses." The tricks he picked up there, combined with further experimentation, gave him a smoked salmon he can live with.

"It isn't perfect," Des remarked quickly, making light of the fact that it is often compared favorably with Scottish salmon, considered the world's best, and that it is Ducktrap's best-selling product.

"It's good, but we're still workin' on it. It's such a personal taste, like caviar and wine."

Des wants to use the best at Ducktrap, and experience has taught him that for smoking, farmed Atlantic salmon is more to his liking than its wild Pacific cousin. The farmed salmon is fattier, and it's available every day in uniform shape and size, things he could never count on with wild fish.

After more than ten years in the smoked fish business, Des feels a cautious measure of confidence. "We've pretty much experimented with everything, and I don't see us adding too many new items," he said. "But we did try this catfish the other day." He unwrapped a boneless fillet that once swam in a pond in the Mississippi Delta. The fillets are smoked over mixed fruit-woods, either plain or doused in a fiery red herb-redolent Cajun spice mix.

"We don't even have packaging for these," he said, slowly slicing the Cajun version. "We're not sure about it at all."

But when he popped a piece in his mouth, his eyes lit up. "It's really pretty good, isn't it?" he asked. "Yeah, we're excited about this one."

Autumn Bluefish

This is Des's simple elegant bluefish. The marinade is quite acidic, to balance the fattiness of the fish, and you will find that the mustard is an ideal flavoring. If you can't find bluefish, try this with salmon.

3 pounds bluefish fillets, with skin on

MARINADE
2 tablespoons balsamic vinegar
3 tablespoons coarse-grained mustard, such as Creole
¼ cup extra-virgin olive oil
1 cup dry white wine, such as Sauvignon Blanc
Salt and freshly ground black pepper to taste
1 cup wood chips

1. Rinse the bluefish fillets. Remove the skin by running the blade of a sharp flexible knife between it and the meat. Remove the pinbones from the center of the fillet, by cutting them out. Remove as much as possible of the wide, shallow layer of dark meat on the skin side of the fillet.

2. In a medium-size bowl, whisk together the balsamic vinegar and the mustard until combined. Whisk in the olive oil in a thin stream, then whisk in the wine. Season with salt and pepper.

3. Lay the bluefish fillets in a large non-corrosible dish with sides that are at least 2 inches high. Pour the marinade over the fish, and turn the fillets so they are coated on both sides. Loosely cover with waxed paper and aluminum foil and refrigerate for at least 1 hour, or up to 8 hours.

4. Build a good-size fire in a barbecue grill. Soak the wood chips in 2 cups water. When the coals glow red and a few flames are still licking at them, squeeze the water from the wood chips and add them to the fire. Thoroughly oil the grill rack, using a paper towel dipped in vegetable oil, and place the rack about 4 inches above the coals. Place the bluefish on the rack and cover the grill, leaving the vents open. Cook until the fillets are opaque through, which should take only 8 minutes. (You don't need to turn the fillets.) Remove the fillets from the grill, and serve immediately.

6 SERVINGS

Des and Lucinda's Twice-Baked Potatoes

Like old friends wearing new clothes, these potatoes emerged from the oven at Des and Lucinda's house. I say old friends because twice-baked potatoes are a familiar dish, though the potatoes I remember from my college days were usually laden with Cheddar cheese, butter, and any number of other odd ingredients. These, on the other hand, are light and fluffy, delicately flavored with fresh Parmesan and perfect alongside Des's grilled bluefish.

I don't call for salt here because Parmesan is so salty, but use your own judgment. Also, you will find guests eating more than one, so be prepared with extras!

6 large russet potatoes, scrubbed
¾ cup half-and-half
3 tablespoons unsalted butter, cut into pieces
¾ cup (loosely packed) freshly grated
    Parmesan cheese
Freshly ground black pepper to taste

1. Preheat the oven to 400°F.

2. Place the potatoes on a baking sheet, and poke several holes in them so they won't burst during cooking. Bake on the center rack of the oven until their skins are crisp and the insides are tender through, 45 to 50 minutes. (The baking time will vary depending on the potatoes—the older they are, the longer they take to bake.)

3. Remove the potatoes from the oven, and as soon as they are cool enough to handle, cut each one in half lengthwise and scoop out the interior, leaving the skins and a very thin layer of potato intact. Don't worry if you have minor incidents of tearing the skin; just be as careful as possible.

4. Using a potato masher, a fork, or the regular mixing attachment in a heavy-duty mixer, break up the potato pulp. When it is smooth, gradually add the cream, whisking until evenly incorporated. Add the butter and ½ cup of the cheese, whisk, and season with pepper. The butter and cheese will melt into the potatoes. Gently spoon the filling into the potato skins, mounding it slightly above the edges.

5. Sprinkle the potatoes with the remaining cheese, and bake until they are hot through, about 10 minutes.

6. Preheat the broiler

7. Place the potatoes under the broiler and cook until they are deep golden on top,

6 to 8 minutes. Serve immediately.

6 TO 8 SERVINGS

Lucinda's Salad Dressing

This is Lucinda's standard salad dressing, winter or summer. It is luscious, tart, and redolent with herbs—a nice change from a simple vinaigrette. It is also delicious as a dip with fresh vegetables, and it will keep for a day or so in the refrigerator. Just whisk it to recombine the ingredients before serving.

This recipe makes enough dressing for two large salads. Use a variety of greens including watercress, arugula, escarole, and red-leaf lettuce. Tearing the lettuce into small pieces allows the dressing to fully coat them, and it greatly improves the flavor.

1 tablespoon balsamic vinegar
3 tablespoons freshly squeezed lemon juice, or more to taste

2 teaspoons Dijon mustard
1 tablespoon plain yogurt
¾ cup extra-virgin olive oil
2 cups (loosely packed) fresh basil leaves
⅓ cup (loosely packed) fresh dill leaves
1 clove garlic, minced
1 ripe avocado, pitted and peeled
Salt and freshly ground black pepper to taste

1. In a large bowl whisk together the vinegar, lemon juice, mustard, and yogurt. Slowly add the olive oil in a thin stream, whisking so the mixture emulsifies. Set aside.

2. Place the herbs, garlic, and avocado in a food processor or blender, and process until they are combined but still somewhat chunky. Slowly add the olive oil mixture, processing until combined. There will still be some small chunks in the dressing. Season to taste with salt and pepper.

3. Serve over mixed salad greens or as a dip.

1 TO 1½ CUPS

Rhubarb Pie

There's something about the tartness of rhubarb that is perfect after a seafood dinner. I make this pie often in spring and summer, when rhubarb is at its peak. I also make it during the winter, with the rhubarb I manage to save and freeze. It's a real tonic in any season, and it's perfect with Des' bluefish.

Double-Crust Pastry Dough
(recipe follows)
¼ cup unbleached all-purpose flour
1 cup sugar
Minced zest of 1 orange
Heaping ¼ teaspoon ground mace
1 large egg
1 tablespoon water
8 cups diced rhubarb

1. Roll out 1 of the pastry dough disks to fit a 9- or 10-inch pie plate. Line the plate with it, leaving an inch of dough hanging over the edge. Roll out the second disk, transfer it to a baking sheet, and refrigerate both top and bottom, uncovered, for at least 1 hour.

2. Preheat the oven to 400°F.

3. Mix the flour, sugar, orange zest, and mace together in a small bowl. In another bowl, whisk together the egg and the water for the egg glaze. Set it aside.

4. Sprinkle one fourth of the flour mixture on the bottom of the chilled pie shell. Top with one fourth of the rhubarb, and continue layering the remaining rhubarb and flour mixture. Cover with the dough top. Fold the edges of the bottom dough up and over the dough top, and crimp the edges. Brush the top with the egg

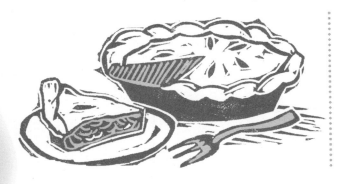

glaze, make at least 8 small slits in it to allow steam to escape, and place the pie plate on a baking sheet.

5. Bake the pie in the bottom third of the oven until the crust is golden and the filling is bubbling through, about 55 minutes. Remove it from the oven and let it cool to room temperature before serving.

6 TO 8 SERVINGS

Double-Crust Pastry Dough

*T*ender and buttery, this is a no-fail pastry dough recipe. Be sure the butter is well chilled and work quickly with the ingredients to avoid toughening the pastry.

2 cups unbleached all-purpose flour
½ teaspoon salt
15 tablespoons unsalted butter, chilled, cut into
    small pieces
3 to 5 tablespoons ice water

1. Place the flour and salt in a food processor and process briefly to mix together.

2. Add the butter to the flour, and using short pulses, process until the mixture ranges in size from peas to coarse cornmeal.

3. Slowly pour in 3 tablespoons of the ice water, and using short pulses, incorporate it into the flour mixture. If the dough is still very dry, add enough of the remaining water so the dough holds together in a loose ball.

4. Transfer the dough to a large piece of waxed paper. Divide it in half and press each half out to form a disk about 5 inches across. Wrap them separately and tightly in waxed paper, and refrigerate for at least 1 hour. (If you make this the night before, wrap the dough in aluminum foil also. Remove it from the refrigerator about 30 minutes before you plan to roll it out.)

PASTRY DOUGH FOR ONE 9-OR 10-INCH
2-CRUST PIE

Swordfish on the Docks

A Freedom Tasting
in America

A huge Soviet ship sat in the harbor of San Pedro, California, its hold empty. The crew was restless. Back home in the Soviet Union, political upheaval was changing the face of their country to such a degree that they had no idea what they would find when they returned.

The crew had strict orders from home not to leave the port. And while there, they were confined to the ship and to the immediate dock where it sat. Their only contact with America was the crew of longshoremen unloading the ship, who made every effort to communicate with them.

The San Pedro longshoremen have a longstanding summertime tradition. When they finish unloading a ship, they celebrate with a barbecue on the dock. After days of working around the Soviet seamen and sympathizing that they sat so close to freedom without being able to explore it, they planned a special celebration. They wanted to give the Soviets a taste of America.

The longshoremen dragged a 55-pound steel barrel that had been cut in half onto the dock and built a fire in it with "dunnage," scraps of hardwood used to wedge cargo in the hold. Each person scrambled to his or her task, assembling the essentials of the barbecue: wine, long loaves of bread from one of the city's numerous Italian bakeries, the fresh, fresh swordfish that was landed just hours before.

"These barbecues are a tradition," said Gretchen Williams, a longshoreman. "They're usually really simple. The only absolutes are the fish and the wine. If you get fancy, you have a salad."

SHARING THE WEALTH, AMERICAN STYLE

Today's celebration qualified as fancy. They enjoyed salad and a big bowl of San Pedro basting sauce, a zesty mixture of parsley, garlic, olive oil, and lemon juice.

The cooks cut the swordfish into inch-thick steaks, and when the fire burned hot and pure, put them on the grill. They slathered the steaks with the sauce, and in twenty minutes a feast for dozens was ready.

The swordfish was succulent, firm, and meaty, the fresh and lively sauce a perfect foil. Americans and Soviets together washed it down with the wine in the warm, clear hours of the afternoon, celebrating until the sun set. Even on the short leash allowed to them while docked in America, the Soviet crew was able to taste something foreign, something called freedom. But they would really learn about that only when they got home.

San Pedro Swordfish

If you live in San Pedro and you're barbecuing fish in the backyard or on the beach, chances are this is the sauce that will drench it. A simple mixture of olive oil, lemon juice, parsley, and lots of garlic, this local favorite enhances any fish—grilled, steamed, or otherwise prepared.

When turning fish on the grill, do so with care. The best method is to slip a long, wide spatula underneath and then smoothly but quickly flip it over.

4 swordfish steaks, 8 to 10 ounces each
½ cup olive oil
6 cloves garlic, minced
⅔ cup minced Italian (flat-leaf) parsley leaves
5 tablespoons freshly squeezed lemon juice

1. Rinse the fish steaks with cold water, and pat them dry. Refrigerate loosely wrapped in waxed paper until ready to cook.

2. Prepare a fire in a barbecue grill. When the coals are red and dusted with ash, spread them out. Lightly oil the grill rack, using a paper towel dipped in vegetable oil, and place it about 4 inches above the coals.

3. In a small bowl, whisk together the olive oil, garlic, parsley, and lemon juice.

4. Place the fish steaks on the grill, and brush them generously with the sauce. Cover the grill, and cook until the fish is opaque through, about 4 minutes per side.

5. Serve the fish immediately, and pass the remaining sauce separately.

4 SERVINGS; ABOUT 1 CUP SAUCE

Focaccia

In San Pedro, delicious fresh focaccia can be purchased from any number of the city's many Italian bakeries. According to Gretchen Williams, focaccia is typically served at a San Pedro swordfish barbecue.

I make my own focaccia, and to accompany swordfish I choose a simple herb topping, but you can top the dough with just about anything you like. Try sprinkling it with lightly cooked onions—or minced garlic, freshly ground black pepper, chile oil, or San Pedro sauce. Use your imagination, and serve this either as an appetizer or alongside the meal.

1 teaspoon active dry yeast
1 cup lukewarm water
3½ cups unbleached all-purpose flour
¼ cup plus 1 tablespoon extra-virgin olive oil

Cornmeal or flour
2 tablespoons fresh rosemary leaves,
    or 2 teaspoons dried
2 teaspoons kosher (coarse) salt or coarse sea salt

1. In a large bowl, dissolve the yeast in the lukewarm water. Add 1 cup of the flour, stir, and then stir in the ¼ cup olive oil. Add the remaining flour 1 cup at a time, stirring after each addition. If the dough gets too stiff to stir, turn it out onto a floured work surface and knead in the remaining flour by hand. Don't add more flour than called for unless the dough is very wet. It should be soft, tender, and somewhat sticky, but it shouldn't stick to your hands.

2. Place the dough in a bowl and cover it with a damp kitchen towel. Leave it in a draft-free spot until it has doubled in bulk, about 1¼ hours.

3. Punch down the dough, cover, and let it rise again until almost doubled in bulk, about 1 hour.

4. Preheat the oven to 400°F. Thoroughly sprinkle 2 baking sheets with cornmeal or flour.

5. Divide the dough into 2 pieces. Roll each out to form a ¼-inch-thick rectangle or round. Using your fingertips, make several indentations in each one. Brush the dough with the remaining tablespoon of olive oil, and sprinkle with the rosemary and the coarse salt. Bake in the center of the oven until the bread is golden and slightly puffed, about 15 minutes. Serve immediately.

2 FOCACCIAS;
ABOUT 8
SERVINGS

Mediterranean Vegetable Salad

As Gretchen Williams says, "If you want to get fancy, add a salad." Inspired by the Italians who've made such a mark on San Pedro, the marinated vegetables in this salad add a Mediterranean flair that goes perfectly with the sunny clime of southern California. Make it wherever you live—it will bring a bit of sun to your meal.

3 tablespoons extra-virgin olive oil
1 tablespoon best-quality red wine vinegar
1 cup Rose's Christmas Salad Vegetables
  (page 179)
Salt and freshly ground black pepper to taste
10 cups torn mixed salad greens, such as escarole,
  arugula, red leaf lettuce, and mâche

Whisk together the olive oil and vinegar in a large bowl. Add the marinated vegetables, toss, and season with salt and pepper. Add the salad greens. Toss thoroughly until all the greens are coated with the dressing and the marinated vegetables are distributed throughout the salad. Serve immediately.

4 TO 6 SERVINGS

The Fish Peddlers

A CANALSIDE
HALLOWEEN PARTY

Chick and Vickie Fuller felt like pioneers fifteen years ago, when they decided to leave their corporate-track jobs and work for themselves. Chick, having grown up on the west coast of Florida with a fishnet in his hand, immediately thought of going into the fish business, and Vickie was game to join him.

The Fullers chose Fort Lauderdale as a place to settle and the budding new community of Sunrise City as the ideal spot for their shop.

"When we built our store, this was all undeveloped," Chick said, sweeping his arm to include what is now a traffic-choked thoroughfare and a mall that holds everything from a high-quality Italian delicatessen to a bakery that looks as if it came straight from New York's Delancey Street.

"I guess we anticipated this growth," he said modestly. "I knew there were some well-known people investing out here, and I knew there was nothing like our store anywhere near, so it seemed logical."

Logical—and unbelievably successful. What Vickie and Chick now preside over is a small ichthyological dynasty. "We struggled for a year and a half and lost every cent we put into this business," Vickie said. "We'd be up at 4 A.M., drive to the west coast to pick up fish, then be back to open our store by 9:00 every morning."

They really didn't know much about fish, but what almost finished them those first few years—and has made them successful today—is what they *did* know. "If it isn't fresh, we won't sell it," Chick said firmly. "I grew up knowing about fresh fish."

"When we started, that meant if it was the end of the day and we still had fish, we either ate it or threw it away," Vickie said, laughing. "We ate a *lot* of fish. Now we know more and understand that certain kinds of fish might keep a day, or even two."

The Fish Peddler was so full of customers on the Saturday afternoon when I was there that it was difficult to look through the crowd at the gleaming fish that lay in the case.

"This isn't busy for us," Chick insisted. "You should see us on a Monday." As I exclaimed over the fish and the remarkable cleanliness and freshness of the store, Chick shrugged. "It's about an 'eight' today. I like to see it at a 'ten,' but we've been out of town for a couple of days." Obviously he and Vickie are perfectionists.

What the Fishmonger Eats

When we stayed with the Fullers at their comfortable canalside home in Fort Lauderdale, we enjoyed some of the finest seafood I've ever eaten. Friends arrived and Vickie shooed all of us out to the deck, where Chick prepared to make the first course. He cooks comfortably with an audience, and his dream is to open a restaurant in some out-of-the-way spot where he can cook for small groups, preparing whatever he feels like. In the meantime, he contents himself with dinners at home.

Chick had marinated some tuna steaks in butter and spices. When the cast-iron skillet he was heating on the grill started to smoke, he threw in the tuna and quickly seared it on each side. Smoke from the marinade spun off the pan, and the tuna emerged from it golden brown and spicy on the outside, still cool in the center. Normally I look askance at such a preparation—I've always insisted that I like my tuna either uncooked or cooked all the way through—but I loved it. It was tender and succulent, and the spices enhanced its flavor.

Chick had also mixed up a smoked fish dip, and before dinner we all relaxed by the canal, enjoying these appetizers, the warm evening, and the sound of the boat stays clanging. It was Halloween, and as night fell, jack-o-lanterns and luminaria lit the darkness.

When we sat down to dinner inside, we feasted on chilled stone crab claws that were steamed that day on the dock, relishes, and Vickie's slaw. We fell right in with the Fullers and their friends, all of us enjoying a wonderful meal.

Southern Smoky Fish Dip

This simple, and simply delicious, dip is a specialty at the Fish Peddler. Owner Chick Fuller, who originated the dip, likes it so much that he brings it home to serve before dinner, which is where we tried it. Smooth yet full of texture, it keeps a long while in the refrigerator and is perfect for impromptu occasions. I like to use hot-smoked salmon (salmon that has been cooked by the heat of burnished wood chips), which I order from Mutual Fish in Seattle, but any firm hot-smoked fish will do wonderfully.

Try to find cream cheese that doesn't contain guar gum, a stabilizer. There is nothing wrong with it, but the texture of cream cheese without it is creamier.

I like to serve this with carrot disks, celery sticks, strips of fresh fennel bulb, scallions, and any other fresh seasonal vegetables. It is also wonderful with good-quality crackers.

Try it on a piece of toasted country bread for a quick snack, with thin slices of cucumber for a summer sandwich, or straight from the refrigerator on the end of your finger.

1 pound cream cheese, at room temperature
½ cup sour cream
1 tablespoon freshly squeezed lemon juice
12 ounces skinless hot-smoked fish, such as

salmon, sturgeon, bluefish, or mackerel, cut
into 1-inch chunks
Several drops Tabasco sauce, or to taste

1. Place the cream cheese and the sour cream in a food processor and process until smooth. Add the lemon juice and process again. Then add the fish and process until it is thoroughly distributed. The dip may still be chunky, which is fine. Season with Tabasco.

2. Transfer the dip to an attractive bowl or dish, and serve. Covered and refrigerated, this will keep for up to 3 weeks.

4 CUPS

Bahamian Fish Chowder

Chick Fuller described this light, clear chowder as "revivifying and macho." The "macho" part surely refers to the traditional manner in which it is eaten in the Bahamas: for breakfast, with a fish head floating on top.

I've eaten this chowder with and without the head, and I prefer it a thousand times over without the head. It's not the head I mind, it's the many bones that come from it, which you end up chewing around and trying not to swallow. One way to avoid this is to use very large fish heads, from an 8- to 10-pound very fresh snapper for example. They won't fall apart so easily in cooking. The other is to just leave out the heads and imagine the effect. If you want to try it with the head, however, do so and enjoy!

When preparing the bones to make stock, rinse them very, very well, brushing along the backbone if necessary to remove any blood clinging to it. When making the stock, be diligent about skimming off the foamy impurities that rise to the surface. Also, fresh thyme is essential in this recipe—dried thyme just doesn't give it the appropriate perfume.

The heavenly aroma that fills your kitchen will have your mouth watering in anticipation of this very special chowder.

An Island Discovery

Chick and Vickie unearthed this chowder in the Bahamas some time ago, when they were poking around a market under the bridge linking Nassau and Paradise Island.

"The ladies there sell fresh fruits and vegetables, conch and conch salad, and there are little boats tied up there selling snapper," Chick said. "It's a tourist attraction, but only the locals buy there."

It was early morning, and as they looked around they asked all about the fish in the area and traded fishing stories with the vendors. When it got to be breakfast time, Chick asked the woman they were talking with where they should go.

"You want a real Bahamian breakfast?" she asked. They did, and she directed them to a bar several blocks away. "Go through it and to the back, and you'll find some tables," she said.

OUTSIDER FITS IN

"That bar was full of the seediest characters," Chick said. "I think they thought we were drug enforcement officers, but when Vickie said she wanted a fish head in her soup, they loosened up." A bowl of chowder and a couple of beers later, the chef came out to show them how it was made.

Now Chick makes the chowder at home, usually when they have a bunch of guests over on a Sunday morning. As a fish merchant, he has a ready supply of the best fish east of the Mississippi, and he puts everything into the chowder, heads and all. There's nothing like it, especially if you're sitting at the Fullers' table, watching boats ply the canal outside. Whether or not it's macho I can't say, but it is certainly revivifying.

FISH STOCK
4 pounds fish bones (frames, heads, and tails)
4 tablespoons (½ stick) unsalted butter
4 medium carrots, coarsely chopped
2 large onions, coarsely chopped
4 celery ribs with leaves, coarsely chopped
5 quarts cold water
2 bay leaves
4 parsley stems
2 sprigs fresh thyme
20 peppercorns
4 teaspoons salt

CHOWDER
4 tablespoons (½ stick) unsalted butter
1 cup fresh thyme leaves

1 cup (loosely packed) Italian (flat-leaf)
    parsley leaves
8 small russet potatoes, peeled and quartered
4 scallions, green tops only, very thinly sliced
Freshly ground black pepper to taste
4 fish heads, preferably snapper or rockfish,
    halved vertically (optional)
4 pounds skinless fish fillets, preferably snapper,
    cod, petrale sole, or rockfish, pinbones
    removed, cut into 2-inch chunks

GARNISH
4 scallions, green tops only, thinly sliced
    (optional)
2 tablespoons fresh thyme leaves (optional)

1. First, prepare the stock: Rinse the fish bones well under cold running water, and set them aside. In a large saucepan, melt the butter over medium heat. Add the carrots, onions, celery, and 2 cups of the cold water. Stir, cover, and cook until the vegetables are slightly softened, about 10 to 12 minutes.

2. Add the fish bones, herbs, seasonings, and remaining cold water. Increase the heat to medium-high, cover the pan, and bring to a boil. Reduce the heat to low, remove the cover, and simmer, skimming off any foam that rises to the surface, for 18 minutes. Remove from the heat. Strain the stock and discard the solids. Set the stock aside.

3. Make the chowder: Melt the butter in a large stockpot over medium-high heat. Add the thyme and parsley, and cook until the parsley turns dark green, about 5 minutes. The herbs should sear just slightly, so don't worry that you are overcooking them.

4. Reduce the heat to medium, and add half the potatoes in one layer. Top them with the scallions, and cover with the remaining potatoes. Season the potatoes generously with pepper, cover, and cook, stirring occasionally, until tender, with no hard core when pierced with a knife or skewer, about 20 minutes. It is not unusual for the potatoes to brown just slightly.

5. Place the fish heads, if you are using them, on top of the potatoes. Add 2 cups of the stock, cover, and cook until the potatoes are very soft, about 30 minutes.

6. Add the fish to the pot, pour in the remaining stock, and bring to a gentle boil. Keeping the stock at a high simmer, cook just until the fish is opaque through, about 8 min-utes. Be careful not to bring the stock to a full boil. Adjust the seasonings to your taste.

7. Serve immediately, with a piece of fish head atop each bowl if you used them. Garnish with the additional scallions and thyme leaves, if desired.

8 GENEROUS SERVINGS

Chick's Seared Tuna

Chick Fuller cooked this tuna on the deck of his house, overlooking his fishing boat, which bobbed lightly on the canal. Smoke poured into the air when he threw the fish into the pan, but it was over in moments and the result was this tender, gently spiced tuna. I've had seared tuna before, but I never appreciated it as much as I did that warm autumn evening in Fort Lauderdale.

I've since prepared this inside on the stove, and while it smokes things up for a while, the smoke does dissipate and surprisingly leaves no aroma in the house. Decide what you can tolerate, but I'd say that for these results, a bit of smoke is a small price to pay!

You will need a cast-iron skillet, and if you plan to prepare the tuna indoors, remember to disconnect your smoke alarm or you'll have the fire department at your door within moments! You may also want to warn the neighbors, in case they see smoke.

You can serve the tuna as a main course, or cut it into small pieces for an appetizer.

4 tuna steaks, 7 ounces each
1 teaspoon dill seed
2 teaspoons coarsely ground black pepper
¼ teaspoon cayenne pepper, or to taste

1½ teaspoons celery salt
2 cloves garlic, pressed through a garlic press
8 tablespoons (1 stick) unsalted butter, melted

1. Rinse the tuna and pat it dry.

2. With a mortar and pestle or in a small grinder, combine and crush the dill seed, black pepper, cayenne, and celery salt. The dill seed should be crushed into smaller pieces, not powdered. Transfer the spices to a small bowl, add the garlic, and stir. Then whisk in the melted butter.

3. Pour the marinade into a noncorrosible (preferably glass or enamel) shallow baking dish. Add the tuna, turn it to coat it on both sides, cover the dish, and refrigerate until the butter is well congealed, at least 30 minutes. You may do this the night before you plan to cook the tuna.

4. Place a cast-iron skillet over a burner turned on high, and let it heat until it has a grayish cast to it and is very, very hot. Remove a tuna steak with its congealed butter from the marinade dish and place it in the skillet. You may do two steaks at a time, or however many will fit in the skillet without crowding. A lot of smoke will curl out from under the steak, but don't be concerned. Cook the fish just until it is darkened on one side, about 45 seconds. Then turn it and cook until it is darkened on the other side, another 45 seconds. The fish won't really be blackened; it will be golden to dark on the outside, cool and tender inside. You may adjust the amount of time you cook the tuna, keeping in mind that the longer you leave it in the skillet, the tougher the surface will be. Certainly don't leave it any longer than 1 minute per side, and even that is pushing it.

5. Place each tuna steak on a warmed dinner plate, and serve immediately.

4 SERVINGS (8 APPETIZER SERVINGS)

Vickie's Southern Slaw

*V*ickie Fuller grew up enjoying this juicy slaw, and she can still eat it by the bowlful. After I'd tasted it I understood, because it has a freshness that makes you want to keep eating spoonful after spoonful.

The secret is ripe tomatoes. They must be full of juice, which will blend with the mayonnaise to make a rich, tart dressing for the cabbage. The mix of cabbages is important, too, for the salad's texture.

Chick made this slaw several hours before dinner, so it was mellowed and flavorful by the time we sat down. The pale pink tinge contributed by the tomatoes makes it lovely as well as luscious.

1 small Napa cabbage (22 ounces), trimmed
1 small green cabbage (1 pound), trimmed
½ red onion, cut crosswise into paper-thin slices
½ white onion, cut crosswise into paper-thin slices
2 scallions, finely chopped

1½ cups best-quality mayonnaise
1 tablespoon cold water
Salt and freshly ground black pepper to taste
4 medium tomatoes (3 ounces each), peeled

1. Cut each cabbage lengthwise into quarters, remove the core, then cut them crosswise into paper-thin slices. Separate the rings of the onions. Toss the cabbage, onions, and scallions in large bowl until they are well mixed.

2. In a small bowl, whisk the mayonnaise with the cold water until it is smooth. It will still be very thick. Season it with salt and generously with pepper.

3. Dice the tomatoes and add them, along with their seeds and juice, to the cabbage; toss again. Add the mayonnaise, and using two wooden spoons, toss until the vegetables are thoroughly coated. Cover, and refrigerate for at least 2 hours before serving.

4. About 15 minutes before serving, remove the coleslaw from the refrigerator. Toss, adjust the seasoning, and serve.

10 TO 12 SERVINGS

The World's Best Cornbread

By 6 A.M. Sunday morning Chick Fuller was up, dressed, and in the kitchen surrounded by fish heads, flour, and vegetables. He was making breakfast, and I could tell it wasn't going to be eggs and bacon. "I'm preparing the stock for the chowder we're having for breakfast," he said with a satisfied grin.

He turned to the counter and started sifting and whisking. "This is the cornbread that goes with it," he added.

Chick baked the cornbread in a cast-iron skillet, and that's what I use too. There's nothing like it for giving a nice crust that seems to seal the bread and make it extra-moist and tender inside.

---

2 cups yellow cornmeal
½ cup unbleached all-purpose flour
1 tablespoon baking powder
1 tablespoon sugar

1 teaspoon salt
2 large eggs
6 tablespoons mild vegetable oil, such as safflower
1½ cups milk

---

1. Preheat the oven to 400°F.

2. Place the cornmeal in a large bowl. Sift the remaining dry ingredients on top of it. Combine them, using a fork.

3. In a large mixing bowl, whisk together the eggs, 2 tablespoons of the oil, and the milk until thoroughly combined. Make a well in the dry ingredients, and pour the liquid ingredients into it. Gradually stir the dry ingredients into the liquids, working quickly.

4. Pour the remaining 4 tablespoons oil into a 10-inch cast-iron skillet, and heat it over medium-high heat. When a wisp of smoke comes off the oil, drain out all but a thin layer (don't drain the oil into a container that is wet inside). Immediately pour the batter into the skillet. Transfer it to the center of the oven, and bake until the cornbread is golden and springs back when touched, 15 to 20 minutes.

8 SERVINGS

Key Lime Cream Pie

*V*ickie Fuller serves a range of desserts when she entertains, and key lime pie is among them. This pie differs from many key lime pie recipes in that it is light and luscious yet still has a great deal of body. The recipe says it will serve eight, but don't be surprised if four hungry people devour the whole thing!

This should be eaten the day it is made. Citrus does not improve with time—it develops a metallic flavor after twenty-four hours—so be sure you've got a hungry crowd on hand! Bottled key lime juice is available in many specialty shops and natural food stores. It has a deeper more intense lime flavor than juice from regular limes, but this pie is luscious with any lime juice.

FILLING
6 tablespoons (¾ stick) unsalted butter
10 tablespoons (½ cup plus 2 tablespoons) key
    lime or regular lime juice
4 large egg yolks
1 large whole egg
1½ cups sugar

1 cup heavy (or whipping) cream, chilled

1 prebaked 9-inch pie shell
(recipe follows)

GARNISH
3 paper-thin slices key or regular lime, cut in half

---

1. Fill the bottom of a double boiler with water to reach about ¼ inch below the top section, and bring it to a vigorous simmer over medium-high heat. Combine the butter and 9 tablespoons of the lime juice in the top of the double boiler, and heat over the simmering water just until the butter has melted. Remove the top section from the heat. Leave the bottom of the double boiler, covered, over low heat so the water stays at a gentle simmer.

2. Using an electric mixer, whisk the egg yolks, the whole egg, and the sugar together in a bowl until the mixture is pale yellow, thick, and fluffy, which will take 3 or 4 minutes. Add the mixture to the melted butter and lime juice

in the top of the double boiler, and set over the bottom. Make sure the water is simmering vigorously; you may want to increase the heat under it. Whisking the mixture constantly, cook until it thickens, which will take 8 to 10 minutes. Remove the pan from the heat and transfer the mixture to a bowl so it will stop cooking. Let it cool to room temperature.

3. Whip the cream until it is thick enough to form soft points. Whisk in the remaining 1 tablespoon lime juice. Then fold the cream into the cooled lime mixture. Turn the mixture into the baked pie shell, and chill, loosely covered with waxed paper, for at least 1 hour or up to 4 hours. Remove the pie from the refrigerator about 15 minutes before you plan to serve it.

4. Garnish the pie with the lime slices, and serve.

8 SERVINGS

One-Crust Pastry

This pastry will fit a 9- or 10-inch pie plate. It is crisp and tender, and simple to make. Be sure to chill the dough for at least an hour; then take it out of the refrigerator about 15 minutes before you plan to roll it out.

1½ cups unbleached all-purpose flour
½ teaspoon salt
1 tablespoon sugar
6 tablespoons (¾ stick) unsalted butter, chilled, cut into small pieces
2 tablespoons lard, chilled, cut into small pieces
2 to 3 tablespoons ice water

1. Place the flour, salt, and sugar in a food processor, and process briefly to mix together.

2. Add the butter and the lard, and using short pulses, process until the mixture ranges in size from peas to coarse cornmeal.

3. Slowly pour in the ice water, and

using short pulses, incorporate it into the flour mixture. Add enough water so the dough holds together but does not form a ball.

4. Transfer the dough to a large piece of waxed paper and press it out to form a disk about 5 inches across. Wrap it tightly in waxed paper, and refrigerate it for at least 1 hour, or preferably overnight. If you are leaving it overnight, wrap the dough also in aluminum foil.

5. For a 9-inch pie plate, roll out the dough on a lightly floured surface to form a 10-inch round (for a 10-inch pie plate, roll it out to form an 11-inch round). Line the pie plate with the dough, pressing it gently into the plate, and carefully crimp the edges. Cover and chill for at least 1 hour or up to 8 hours. If you like, you can wrap the pie shell in aluminum foil and freeze it at this point. Do not thaw before baking.

6. To prebake the pie shell, preheat the oven to 400°F.

7. Line the dough with parchment paper or aluminum foil, and fill it with pastry weights or dried beans. Bake until the edges begin to turn golden, 12 to 15 minutes. Remove the weights and the paper or foil, and continue baking until the bottom of the pastry is golden, another 10 minutes.

8. Cool the pie shell on a wire rack, and proceed with the recipe.

PASTRY FOR A ONE-CRUST 9- OR 10-INCH PIE OR A 10½-INCH TART

Grand Oyster Gala at Sotterly

A CULINARY STEP BACK IN TIME

Built in 1717, Sotterly Mansion is the oldest continuously working plantation in the United States. The gracious home and its small outbuildings are surrounded by rolling fields where tobacco, vegetables, turkeys, and a host of other agricultural products are produced.

The plantation, located in Solomon, Maryland, has been owned by many families in its long history. Purchased in the early 1900s by the daughter of financier J. P. Morgan, it remains today in the same family. The current owner, Morgan's granddaughter Mabel Ingalls, turned Sotterly into a private foundation and it is now open to the public.

FOOD BY DESIGN

William Taylor, who calls himself "the American Dinner Designer," lives near the mansion in the bucolic little Eastern Shore community of Hollywood, Maryland (see Index for his potato salad recipe). A designer by profession—he worked for twenty years in Washington, D.C., as display director for a large department store—Taylor moved to St. Mary's County in the 1970s to open a small design shop. An aficionado of food and cooking, Taylor gradually developed into a professional food designer. "Don't ever call me a caterer," he said. "That's the kiss of death for someone who does what I do."

And it's true that Bill, whose energy radiates in a kind of electric field, does far more than just cook food for the parties he organizes. He has endless curiosity about the historical context of food, and spends as much time poring over old cookbooks and testing historic recipes as he does arranging parties and chopping vegetables.

Eighteen years ago Bill discovered Sotterly and obtained permission to hold parties there. Since then he has made the place famous, locally and beyond, with his often fanciful and always extravagant dinners. We attended his tenth annual Grand Oyster Gala there, and it was no exception.

IN THE MOOD FOR OYSTERS

When we walked up to the grand old mansion, which was lit from within and without, a crowd was already enjoying oysters on the veranda. Bill, dressed elegantly in a gray linen suit, ran over to greet us and immediately steered us to the raw bar.

"This fellow here harvested all the oysters, and he's here to shuck them and answer any questions you have," Bill said, disappearing into the kitchen.

We sampled the briny oysters on the half shell, learning they'd come from the mouth of the Potomac, and then moved along a few steps down the veranda where a hot hors d'oeuvre was being prepared. There, a young gentleman in tails was intently sautéing oysters with garlic and lemon for an oyster pan roast. I was given a small plateful, and the oyster I popped into my mouth was hot, plump, and garlic-laced.

We mingled with the other sixty people who were attending the gala. "We always ask Bill for tickets," said one woman who has attended each year, "but he makes us call just like everyone else." Places are highly sought after, and within days of the gala people are calling to reserve them for the following year.

"I started this in homage to the oyster, and I wanted to give people a chance to dine on oysters," Bill said. "Usually what people get when they come to this area is what I call 'county fair' oysters that are fried or stewed or put in a sandwich. The gala is the 'other side' of eating oysters."

OYSTER DÉJÀ VU

It gave me a chill to peek inside and see the period furnishings as I slipped cool Chesapeake Bay oysters into my mouth on the veranda of this gracious antebellum mansion. Sotterly has been restored down to the doorknobs, and I had a vision of women in full gowns and men in breeches strolling through the rooms as they must

have centuries ago. Oysters were as valued then as now, and chances are early residents of Sotterly had oyster galas as well.

"I'm sure they did," Bill agreed when I told him my vision. "Oysters from this area have always been valued as far away as New York, and people have always celebrated them. The people who lived here and who visited the mansion were gentry, fine people from England and beyond, and they had wonderful parties. I'm trying to re-create some of that here."

The menu Bill created for that evening was testament to the region's abundance, and to its history. He served oysters on the half shell and the Oyster Pan Roast outdoors. Then, after the guests had settled in the long dining room, which twinkled with light bouncing off the chandeliers and crystal, we were presented with Oysters Galway, Chesapeake Oyster Stew, tiny oysters en brochette, a dressed up oyster po' boy, cool and refreshing Oyster-Stuffed Tomatoes, Grand Marnier Parfaits, petit fours, and coffee. Bill, who knew most of the guests personally, gave a brief talk before the dinner began, describing the effort involved in preparing the feast. He had procured 2,640 oysters for the gala, some in the shell, some already shucked.

WHO'S COUNTING?

"Every year I order at least that many, and I never seem to have too many or too little," he said. "If there are any leftovers I just shuck 'em and take 'em home in a jar." For the Oysters Galway, which needed to be freshly shucked and on the half shell, the

The Leonardtown Oyster Festival

A hush falls over the crowd as six people—two women and four men—mount the small stage and take knives into their hands. They stand poised, tense, ready to pounce at the first sign. The signal is given, and knives, wrists, and hands fly as each person attempts to shuck as many oysters as possible, as tidily as can be managed. It's the national oyster-shucking contest, held each year at the Leonardtown Oyster Festival, and the heat is on.

The first round is over, the crowd cheers deliriously, and another group mounts the stage as those who've just finished slump off, exhausted. The national championships continue through Sunday, with competitors from as far away as Seattle and as close-by as Baltimore. Sunday afternoon the champion is announced amid much fanfare, and congratulations are given by King Oyster, a stately gentleman wearing a red velvet cape and impressive gilt crown.

But there's more. The national champion must test his or her mettle at the international championship in Galway, Ireland, later in the year, sent there in the company of King Oyster by the Rotary Club, which sponsors the Oyster Festival in Leonardtown.

WORK BUT EAT, TOO

While the championships are being held on one side of the fairgrounds, across the street in the middle school a handful of cooks are tensely waiting their turn to transform oysters into luscious

waterman who brought them went right to work shucking them just moments before the guests arrived. Bill had his staff ready to top them with butter, sprinkle them with herbs, and pop them in the oven so they could be served hot the moment we sat down.

We attended the gala with our friends Andy and Marie Keech, who are always in the mood for a feast. Marie carefully counted the dishes in the annual National Oyster Cook-off. In the kitchen six men are already determinedly whisking, mixing, tasting, and arranging their best oyster dishes.

An elderly man whisks egg whites for a light soufflé he will put atop oysters before broiling them; a younger man is toasting French bread and preparing a pepper and onion mixture for bruschetta with oysters; and a muscular young chef from Baltimore is whipping up his specialty, deep-fried Cajun oyster puffs.

They sweat, they're nervous, and when the timer goes off and their time in the kitchen has ended, they heave a collective sigh of relief and put a finishing touch on their dishes. Off in another room the judges await, forks in hand. The dishes are judged, then quickly carried down the hall to the room where the public has been invited to come and taste. The chefs know the toughest judg-

ing still awaits as people line up, plates in hand, to sample.

On the fairgrounds hundreds of booths are set up, and most of them sell oysters. You can get them scalded in a bag and served with melted butter, deep-fried and served with cocktail sauce, in lip-searing stews, sandwiches, and soups. Everyone walks around with paper cups full of fried oysters, popping them into their mouths and washing them down with soda or hot apple cider.

From the Grand Oyster Gala to meandering the fairgrounds with a cup of fried oysters, the Oyster Festival and a visit to St. Mary's County are a true celebration of the oyster. The festival is always held on the third weekend in October. For more information, call (301) 863-5015.

number of oysters we consumed, arriving at thirty-five each. We were astonished when she gave us the count. Cooked or on the half shell, they slip down so easily you hardly notice.

We left the gala satiated but not stuffed. Bill had planned the evening well and carefully, so that we would enjoy each oyster down to the last bite.

The Chesapeake oyster has had a checkered history, filled with abundance and drought. It is on the upswing now, and I, for one, am willing to report after that evening that it is in fine, healthy, plump, and delicious form.

Long may it prosper, I thought as I walked outside into the cool night air. And long may Bill Taylor put on his Grand Oyster Gala.

Cheddar Cheese Tarts

*T*hese have nothing to do with oysters except that they go uncommonly well alongside, particularly when served outdoors on a slightly chilly but comfortable autumn evening. Bill Taylor served these along with oysters on the half shell and an oyster pan roast, and they were an ideal accompaniment.

They're a little burst of flavor in a mouthful and they couldn't be easier to make. You can bake the tarts two hours before you plan to serve them, and then serve them at room temperature or slightly warmed. You will need three dozen small tart molds.

Double-Crust Pastry Dough
   (page 108)
3 large eggs
⅓ cup best-quality mayonnaise
1 teaspoon Worcestershire sauce
¼ teaspoon Tabasco sauce, or to taste

Pinch of salt
Ground white pepper to taste
3 cups (about 9 ounces) grated sharp
   Cheddar cheese
Cayenne pepper to taste

1. Preheat the oven to 425°F.

2. Have ready 36 small (2-inch) tart molds. Remove one of the pastry dough disks from the refrigerator and roll it out to ⅛ inch thick. Using a 2¼-inch cookie cutter, cut out as many rounds as possible from the dough and gently line the tart molds with them. Repeat with the second disk to line all 36 molds. Prick the bottoms of the dough, and chill for 15 minutes. Then bake the pastry shells in the center of the oven until they begin to turn golden, about

9 minutes. Remove them from the oven and set aside to cool. Leave the oven on.

3. In a large bowl whisk the eggs until they are frothy. Add the mayonnaise and whisk

until combined. Then add the Worcestershire sauce, Tabasco sauce, salt, and white pepper, and whisk until combined. Using a wooden spoon, stir in the grated cheese and mix well. Add cayenne pepper and adjust the seasoning.

4. Fill each tart shell with enough of the cheese mixture to reach just to the edge of the pastry. Bake the tarts on the center rack of the oven until they are puffed and golden, 10 to 11 minutes. Remove from the oven and let cool slightly before serving.

36 TARTS; 8 SERVINGS

Oyster Pan Roast

wonder if appetizers in past centuries were as good as those Bill Taylor conceived for the gala. His Oyster Pan Roast was a wonder of plump oysters swimming in their juices, seasoned with butter and garlic. I could have made a meal of them, and have done so several times since then.

There is nothing complex about an oyster pan roast, an old-time dish that appears in every region where oysters are found. It differs little from coast to coast, doubtless because it needs no improvement. It's easy and elegant—just be sure to use the freshest possible oysters.

This recipe makes eight appetizer servings, and as Bill says, it's important to "get your hands in the seafood." When he makes it, a process that takes no longer than a minute, he heats the pan until it is good and hot, adds the butter and the garlic, stirs, then throws in a handful of oysters and shakes them around until they plump up and the edges curl. "That's it," he said. "You serve it with some bread and it's the best thing you ever ate."

8 tablespoons (1 stick) unsalted butter,
cut into 8 pieces
4 cloves garlic, minced
1⅓ pounds (about 48) freshly shucked oysters

1. Melt the butter in a large skillet over medium-high heat. Stir in the garlic, and cook until the butter foams and the garlic begins to turn slightly translucent, 1 to 2 minutes. Then add the oysters and cook, stirring constantly or shaking the pan, until they are plump and beginning to curl at the edges, 1 to 2 minutes.

2. Turn the oysters out into a warmed serving bowl or individual bowls, and serve with plenty of crusty bread.

As the oysters plump, they release the liquor inside them, creating a wonderfully juicy sauce. Fresh crusty bread is a must, and you might consider serving this in small bowls, with a large soupspoon!

8 APPETIZER SERVINGS
(4 MAIN-COURSE SERVINGS)

William Taylor's Oyster Galway

Galway is the town in Ireland that hosts the international oyster-shucking contest each year. From its many years of sending the national champion, Leonardtown has developed ties with Galway, and the residents feel a kinship with their Irish friends. In honor of the town, Bill Taylor named this dish Oysters Galway. "The bit of green—and the whisky—is the Irish in it," he explained.

This serves eight as an appetizer, two to four as a main course—but you can increase the amounts proportionately if you're serving a larger crowd.

9 tablespoons (1 stick plus 1 tablespoon)
   unsalted butter, at room temperature
1 small clove garlic, minced
⅓ cup Italian (flat-leaf) parsley leaves
3 scallions, green tops only

24 oysters, in the shell, scrubbed
4 cups kosher (coarse) salt
¼ cup freshly grated Parmesan cheese
1½ tablespoons Irish whisky

1. Preheat the oven to 450°F.

2. In a medium-size bowl, whisk the butter until it is soft. Add the garlic and mix.

3. Chop the parsley and the scallion greens together until they are finely minced.

4. Shuck the oysters, leaving each oyster in the bottom shell and being sure to loosen the muscle that attaches it to the shell. Divide the kosher salt between two 8½ × 12-inch baking pans, and place the oysters on the salt, balancing them so their juices don't run out.

5. Place a small spoonful of the garlic butter atop each oyster, and then sprinkle the minced herbs over them. Sprinkle them evenly with the Parmesan cheese, and place the pans in the top third of the oven. Bake until the butter has melted and the oysters are hot through and curling slightly at the edges, about 5 minutes.

6. Remove the oysters from the oven, and drizzle the Irish whisky over them. Serve immediately.

8 APPETIZER SERVINGS

Oyster-Stuffed Tomatoes

This was the final oyster course at Bill Taylor's Grand Oyster Gala. Ripe, flavorful tomatoes filled with a refreshing mixture of cool cucumbers, tomato, and warm just-poached oysters, they were the ideal end to the extravaganza. Like much of Bill's food, they are an ode to simple, fresh flavors. It takes a profound understanding of foods to do so little to them and have their best characteristics emerge.

I like to serve the stuffed tomatoes individually, as an appetizer, or as a main course for lunch, when I serve two to each person.

8 medium (3 ounces each) ripe tomatoes
1 medium cucumber,
    peeled and halved lengthwise
1 small onion,
    cut into small (⅛-inch) dice
32 oysters, in the shell, shucked, with their liquor

¼ cup extra-virgin olive oil
1 tablespoon freshly squeezed lemon juice
2 teaspoons balsamic vinegar
Salt and freshly ground black pepper to taste
1 handful Italian (flat-leaf) parsley leaves
    and/or 1 handful arugula leaves, for garnish

1. Slice the top off each tomato, and using a grapefruit knife, scoop out the pulp, being careful not to pierce the tomato shell. Reserve the tomato pulp, but discard the seeds. Place the tomatoes upside down on a wire rack over a pan or the sink, and let them drain for at least 30 minutes. Chop the tomato pulp into small (⅛-inch) dice and place in a medium-size bowl.

2. Remove the seeds from the cucumber by carefully scooping them out with a teaspoon. Cut the cucumber into thin (⅛-inch) lengthwise strips; then cut the strips crosswise into small (⅛-inch) dice. Add the cucumbers to the chopped tomatoes, add the diced onions, and toss gently. Cover and set aside.

3. Place the oysters and their liquor in a medium-size saucepan, and bring to a simmer over medium heat. Cook just until the edges of the oysters curl and they begin to plump, about 2 minutes. Remove the pan from the heat, and using a slotted spoon, transfer the oysters to the bowl with the vegetables, and toss gently.

4. In a small bowl whisk together the olive oil, lemon juice, balsamic vinegar, and salt and pepper. Pour over the oysters and vegetables, and toss gently but thoroughly. Adjust the seasoning.

5. Sprinkle the inside of each tomato shell with a pinch of salt and pepper.

6. Using a slotted spoon, fill the tomatoes with the oyster and vegetable mixture, making sure that each tomato has a nice-looking oyster on top. Either serve immediately or cover and chill.

7. To serve, place a tomato in the center of a plate, and arrange the parsley and/or arugula leaves flat against the plate around the base of the tomato, like flower petals.

8 APPETIZER SERVINGS

Grand Marnier Parfaits

The dénouement of William Taylor's oyster gala was this light, refreshing dessert, which I thought was a perfect choice after eating thirty-five oysters prepared half a dozen ways. It's what I call a "frou-frou" dessert, coming as it does to the table all dressed up for a party.

I like to serve this in a tall, graceful beer glass, though any slender glass will do—even a champagne flute. The number of servings will vary according to the size of the glass you choose. If you don't want to fancy this up, just serve it in a glass bowl, with orange wedges around the edge.

I buy vanilla ice cream and make the frozen yogurt. You can also buy frozen yogurt, if you like. If you are going to make the yogurt, it's best to do so the day you plan to assemble the parfaits, because if it is left too long in the freezer it gets very, very hard and difficult to scoop.

½ cup Grand Marnier or
*   Cointreau, chilled*

FROZEN YOGURT
1 pound full-fat plain yogurt
Minced zest of 2 oranges
¾ cup granulated sugar
1 teaspoon vanilla extract

PARFAITS

1½ cups heavy (or whipping) cream, chilled
2 tablespoons confectioners' sugar
1 teaspoon vanilla extract
1 quart best-quality vanilla ice cream

GARNISH
1 orange, peeled, pith removed, cut into sections

1. The night before you plan to make this, place the Grand Marnier or Cointreau in the freezer.

2. To make the frozen yogurt, whisk together all the ingredients in a large bowl and freeze in an ice cream maker according to the manufacturer's instructions.

3. Combine the cream with the confectioners' sugar and the vanilla in a large bowl, and whip until it is thick enough to hold a point.

4. Place 1 small (¼ cup) scoop of frozen yogurt in the bottom of each glass. Top with 2 small scoops of vanilla ice cream. Then add 2 small scoops of frozen yogurt and another 2 scoops of vanilla ice cream. Top with the whipped cream, using a pastry bag and a star tip, or just scoop it on with a spoon. Place the parfaits in the freezer to chill. They can be made to this point up to 2 days in advance.

5. Remove the parfaits from the freezer 30 minutes before you plan to serve them. Cut each orange section in half lengthwise. Just before serving, drizzle each parfait with 1 tablespoon of the chilled Grand Marnier or Cointreau, and garnish with 2 halves of an orange section. Serve immediately.

8 SERVINGS

Natchez Catfish Fry

UNLOCKING THE SECRETS

It was late fall when we visited the Vasser estate right outside Natchez, Mississippi, for the occasion of a catfish fry. Eugenie Vasser, who undertook to show us as many southern seafood celebrations as she could possibly pack into a week, insisted we couldn't leave the South without a visit to Natchez and her mother's house.

When we arrived, the table was already groaning under the weight of the dishes that Elizabeth Wilson, who has cooked for the Vasser family for thirty-five years, had been preparing since morning. The food was simple home cooking, so much so that when Elizabeth fully understood the purpose of our visit she said, "Oh, I wish I'd known what you were up to. I'd'a done some real special things."

NO APOLOGIES NECESSARY

I was so glad she hadn't because what we sat down to that chilly afternoon was a real, traditional Natchez fish fry—a mound of delicately fried spicy catfish, sweet potatoes, toothsome mustard greens, snap beans with potatoes, potato salad, coleslaw, eggplant cakes, spareribs, and yellow squash.

Elizabeth apologized about not having made French fries. "I already had too much white in the meal," she said. "I needed more green, so I added the mustard greens."

Eugenie grew up eating Elizabeth's

food and she claims she learned everything she knows about cooking from her.

"My mother didn't know a thing about cooking, so I'd spend my time in the kitchen with Elizabeth, watchin' what she was doin'," Eugenie said. "I still do when I come home to visit."

"I just cook what I know to cook," Elizabeth claimed.

It may be as simple as that to her, but you'll discover that this woman knows how to unlock the secrets of flavor. Somehow she manages to coax the best from a simple sweet potato, a mess of greens, yellow squash, and other garden vegetables. And as for her catfish . . . read on.

Southern Fried Catfish

The crisp fried catfish fillets we ate at Gloria Vasser's home in Natchez, Mississippi, were without a doubt the best I've had anywhere. Elizabeth Wilson fried them slowly in about half an inch of oil until they were a very deep golden brown, drained them on brown paper, and served them just warmer than room temperature. They were incredible.

Part of the secret, of course, is to use really fresh catfish fillets. But I think the other part is knowing in your bones, the way Elizabeth does, just how much flour and cornmeal to put on them, how long to fry them, and at what temperature. She's been frying catfish for so many years she doesn't think twice about it, or question that what she produces is good, good, good.

I have found that an equal mixture of flour and cornmeal, generously seasoned with salt and pepper, gives a result closest to what we ate in Natchez. Because catfish fillets can be watery, I pat them dry and dip them quickly in milk before dredging them in the flour and cornmeal. Serve the catfish with the tartar sauce.

3 pounds skinless catfish fillets
¾ cup unbleached all-purpose flour
¾ cup yellow cornmeal
1½ teaspoons salt

Freshly ground black pepper to taste
1 cup milk
1½ cups mild vegetable oil, such as safflower
Fresh Tartar Sauce (recipe follows), for serving

1. Rinse the fillets with cold water, and pat them dry. Refrigerate loosely wrapped in waxed paper until ready to cook. Line a baking sheet with unprinted brown paper bags, and set it aside.

2. Mix the flour and cornmeal together on a piece of waxed paper. Season with the salt and a generous grinding of pepper, and mix well. Pour the milk into a shallow dish.

3. Pat the catfish fillets with paper towels to remove any excess liquid. One fillet at a time, dip them in the milk and then dredge them in the flour mixture, gently patting it onto them. Let them sit for 10 minutes on a wire rack, and then dredge them again.

4. Heat the oil in a large cast-iron or other heavy skillet over medium-high heat. When the oil is shimmering, add two fillets, or as many as will fit without crowding the pan and making the fat boil up too high. Cook until they are golden on one side, about 3 minutes. Using a perforated spatula, turn the fillets and cook until the other side is golden and the fish is cooked through, another 3 to 4 minutes. Transfer the fish to the lined baking sheet to drain. Keep warm in a low oven until ready to serve.

5. Repeat with the remaining catfish, and serve immediately with Fresh Tartar Sauce.

6 TO 8 SERVINGS

Fresh Tartar Sauce

This is a fresh, zingy tartar sauce that goes perfectly with crisp fried fish. (You can also use it as a dip for fresh vegetables.) It will keep for about four days, tightly covered, in the refrigerator. Do note that this sauce contains raw eggs. Recently some uncooked eggs have been a source of salmonella, a serious infection. If you are unsure of the quality of the eggs you buy, it's best to avoid recipes using them raw. You can always use high-quality commercial mayonnaise.

2 large egg yolks, at room temperature
2 tablespoons freshly squeezed lemon juice
Salt and freshly ground black pepper to taste
1 cup olive oil
1 large dill pickle, minced

1 tablespoon drained capers
½ small onion, minced
1 clove garlic, minced
Several drops Tabasco sauce, or to taste

1. Place the egg yolks in a food processor. Add 1 tablespoon of the lemon juice and a sprinkling of salt and pepper. Process until thoroughly combined.

2. With the machine running, slowly add the olive oil through the feed tube in a very thin stream. The mixture will emulsify and become quite thick. When the olive oil is fully incorporated, add the remaining 1 tablespoon lemon juice.

3. Scrape the mayonnaise into a medium-size bowl. Add the remaining ingredients and mix well. Taste and add more salt, pepper, and Tabasco, if desired. The mayonnaise will keep for a week, covered, in the refrigerator.

MAKES ABOUT 1⅓ CUPS

Mississippi Yellow Squash

If you are wedded to the concept of crisp-cooked vegetables, you may shudder at this recipe—but don't, for a wonderful transformation takes place as the squash and onions cook together. A flavor one would never guess existed in yellow squash emerges to a full, round depth. In fact, this is so delicious that you may find yourself ignoring everything else on the table in its favor!

1 medium onion, coarsely chopped
¾ cup water
4 medium yellow summer squash, trimmed and
    cut into ½-inch rounds
Salt and freshly ground black pepper to taste
2 tablespoons unsalted butter

1. Combine the onion and the water in a medium-size saucepan, and bring to a boil over medium-high heat. Reduce the heat to medium, cover, and cook until the onion is soft, 10 to 12 minutes.

2. Add the squash, season generously with salt and pepper, stir, and cover. Cook until the squash is tender, about 25 minutes, shaking the pan occasionally so it cooks evenly.

3. Drain the vegetables and return them to the saucepan. Stir in the butter. When the butter has melted, remove the pan from the heat, adjust the seasonings, and serve.

6 SERVINGS

Elizabeth's Lay-ros (Eggplant Cakes)

Tender, succulent, and mild, Elizabeth Wilson's lay-ros are a treat, and they make a wonderful accompaniment to just about anything I can think of.

These really are best made in summer and fall, when the eggplants are full, their skins so tight they look as if they'll burst. (Burst they will if they're baked in the

Mystery Pancakes

N ow you come here and take'a taste of this," Elizabeth Wilson said as she handed me a flat, soft disk that looked like a green pancake. I took a bite and experienced the most unusually wonderful texture and subtle flavor.

"Now, you tell me what that's made of," she demanded with a twinkle in her voice. I tasted it, I smelled it. I had no idea.

"That's eggplant," she said, laughing at the look on my face. "My mama always made those and she called 'em lay-ro."

I looked at my friend Eugenie Vasser. "Just last week I was reading about a chef in New York who was making waves with his eggplant pancakes," she said. "Wouldn't you know Elizabeth has been making them all her life!"

The last place I expected to be served one was in the heart of Mississippi at a traditional catfish fry. Well, I thought, these dishes do originate somewhere.

oven without being pricked all over to let the steam escape, so don't omit that step.) Choose very firm, evenly colored eggplants without blemishes or soft spots.

You can bake the eggplant the night before, remove the skin, and refrigerate the flesh overnight.

1 large (1¾-pound) eggplant
1½ tablespoons unbleached all-purpose flour
¼ teaspoon baking powder
2 large eggs
1 clove garlic, minced
Salt and freshly ground black pepper to taste

1. Preheat the oven to 425°F.

2. Using a cake tester or a trussing needle, prick the eggplant all over. Place it in a baking dish and bake until it is nearly soft throughout, 40 to 50 minutes. The cooking time will vary with the size and freshness of the eggplant—one that is fresh from the garden will roast more quickly than one from the supermarket.

3. Remove the eggplant from the oven, cut it in half lengthwise, and cover it with a kitchen towel to steam. When it is cool enough to handle, peel off the skin, trim the ends, and either mince the flesh or process it in a food processor until it is chunky.

4. Sift the flour and baking powder together onto a piece of waxed paper. Whisk the eggs in a medium-size bowl. Add the eggplant, the garlic, and then the flour mixture, whisking well. Season generously with salt and pepper.

5. Heat a large nonstick skillet over medium heat. When it is hot, drop spoonfuls of the batter onto it (about 2 tablespoons each) flattening the batter out slightly. Cook until the pancakes begin to look firm on top and are lightly browned underneath, about 3 minutes. Turn, and continue cooking until they are golden on the other side and are cooked through, another 2 minutes. Serve immediately.

ABOUT 20 PANCAKES; 6 TO 8 SERVINGS

Elizabeth's Sweet Potatoes

*H*ere's another dish from Elizabeth Wilson. I like these sweet potatoes because the preparation is unusual, with the tubers sliced lengthwise so they stay in large pieces yet get very tender and succulent. Frying the sweet potatoes first gives them a golden nuttiness, and the fresh nutmeg and light dusting of brown sugar emphasize their natural sweetness without overpowering it.

Though Elizabeth served this with a fish fry, I like to serve it for the holidays, when something a little different is called for. If you like, add ginger along with the nutmeg—it gives the potatoes added zip.

These may be prepared several hours in advance, then finished on the stove just before serving.

2½ pounds sweet potatoes, peeled
2 tablespoons unsalted butter
2 tablespoons mild vegetable oil, such as safflower
Salt and freshly ground black pepper to taste
¾ teaspoon freshly grated nutmeg

½ teaspoon ground ginger (optional)
2 tablespoons (lightly packed) dark brown sugar
½ cup water

1. Line a baking sheet with unprinted brown paper bags, and set it aside.

2. Slice the sweet potatoes lengthwise into ¼-inch-thick slices.

3. Combine 1 tablespoon of the butter and 1 tablespoon of the oil in a large heavy skillet, and place over medium heat. When it is hot, add a single layer of sweet potatoes and cook until they are golden, 3 to 4 minutes per side. Remove the slices as they brown, and drain on the lined baking sheet. Continue with the remaining slices, adding more butter and oil as needed. (If you are preparing these ahead of time, transfer the cooled potatoes to a baking dish, cover, and refrigerate.)

4. Layer the potatoes in a shallow flameproof baking dish, sprinkling the layers evenly with salt and pepper, the nutmeg, the ginger if you're using it, and the brown sugar, ending with a fine dusting of brown sugar. Pour the water around the edge of the dish, and bring to a boil over medium-high heat. Reduce the heat to medium-low and simmer, uncovered, until the potatoes are tender, about 30 minutes. Serve immediately.

8 SERVINGS

Natchez Greens

These greens were a side dish at the Mississippi fish fry, but they nearly stole the show. Tender, slightly bitter, salty, and a bit sweet, they were so good that all of us went back for more and more.

They're unusual for southern greens because of the bell pepper. As Elizabeth Wilson explained to me, she always cooks them this way but doesn't always leave the pepper.

"If people don't like the pepper, I just take it out," she said. "Otherwise I stir it right in."

I love the combination and always stir it in. Pepper turns sweet when it's cooked slowly, just the way greens do. The added sugar brings the flavors together. If you want a hint of color, substitute a red bell pepper for the green one. And in good southern tradition, you may want to serve hot sauce and vinegar alongside, for those who like those condiments.

2 large (20-ounce) bunches mustard greens,
   collard greens, or kale, rinsed and stemmed
1 cup water
1 tablespoon sugar

3 ounces salt pork or bacon, rind removed,
   rinsed, and cut into 1 × 1½-inch pieces
1 green or red bell pepper, cored, seeded, and cut
   in half
Salt and freshly ground black pepper to taste

1. Tear the greens into pieces. Place the water, sugar, and salt pork in a large saucepan, stir, and add the greens. Cover and bring to a boil over medium-high heat. Reduce the heat to medium, and cook the greens at a lively simmer until they are wilted and have turned a very dark green, 15 to 20 minutes.

2. Place the pepper halves atop the greens, cover, and cook until they are tender and the greens have further reduced, are a paler green, and are very tender, 20 to 30 minutes.

3. Stir the pepper into the greens, breaking it up with a spoon as you do. Season with salt and pepper, and serve immediately.

6 SERVINGS

Joanne's Fruit Salad

This is a salad that almost everyone raised in the South grew up with. Joanne Clevenger, owner of the Upperline Restaurant in New Orleans, remembers this dish, along with nearly every other dish she ate as a child.

The salad is a natural after a seafood dinner because of its light, simple flavor. It is sweet and just the tiniest bit tart from the oranges. It benefits greatly from fresh coconut, so try to find one if you can.

I like the simplicity of this salad, but you can add as many different varieties of fruit as you like. A southern friend of mine remembers this salad coming to the table with canned peaches, peeled grapes, and fresh or canned cherries, depending on the season.

We didn't have a dessert at the Vassers' catfish fry, but when I make those wonderful dishes, this is what I serve afterwards. And I've found myself serving it quite often at other times, particularly in winter when coconuts are plentiful (at least where I live) and everyone craves fresh fruit. It's fresh and beautiful, simple and impressive.

1½ cups (5 ounces) grated coconut, fresh or unsweetened packaged
10 oranges
3 large bananas
1 cup toasted pecans (see Note)

1. If you are using a fresh coconut, pierce the eyes, drain out the milk, and whack the shell with a hammer or the blunt edge of a chef's knife. (Coconut juice is lovely to drink, or mix it with other fruit juices.) Use a sharp knife to pry the coconut meat from the shell. Peel the coconut meat with the knife or a vegetable peeler, then grate it, in chunks, in a food processor or with a hand grater.

2. Peel the oranges, removing all the white pith, and slice them into thin rounds. Remove any seeds. Slice the bananas into ¼-inch-thick rounds.

3. Combine the oranges and bananas in a large serving bowl, and toss gently. Add the coconut and the pecans, toss, and serve immediately.

8 TO 10 SERVINGS

Note: To toast pecans, preheat the oven to 350°F. Spread the nuts in a single layer on a baking sheet, and bake until they are golden, stirring once, about 12 minutes. Let cool thoroughly before using.

On Bayou Petit Caillou

JAMBALAYA AND SHRIMP IN CAJUN COUNTRY

Peter Broussard, a resident of Houma, Louisiana is a fisherman and cook extraordinaire, well known on Bayou Petit Caillou for his jambalaya. Raised along the bayous, where fishing was as popular as baseball for a young man, Pete comes from a large Cajun family with a mother who, as his brother George put it, "had the magic pot." She cooked big meals for her seven children, and no matter how many people stopped by, there was always plenty to go around.

Their father, however, prepared the family meals on the weekends, and it was he who taught the boys how to cook. Like all Cajuns, they learned to begin most dishes with the "holy trinity" of onions, bell peppers, and celery, the basis of Cajun food from jambalaya to étouffée.

Pete is the keeper of the family recipes and he cooks every weekend out at the fish camp he and his wife, Boo, own on Bayou Petit Caillou, just thirty miles south of Houma. Every Friday after work they drive there, go out to a restaurant for supper, and spend Saturday fishing. Saturday night Pete cooks steaks and come Sunday he incorporates whatever fish they've caught into a big Cajun supper.

"I don't do anything special," he said modestly. "It's just the kind of cooking I know how to do."

Pete's friends know his habits and they tend to visit on Sunday afternoon, so he's gotten used to cooking for groups.

When we visited the fish camp with Eugenie Vasser and a group of friends, we found Pete in the kitchen, deep into several Cajun dishes. He had white beans in one pot, étouffée in another, the ingredients for jambalaya on the table, and a pot of crab gumbo heating on the stove.

COOKING UP A STORM

It was a howling November night, and there was an edge of nervousness in the group. We all hoped the storm wouldn't turn ugly and take the camp down with it. Our fears were reasonable as we learned when the neighbors came over for supper. The house next to theirs had been smashed by a tornado the night before, its roof laid not-so-gently on

their own house. Just two months before that, Hurricane Andrew had ripped through the bayous, flattening, flooding, and uprooting. Pete and Boo's house is built high off the ground, so the living area wasn't affected, except for wine glasses that were shaken loose from their shelf. But the first floor, which is like an open basement and which sheltered the heater and numerous pieces of outdoor furniture and barbecue grills, was swept bare.

As Pete hovered over his dishes on the stove, a dozen of us stood around the

center island drinking Gewürztraminer and eating handfuls of dried shrimp that Pete called "Cajun popcorn."

Pete continued to work methodically, always going back to the onions bubbling in oil. I watched those too, as they went from white to gold to dark, dark brown, which took an hour or more. The darker they got, the closer he watched, until just before they burned he tossed in the peppers and celery and a good dash of water.

"The secret to a good jambalaya is those onions," Pete said triumphantly.

"They've gotta be so dark they're almost burned, and they've gotta brown evenly. If the pieces brown on the outside before they brown on the inside, the heat's too high. Ya' just gotta play with it."

Pete added the rice and more water, seasoned it, put the top on, and turned to the table. There sat a gorgeous platter of boiled shrimp, potatoes, onions, and heads of garlic that Steve Mallernee had just brought inside. A Cajun shrimp boil, complete with Steve's Spicy Cocktail Sauce was the prelude to Pete's jambalaya feast.

Debbie's Shrimp Boil

When we were at Pete Broussard's camp on Bayou Petit Caillou, Debbie Mallernee supervised while Steve Mallernee and George Broussard prepared this shrimp boil. The cooking took place in the sheltered area under the house, and it was cold. With the rain slicing in around them, they huddled near the warmth of the boiler. We could hear them laughing, sneezing as the spices came out of the bag, worrying that they hadn't added enough, that it wasn't cooked enough, that it was cooked too much. My husband, Michael, was photographing the process and they were all clowning around.

Then it went quiet, and I investigated. There they all were, transfixed by this big pot of shrimp and vegetables just sitting there. "We're lettin' 'em absorb flavor," Steve said seriously, as they stood around the pot in a meditative state.

About fifteen minutes later they came upstairs with a huge, gorgeous platter they'd arranged. Debbie put a few finishing touches to it, and we all dug in.

You can expand or reduce this mini version of the shrimp boil to accommodate the number of people you have on hand. You can beef it up with hot peppers, more cloves and mustard seed, whatever you like to add. Or you can use your own spice mixture. Just be sure to add a jot of cayenne to give it a true Cajun kick.

3 pounds medium shrimp, in the shell
3 bags Zatarain's Crab and Shrimp Boil
    seasoning, or ½ cup pickling spice
6 tablespoons salt, preferably sea salt
2 teaspoons cayenne pepper, or to taste
6 small onions, peeled
6 small potatoes, unpeeled, halved lengthwise
6 ribs celery, trimmed and cut into 5-inch lengths
6 carrots, trimmed and cut into 5-inch lengths

4 artichokes, leaves trimmed, halved lengthwise
1 lemon, halved
4 whole garlic heads
4 cups ice cubes

FOR DIPPING:
8 tablespoons (1 stick) unsalted butter, melted
2 tablespoons freshly squeezed lemon juice
Steve's Spicy Cocktail Sauce (recipe follows)

1. Rinse the shrimp with cold water, and pat them dry. Refrigerate loosely wrapped in waxed paper until ready to cook.

2. Pour 2 gallons of water into a large kettle or soup pot. Place the boil seasoning or pickling spice on a square of cheesecloth, and tie it up to form a bag. Add them, along with the salt and pepper, to the water, and bring to a boil. Boil for 10 minutes. Then add the onions and boil for another 10 minutes. Add the remaining vegetables, the lemon, and the garlic, and boil until the potatoes and artichokes are tender, 15 to 20 minutes. (An artichoke leaf will detach easily.)

3. Add the shrimp and return the water to the boil. Remove the kettle from the heat, throw the ice cubes into it, and cover it. Let it sit for 10 to 15 minutes, so the shrimp and vegetables absorb the flavors of the cooking liquid.

4. In a small bowl, mix together the butter and the lemon juice.

5. Drain the shrimp and vegetables, transfer them to a large warmed platter, and serve immediately. Pass Steve's Spicy Cocktail Sauce and the butter-lemon sauce alongside.

6 SERVINGS

Steve's Spicy Cocktail Sauce

Steve Mallernee, a physician by day (and sometimes night), member of the Order of Endemion during Mardi Gras, and lover of fine food and good times, made this dip when we were all out at Pete Broussard's camp south of Houma, Louisiana. Steve carefully mixed and tasted his dip until it was, as he put it "just shy of where the horseradish makes you feel like you're blowing smoke outta your ears."

This version doesn't quite fit the description, but you can certainly make it that hot. I like it with some bite, and I serve extra hot sauce and horseradish alongside so everyone can heat up their own.

Tightly covered, this will keep for a week or so in the refrigerator. The horseradish loses power over time, so you may want to stir in more after you've let it come to room temperature and had a taste.

¾ cup good-quality ketchup
3 tablespoons prepared horseradish
1 teaspoon hot sauce (preferably
    Crystal or Louisiana brand), or
    to taste
2 tablespoons freshly squeezed lemon
    juice
½ teaspoon Worcestershire sauce

Whisk all the ingredients together in a medium-size bowl. Taste for seasoning, and serve.

ABOUT 1 CUP

They Came from Acadia

It was more than the southern heat on the bayou that made us feel warm, for we were welcomed into the heart of a group of spirited Cajuns who treated us proudly to their daily fare. Cooks from birth one and all, raised on the bayous that teem with fish and shellfish, they prepared their favorite home-style Cajun specialties from shrimp boil to gumbo and crawfish étouffée.

These Cajuns are proud—as proud of their individual tricks for making jambalaya and a spicy crab boil as they are of their rich heritage. They live their Cajun-ness every day through love of family and friends, a keen appreciation for good simple food, dedication to work, and a readiness to let it all go and have a rowdy good time.

Cajuns are descendants of the Acadiens, the French settlers of the coastal region of eastern Canada. Acadia, a harsh and beautiful land, prospered during the 17th century. In the mid-1700s, however, the English defeated the French and took their land, renaming it Nova Scotia.

ACADIEN DIASPORA

The mix of English and Acadiens was not a good one, and the Acadiens were soon banished, sent to New England and as far south as Georgia. Some returned to France.

A small group went to New Orleans. The

steamy, exotic climate and the abundant fish and game suited them, and the Acadiens—soon shortened to "Cajuns"—flourished once more. Many settled deep in the heart of the country on the bayous where they plied their trades of fishing and agriculture. They were cut off from easy access, which allowed them to maintain and develop their traditions, language, and culture.

Highly adaptable, the Cajuns used all that was available to them in this rich new land. From peppers to speckled trout, crawfish, and alligator, they incorporated all they found into a gutsy cuisine. Rich with flavor and texture, it is spicy, sometimes hot, often richly colored from slow-cooked onions and a darkened roux used in soups and stews. It has its roots in France, but it is a tradition unto itself.

The Cajun language, an ancient French very different from that spoken in France today, has been softened and modified by time. It has developed into a beautiful singsong French dialect with many English words and pronunciations. But many Cajuns fear their language will be lost.

"Only the old people really speak it," said Mike Morris, a Cajun sales representative and tour guide for Tabasco, Inc. "I can understand it, but my kids don't have any idea about it. They didn't learn it and I didn't encourage them to. Now I think it's a little too late."

STOKING FOOD TRADITIONS

Perhaps making up for what they fear to lose, Cajuns keep their culinary tradition alive. Though country fare, Cajun cooking requires flair and skill. According to Debbie Mallernee, both male and female Cajuns cook, and whoever makes a dish best makes it all the time, whether it is the husband or the wife. Each teaches their specialty to the children. Every family style has a specific intensity of flavoring and spicing, and identical Cajun dishes made by different cooks never taste exactly alike. If you ask ten Cajuns for their jambalaya recipe, you will get ten different versions.

Cajuns are hardworking, adaptable folk, fiercely emotional, richly endowed with spirit, fire, and loyalty. They need just the tiniest of excuses for a celebration, and few cultures have a better time, despite what life brings. Their credo is: "laissez les bons temps roulez," or let the good times roll.

Pete's Jambalaya

Here is Pete Broussard's renowned jambalaya, a recipe as full of Cajun influences and harmonies as zydeco music. Making it takes a subtle hand, too, and a measure of patience. The onions require about an hour, or perhaps more, to brown properly, and you can't hurry them along. Watch them, stir them frequently, and always keep them in an even layer on the bottom of the pot. If the outer edges of the pieces are browning faster than the middle, reduce the heat. If you don't think they are browning enough, increase it. You may need to play with the heat as they cook, to keep them browning evenly.

The subtlety comes in with the seasoning, which should be full but not hot. Go easy on the cayenne.

If you wish, marinate the shrimp in hot sauce or a bit of oil and herbs. I like them plain, because I like their pure taste balanced by the warm and herby rice.

Like Pete, I use Tony Chachère's Creole Seasoning when I make jambalaya. A mixture of salt, cayenne pepper, and spices, it is generally available at specialty groceries throughout the country.

½ cup olive oil
5 large onions, diced
1 green bell pepper, cored, seeded, and diced
3 ribs celery, diced
5 to 5¼ cups water
4 cloves garlic, minced
3 cups long-grain white rice
1 large branch fresh thyme, or 1 teaspoon dried
2 bay leaves

2 teaspoons salt, or to taste
⅛ teaspoon cayenne pepper, or to taste
Freshly ground black pepper to taste
Freshly ground white pepper to taste
1 to 2 teaspoons Creole seasoning
2 pounds medium shrimp (30 to 35 per pound), shelled
Hot sauce

1. In a large stockpot or saucepan, heat the oil over medium-high heat. When it is hot and shimmering, add the onions and stir until they are thoroughly coated with oil. Reduce the heat to medium and slowly brown the onions until they are very dark, just this side of burned, and substantially reduced in volume. Stir them frequently, keeping them in an even layer in the bottom of the pan. You may need to adjust the heat from time to time to ensure that they brown evenly. This will take about 1 hour.

2. When the onions are browned, add the bell pepper, celery, and ½ to ¾ cup of the water, enough so the vegetables are "soupy." Stir, and cook until the peppers and celery have softened slightly, about 10 minutes. Stir in the garlic. Then add the rice, and stir so it is completely moistened. Add the herbs, the salt, the three peppers, the Creole seasoning, and the remaining 4½ cups water. Cover and bring to a boil over medium-high heat. Reduce the heat to medium-low and cook until the rice is tender and fluffy, about 30 minutes.

3. Arrange the shrimp on top of the rice, cover, and cook until they have curled and turned bright pink, about 10 minutes. Remove the pot from the heat, stir the shrimp into the rice, and adjust the seasoning. Serve immediately, with plenty of hot sauce on the side.

12 SERVINGS (SEE NOTE, PAGE 158)

Pete's White Beans

These beans are a favorite of Pete Broussard's and a staple in any Cajun home. Whenever Pete prepares a meal, white beans are a part of it. His secret for making them delicious? "Boil the hell outta' them," he says, and add water throughout the cooking. He likes his beans to be creamy, and he achieves that by stirring them frequently and mashing them against the side of the pan.

The result of these attentions is smoky, rich-tasting, saucy beans. The final thing Pete does is to enact an old Cajun rule by adding enough black pepper so you can see it in the beans. Stir in the scallions at the last minute, and you have a scrumptious dish.

Pete uses pickled pork or salt meat in his beans. Pickled pork (pork that has soaked in a salt brine) is unobtainable outside Louisiana, and most salt meat isn't worth its weight, at least in a dish like this. I use very high-quality slab bacon in my beans, and I must say they rival Pete's in flavor.

2 pounds navy beans, picked over and rinsed
2 bay leaves
1 large onion, diced
10 ounces slab bacon, rind removed, cut into
    1 × ¼-inch lengths

Salt and freshly ground black pepper to taste
1 bunch scallions, green tops only, trimmed and
    coarsely chopped

1. Place the beans in a large heavy stockpot, cover them with water, and bring to a boil over high heat. Remove from the heat and drain the beans.

2. Return the beans to the pot and cover with fresh water. Add the bay leaves, onion, and bacon, and bring to a boil over high heat. Reduce the heat to medium and cook the beans at a quick simmer, stirring frequently and adding water as they become dry, for about 1 hour. The beans should remain soupy at all times.

3. When the beans are tender, season them generously with salt and pepper. Reduce the heat to low, partially cover, and continue cooking long enough for them to absorb the seasoning, about 30 minutes. Stir the scallions into the hot beans immediately before serving.

12 SERVINGS (SEE NOTE)

Note: The jambalaya and beans make about double the quantity of the shrimp boil, but they can easily be reheated and served the following day.

Eugenie Vasser and a Celebration on Magazine Street

FAVORITE CREOLE FARE, WITH ELEGANCE

There are some people who are able to see endless opportunities in this world to celebrate, learn, and enjoy. Eugenie Vasser is just such a person.

When we were in Louisiana, Eugenie opened doors where we wouldn't have known to look, fed us meals we might only have dreamed of, gave us, through her friends and the special places she knows, an inside view of Louisiana. We traveled together for almost a week, and at each stop she had a celebration planned, dignifying even the most commonplace events with a meal that revolved around traditional foods. Her intent was to show us the depth of her region's culinary wealth.

Eugenie is as southern as her soft, lulling accent. She grew up in Natchez, Mississippi, among privilege and space, and spent languid summer days fishing in the lake on her parents' small estate, swimming with friends in their pool, collecting pecans from under trees that make a canopy almost to the road in front of the house.

The siren call of New Orleans, about 150 miles to the south, drew Eugenie in her early twenties. Confident, outgoing, and ambitious, she dreamed of opening a bistro where New Orleanians could sip wine and satisfy themselves with small, elegant dishes.

Eugenie settled right in on Bayou St. John, in the center of the city, and fell into more good fortune. Her next-door neighbor was an elderly Creole woman who possessed the secrets of her culture's sensuous cuisine and history. She regaled Eugenie with tales of New Orleans at the turn of the century, and wooed her with authentic Creole food.

"We'd sit, eat, and talk. She knew everything there was to know about Creole history and food," Eugenie said. "I practically lived there, and knowing her was how I first got to know so much about the food of New Orleans."

Good fortune continued to court Eugenie as she opened Flagon's Wine Bar and Bistro on Magazine Street, in a revitalized section of the Garden District. She cooked there herself for the first several years, working with a variety of chefs until she found one who embodied her ideal.

THE PERFECT COOK

Steve Calderera is a native of New Orleans who has traveled the country to cook. He and Eugenie have been friends for years. When she discovered he was returning to New Orleans, she offered him the job as chef at Flagon's and gave him carte blanche.

Steve's signature at Flagon's, which has been renamed 3226 Magazine Street, is Creole cuisine. Like Cajun food, it is gutsy: full of flavor, texture, and color. Based on French cuisine, it is influenced by the diverse ethnic groups in Louisiana, including Native American, Italian, German, Asian, and Caribbean. Many define Creole cuisine as Cajun food gone uptown because it is so similar, yet more refined and complex.

Steve learned the essentials of Creole food at home, from his mother. She taught him to coax the fullest flavors from ingredients, to combine them with a light hand, and to give each a *lagniappe*, a little something extra. That something might be a surprise oyster in the gumbo, spiced mashed potatoes at the bottom of a bowl of soup, or the bite of cloves in a rich and luscious gingerbread.

When we arrived in New Orleans after spending several days touring the bayou country with Eugenie, we did so to news of yet another celebration, this one prepared by Steve. With Eugenie, he wanted to welcome us to the city, and he did so with his favorite Creole dishes, served in formal style.

The guests at the party were the same cast of characters we'd been with in

Houma. Regulars at the restaurant, they walked in as though they were entering a friend's living room. Eugenie and her partner, Charlie Gorrondona, welcomed us at the bar with Sazeracs, a typical New Orleans drink, made with Pernod, Bourbon, Peychaud bitters, and sugar.

FROG LEGS, ANYONE?

Debbie Mallernee bypassed drinks for the kitchen, and I followed. "I've got these fresh-caught frogs' legs, and I want Steve to do something with 'em," she said, swishing through the door. Steve, perspiration beading on his forehead, greeted Debbie with a huge smile, stopped to shake my hand,

handed the frogs' legs to his assistant with quick hushed instructions, and gave us a tour of the kitchen. Debbie went out to join the others at the bar. I stayed on to watch the action.

Dressed in whites with a chef's hat perched on his head, Steve didn't waste a move as he went from pot to skillet, twirled to check a salad, sprinkled, chopped, inhaled, checked the color of simmering vegetables, whisked a roux to completion.

A SON'S THANKS

When I asked him about his flavorful gumbos, soups, and sauces, he gave me a modest smile and in a soft voice talked of cooking with his mother—how much he'd learned, how much he referred to that education. "We cooked all the time, and I

was always in the kitchen," he said, going back for just a moment to what must have surely been happy times. "We made roux, we used Creole tomatoes, peppers, onions, and garlic, greens on Fridays, oysters when they were best—we ate wonderful food."

Steve has professional training in French cuisine, and he has traveled and worked throughout the country, which has given his food added refinement and depth. But when he has fun in the kitchen and cooks what he loves best, it is always the food of his roots. His life experience has served to convince him of one thing: that the cooking he learned at home is his favorite. He has also found that it is the food people love the best.

I rejoined the group in the dining room and we were immediately presented with our first course, the frogs' legs fried to a golden crisp. "Steve does these better than anyone, *anyone*," Debbie exclaimed, taking a bite. Caught in a bayou near Houma, they were as meaty as a chicken thigh, as tender as breast meat, with a flavor that combined the two.

An elegant take on a traditional New Orleans snack came next, an oyster po' boy in miniature. Eugenie called it Steve's version of the "Peacemaker," a po' boy traditionally filled with fried oysters. This one had thin slices of Creole tomatoes, a slice of salty country ham, and fried oysters on pillow-soft bread.

Silence fell as we all tasted the next course, a trio of gumbos. One was duck, mirleton, and shrimp, another rich with greens and oysters, the third a sweet, subtle sherried turtle gumbo. All were luscious and no one left a drop.

What came next was a zingy little dish of fried marinated fish. More like a snack, it was irresistible, seductive.

Steve came out of the kitchen to serve the court bouillon of grouper and stayed by the table as we tasted. Deeply modest, he turned away slightly as though worried we wouldn't like it. The accolade began as a low hum, as each of us murmured, "Mmmmm!" Without any prompting we raised our glasses of Chardonnay to this young man who had produced such a stunning feast. The dénouement, the court bouillon, was a culinary triumph, a work of art down to the last drop of broth and bold spoonful of potatoes.

To acknowledge the toast and return the gesture, Steve filled a glass for himself. "Thank you, thank you. It's always a pleasure to cook for people who love to eat," he said. "And thank my mother, my Creole heritage, and New Orleans."

Steve's Escabeche

As we sat at Flagon's Restaurant in New Orleans, the delicacies kept coming from the kitchen, and this escabeche, a beguilingly spiced dish zinging with flavor, was served as an appetizer. It was one of the first recipes I tried when I got home and it made an instant hit—with me because it was fun and easy to make and I love its flavors, and with guests because it is unusual and intriguing with all of its accompaniments.

Escabeche is traditional to Spain and Provence. Under Steve's influence it becomes a hearty Creole dish redolent with spices and herbs. The fish is fried to a golden brown, then marinated, and it absorbs flavor and develops a rich, delicious texture.

Though cracker crumbs are commercially available, I find the results are better when I make my own.

Be sure to bring this dish to room temperature before serving. Tightly covered, it will keep a week in the refrigerator.

2 pounds firm skinless white fillets, such as rock-fish, grouper, striped bass, petrale sole, lingcod, haddock, or cod
1 cup mild vegetable oil, such as safflower
¾ cup cracker crumbs (20 unsalted saltines)
Cayenne pepper to taste
Salt to taste

MARINADE
¾ cup extra-virgin olive oil
¾ cup best-quality white wine vinegar
½ cup freshly squeezed lemon juice
2 teaspoons cumin seeds, crushed

Salt and freshly ground black pepper to taste
Leaves from 1 large bunch cilantro (about ¾ cup, loosely packed)
1 cup celery leaves
½ cup Kalamata olives, pitted and quartered lengthwise

ACCOMPANIMENTS
½ pound feta cheese, crumbled
2 tomatoes, each cut into 6 wedges
1 cup Italian (flat-leaf) parsley leaves, coarsely chopped
1 cup Kalamata olives

1. Rinse the fish in cold water, and pat it dry. Remove any bones. Cut the fish into ¾-inch squares. Refrigerate loosely wrapped in waxed paper until ready to cook.

2. Line a baking sheet with unprinted brown paper bags. Set it aside.

3. Heat the oil in a large heavy skillet over medium heat.

4. Place the cracker crumbs on a piece of waxed paper, and season with cayenne pepper and salt. Roll the fish pieces in the cracker crumbs, and set them aside. When the oil is hot (a few cracker crumbs dropped in it should sizzle furiously), add several pieces of fish and cook, turning the pieces frequently, until they are golden on all sides, about 4 minutes. Be sure not to crowd the pan. Transfer the fish to the lined baking sheet to drain. Repeat with the remaining fish.

5. In a large bowl, whisk together the olive oil, wine vinegar, and lemon juice. Add the cumin, and salt and pepper, and whisk well. Coarsely chop the cilantro and celery leaves, and whisk them into the mixture. Add the olives, stir, and taste for seasoning.

6. Add the drained fish to the marinade, and stir gently to coat the pieces. Marinate at room temperature for at least 3 hours, stirring occasionally. You can hold this, covered, up to 24 hours in the refrigerator.

7. Serve the escabeche on a platter or individual plates with feta cheese, tomato wedges, parsley leaves, and more olives alongside.

10 APPETIZER SERVINGS

Gumbo z'Herbes

In Louisiana, gumbo z'herbes, or gumbo aux herbes, traditionally was made without meat for dinner on Friday, a day of abstinence observed by the region's large Catholic population. It includes at least three different types of greens, and what it lacks in meaty flavor it makes up for in gutsiness and complexity. Of all the gumbos I've eaten, this is my all-time favorite.

There are a few tricks. The first is to cut the greens properly. Steve Calderera, originator of this recipe, cuts them into a chiffonade (very thin strips) and then into 2-inch lengths. The chiffonade brings out a delicacy in the greens. They melt into the broth and give it tremendous flavor.

Another trick is the roux. It is very simple to make, but working with hot oil demands concentration and caution. When you add the flour, do so slowly because flour can contain moisture, which may cause the oil to spit—use a long-handled whisk. And watch carefully as you stir the roux, because it browns quickly. The minute it is medium brown, the color of a brown paper bag, remove it from the heat.

Like any good dish, this gumbo will reflect the taste of whoever makes it. If you can't find the specific greens the recipe calls for, use others—just be sure to have a variety. It is luscious, for example, with beet greens, kale, and collards, or the greens assembled here in the recipe. I don't think the gumbo needs andouille, so I don't add it unless I have an exceptionally delicious one on hand. You can omit it, or if you must have sausage in your gumbo, try kielbasa. The filé powder, a thickener made from ground sassafras leaves, is also optional.

SOUP
1 large andouille sausage (8 ounces), cut into 2-inch lengthwise slices (optional)
2 pounds bok choy, rinsed and trimmed
10 ounces mustard greens, stems trimmed
15 ounces turnip greens, stems trimmed
1 medium purple-top turnip
3 quarts homemade chicken stock

VEGETABLES
2 tablespoons olive oil
½ cup diced onion
½ cup diced green bell pepper
½ cup diced celery
3 cloves garlic, diced

OYSTERS
2 cups mild vegetable oil, such as safflower
¾ cup unbleached all-purpose flour
Salt and freshly ground black pepper to taste
Cayenne pepper to taste

8 ounces shucked oysters (about 20)

ROUX
¼ cup olive oil
¼ cup unbleached all-purpose flour

GUMBO
½ teaspoon Creole seasoning (see Headnote, page 156)
½ teaspoon filé powder (optional)
2 teaspoons Worcestershire sauce
Salt and freshly ground black pepper to taste
6 drops hot sauce, preferably Crystal or Louisiana brand, or to taste
3 drops Tabasco sauce, or to taste
2 tablespoons soy sauce, or to taste

ACCOMPANIMENTS
Hot sauce
Worcestershire sauce

1. If using the andouille, place it in a large heavy skillet over medium-high heat and sauté until it is golden, about 5 minutes. Remove it from the heat and drain the pieces on an unprinted brown paper bag.

2. Cut the stems from the bok choy, and slice them crosswise into very thin (⅛-inch) strips. Cut the bok choy, mustard, and turnip leaves into a chiffonade: Cut small stacks of leaves in half crosswise, combine the two half stacks, and then cut them lengthwise into very thin (¹⁄₁₆-inch) slices. Slice the turnip into very thin (⅛-inch) matchsticks.

3. In a large stockpot, bring the chicken stock to a boil over medium-high heat. Add the turnip and all the greens, including the bok choy stems, and return to a boil. Reduce the heat to medium-low and simmer, uncovered, until the greens are tender, about 30 minutes. Cover and keep warm over very low heat.

4. In a large skillet, heat the 2 tablespoons olive oil. Add the onions, green peppers, and celery. Cook, stirring frequently, until the vegetables have softened and are a caramel color, adjusting the heat so they brown evenly. The onions will brown first, so use them as a guide for the color of the other vegetables. This will take about 20 minutes. Then stir in the garlic and continue cooking until the vegetables are a deep caramel color, about 10 minutes more. They will look almost burned. Set aside.

5. Next, prepare the oysters. In a large heavy saucepan or a Dutch oven, heat the oil until a wisp of smoke comes off it or it registers 375°F on a deep-fat thermometer.

6. Sift the flour with the spices onto a piece of waxed paper. Drain the oysters and dredge them in the flour. Fry the oysters in the hot oil, without crowding the pan, until they are golden, 2 to 3 minutes. Remove the oysters with a slotted spoon and drain them on unprinted brown paper bags. Set aside.

7. Make a roux by heating the ¼ cup olive oil in a medium-size heavy saucepan over medium-high heat. Slowly whisk in the flour a bit at a time and cook, whisking constantly, until the roux turns the color of a brown paper bag, 4 to 5 minutes. Immediately remove the pan from the heat, and stir in the vegetables. Slowly add 2 cups of the soup, and whisk until the mixture has thickened, 3 to 5 minutes. Then pour this mixture into the soup pot. Increase the heat to medium, and let the gumbo simmer to thicken.

8. Stir all the seasonings into the gumbo, and simmer an additional 10 minutes. Adjust the seasonings to your taste.

9. Ladle the soup into large warmed bowls, and add 2 fried oysters to each bowl, pushing them down into the broth. Serve immediately, with extra hot sauce and Worcestershire sauce on the side.

10 SERVINGS (20 APPETIZER SERVINGS)

Creole Oyster Po' Boy

Steve Calderera gives a refined flavor to everything he cooks while keeping its essential character. This po' boy, which he served as an appetizer, was no exception.

This po' boy was a version of the Peacemaker, or La Médiatrice. According to New Orleans legend, men who stayed out carousing all night brought home fried oysters, kept hot in French bread, to their wives. Not even the hardest heart, it was said, could refuse such a gift, and an oyster po' boy became known as the Peacemaker.

This version of La Médiatrice has smoky ham and fresh tomatoes on it. (Steve uses Creole tomatoes, which are large, uncommonly juicy and flavorful, and nearly impossible to get outside of Louisiana. Just select the best tomatoes you can find.)

I have served these as an appetizer, and for a casual meal they are wonderful as a main course. They have the added attraction of being quick and easy to make.

This recipe makes six small po' boys, each with four fried oysters. You can double their size for a main-course sandwich or simply make more of the small ones.

½ cup unbleached all-purpose flour
1 teaspoon salt
Generous amount of freshly ground
    black pepper
Generous pinch of cayenne pepper
½ cup mild vegetable oil, such as safflower
48 medium shucked oysters, drained and care-
    fully picked over

3 loaves Po' Boy Bread (recipe follows) or Italian
    bread, cut into twelve 3-inch pieces
6 tablespoons best-quality mayonnaise, or to
    taste
6 teaspoons Creole (coarse-grained) mustard, or
    to taste
6 ounces best-quality smoked ham, thinly sliced
4 ripe tomatoes, cut into ¼-inch-thick slices

1. Sift the flour, salt, and peppers together onto a plate or a piece of waxed paper.

2. Heat the oil in a large heavy skillet over medium-high heat. Preheat the broiler. Line a plate with unprinted brown paper bags, and set it aside.

3. Dredge the oysters in the flour, shaking off any excess. When the oil is hot and shimmering, sauté the oysters until they are golden on each side, about 3 minutes per side. You may want to do this in batches, to keep from crowding the pan. Be sure to bring the oil back to the appropriate temperature before frying subsequent batches. Drain the oysters on the brown paper.

4. Prepare the sandwiches: Slice each piece of bread in half horizontally. Toast the cut sides of the bread under the broiler until golden. Spread each cut surface with some mayonnaise. Spread the bottom half of each sandwich with ½ teaspoon Creole mustard. Lay the slices of ham over the mustard, and then add the tomato slices. Top with the oysters. Replace the top halves of the bread, and serve immediately.

Eat Those Po' Boys

Po' boys are sandwiches so loaded with filling that you need not only a bib to stop the sauce on its way down but also a safety net to catch all the luscious oysters or shrimp that tumble out as soon as you take a bite.

It wasn't always so. According to Charles Gorrondona, a native of New Orleans who claims to have subsisted on po' boys when he was growing up, they used to be mostly bread with a little bit of filling. "My mother made them with potted meat, and there'd be a thin little layer of meat and lots of bread," he said. "The further along in the month it got, the thinner the layer was. The idea of a po' boy having eight ounces of meat or seafood on it is ludicrous. Po' boys were food for po' people."

Nonetheless, Charlie is one of the first to enjoy a contemporary po' boy, and at Flagon's his plate was clean when he finished Steve's po' boy.

Po' Boy Bread

As I learned from my New Orleans friend Joanne Clevenger, who is the owner of the Upperline Restaurant, the secret to a good po' boy is in the bread. The interior must be tender enough to be packed down by the juices and the filling, absorbing them at the same time. Joanne always pulls out a bit of the interior of the loaf before filling it. This way what remains becomes a kind of casing, keeping all within.

This is a good all-purpose loaf of bread, and I especially like to make it when I'm going to serve po' boys. It contains no salt, and salt isn't missed in the least in a po' boy—in fact, it's better without it. Salt heightens the flavor of bread, makes it lighter, and removes some of the yeastiness. What you want for a po' boy is substance, and salt in the bread would detract from the ingredients inside. This bread is tender inside, crisp outside—ideal for a sandwich.

2 cups lukewarm water
1 teaspoon active dry yeast
5 ½ cups unbleached all-purpose flour
1 tablespoon olive oil

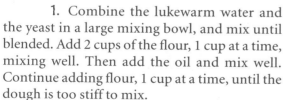

1. Combine the lukewarm water and the yeast in a large mixing bowl, and mix until blended. Add 2 cups of the flour, 1 cup at a time, mixing well. Then add the oil and mix well. Continue adding flour, 1 cup at a time, until the dough is too stiff to mix.

2. Turn the dough out onto a well-floured surface, and knead in the remaining flour until the dough is smooth and satiny. It will be soft, but it should not stick to your fingers when you touch it.

3. Place the dough in a bowl, cover it with a damp towel, and let it rise in a warm (68°F) spot until it has doubled in bulk, 1½ hours. Punch it down and return it to the bowl to rise a second time, 1 hour more.

4. Preheat the oven to 400°F. Line two baking sheets with parchment paper or dust them heavily with flour.

5. Punch down the dough, divide it into three pieces, and roll each piece to form a 13-inch-long loaf. Transfer the loaves to the prepared baking sheets. Press on each loaf gently to flatten it, so it is a flat rectangle rather than baguette-shaped. Let them rise until they have nearly doubled in bulk, 30 to 40 minutes.

6. Make shallow diagonal slashes in the top of each loaf with a sharp knife, and bake the loaves in the center of the oven until they are pale gold and sound hollow when tapped, about 30 minutes.

7. Remove the loaves from the oven and let them cool on a wire rack.

THREE 13-INCH LOAVES

Court Bouillon Blanc

Steve Calderera loves to make this court bouillon (pronounced coo-be-yahn in Louisiana), a traditional Cajun dish that has become, in its elegance, a Creole dish too. In French cuisine, a court bouillon is a simple herb broth. In Louisiana it is as rich as the many cultures that inhabit the state. Here Steve has created a dish that is at once hearty and elegant.

This is a main-course soup with a *lagniappe*, or a little something extra, in the form of highly seasoned mashed potatoes at the bottom. I love it all, from the seasoned broth, to the tender fish, to the delicate, colorful julienne of vegetables.

There are several steps involved in its making, but it is not a difficult dish to prepare. If you can't find a whole snapper or rockfish, use fish fillets; the result will be just as good.

STOCK

7 pounds fresh fish bones, thoroughly rinsed

12 cups very cold water

2 small apples, cored and quartered

2 new potatoes, quartered

2 ribs celery, cut into 1-inch pieces

1 lemon, halved

18 drops Tabasco sauce, or to taste

1 teaspoon Crystal or Louisiana brand hot sauce, or to taste

⅓ cup Zatarain's Crab and Shrimp Boil seasoning, or other quality brand (see Note)

⅛ teaspoon cayenne pepper, or to taste

VEGETABLE MIXTURE

2 tablespoons unsalted butter

2 leeks, white parts only, rinsed well and cut into julienne

Salt and freshly ground black pepper to taste

2 carrots, cut into julienne

2 bunches celery, hearts (tender, pale yellow inner part) only, cut into julienne

2 large tomatoes, peeled, seeded, and diced

FISH

1 whole snapper, rockfish, grouper, or tilapia (4 to 5 pounds), cleaned, head and tail on, or 4 pounds skinless snapper, rockfish, lingcod, petrale sole, or cod fillets

1 lemon, halved

Salt and freshly ground black pepper to taste

1 cup water

1 cup dry white wine, such as Sauvignon Blanc

3 bay leaves

POTATOES

2 pounds new potatoes, scrubbed

3 tablespoons unsalted butter

½ cup milk

Ground white pepper to taste

1 teaspoon Crystal or Louisiana hot sauce, or to taste

Salt and freshly ground black pepper to taste

½ cup (densely packed) Italian (flat-leaf) parsley leaves, coarsely chopped

1. Make the stock: Place the fish bones in a large stockpot, and add all the remaining ingredients. Bring slowly to a boil over medium heat, then reduce the heat and simmer, uncovered, until the bones fall apart when light pressure is applied, 1½ hours. Skim off any foam that collects as it cooks, to remove impurities. Remove the pot from the heat, strain the stock, and set it aside.

2. Prepare the vegetable mixture: Melt the butter in a large heavy skillet over medium-high heat. Stir in the leeks, reduce the heat to medium, and cover. Cook just until they are softened and begin to turn translucent, about 5 minutes. Season with salt and pepper. Remove from the heat and keep warm.

3. Bring a large pot of salted water to a boil. (One tablespoon per gallon is a good ratio.)

Fill a large bowl with ice water and keep it nearby. Add the carrots to the boiling water, return it to the boil, and then, using a slotted spoon, immediately transfer the carrots to the ice water. Return the water to a boil, add the celery, and repeat. When the vegetables are cool, drain them and pat them dry on a kitchen towel. Set them aside, covered with the towel so they don't dry out.

4. Place the tomatoes in a strainer set over a bowl to drain.

5. Preheat the oven to 350°F.

6. If you are using a whole fish: Rub the fish inside and out with the lemon halves, and season it generously inside and out with salt and pepper. Place it in a roasting pan, and pour the water and wine around it. Add the bay leaves to the liquid. Place the pan in the center of the oven and bake until the flesh is opaque, basting every 15 minutes. This should take about 45 minutes. Remove the fish from the pan, reserving the liquid. Carefully pull the skin off the top fillet and remove the fillet from the bones. Turn the fish over, and remove the other fillet. Check the fillets carefully, removing all the bones. Place the fillets in a noncorrosible pan and cover them with enough of the cooking liquid to keep them warm. Set the pan aside.

If you are using fillets, rub them all over with the lemon and season with salt and pepper. Place them in a roasting pan in a single layer, and pour the water and wine around

them. Add the bay leaves to the liquid, and bake in the center of the oven until they are opaque through, 15 to 20 minutes. Remove the fillets from the cooking liquid, and place them in a noncorrosible pan. Pour enough of the cooking liquid over them to keep them warm, and set them aside.

7. For the potatoes: Boil the potatoes in a large saucepan of salted water until they are very tender, about 25 minutes. Transfer them to a large bowl, and using a potato masher or a fork, crush them. Continue crushing the potatoes, mixing in the butter and milk until they are incorporated. Season with the white pepper, hot sauce, and salt and pepper. Stir in the parsley. The potatoes should be smooth but still chunky, and dotted with the red or white of their skins and the green of the parsley.

8. Immediately assemble the court bouillon. Arrange the vegetables, potatoes, and fish near warmed individual serving bowls. Divide the potatoes among the bowls, gently pressing to spread them out over the bottoms of the bowls. Place a piece of fish in each bowl, and then ladle the stock over the fish. Top with the vegetables, and serve immediately.

1O SERVINGS

Note: Crab Boil seasoning is prepared by a variety of manufacturers. If you can't find it, substitute with the same amount of pickling spice.

Creole Ginger Cake

Another gem from Steve Calderera, this cake sings with flavor and spice. Filled with fruit and raisins, showered in confectioners' sugar, and topped with a dollop of whipped cream, it makes a luscious, showy dessert.

This is the perfect dessert for a crowd because it makes a large quantity, and it can be done in advance right down to chilling the cream. If you're having a small gathering, the recipe is easily halved.

It's very simple to make, but don't ever tell anyone because they won't believe it when they see and taste it. The trickiest part is slicing the cake in half horizontally, and that is accomplished using a long, finely serrated knife, with a flexible blade if possible. If circles don't suit you, try triangles, stars, or any shape you like.

I like to use blackstrap molasses, which is more intense than garden variety molasses, and I cut the fruit into very small dice to make it especially attractive.

There are plenty of crumbs left over after cutting out the rounds of cake. Mix them with custard for a quick bread pudding, or eat them plain. They're delicious!

This cake freezes very well.

CAKE
4½ cups unbleached all-purpose flour
4 teaspoons ground cinnamon
5 teaspoons ground cloves
1 teaspoon salt
2 large eggs
1 cup (lightly packed) dark brown sugar
1 cup mild vegetable oil, such as safflower
2 cups molasses
2 cups hot water
3 tablespoons baking soda

FILLING
4 tablespoons (½ stick) unsalted butter
2 tablespoons molasses

½ teaspoon ground allspice
½ teaspoon ground nutmeg
½ teaspoon ground cinnamon
2 tart apples, peeled and diced
2 slightly underripe pears, peeled and diced
1 cup raisins

GARNISH
1½ cups heavy (or whipping) cream
3 tablespoons confectioners' sugar, sifted
2 oranges, peel and pith removed, separated into
   sections

1. Preheat the oven to 375°F. Line two

13 × 9 × 2-inch baking pans with parchment paper. Then lightly butter the pans and dust them with flour. Place a bowl and a whisk in the freezer, to chill for whipping the cream.

2. Make the cake: Sift the dry ingredients together three times onto a piece of waxed paper. In a large mixing bowl, combine the eggs with the brown sugar, and mix until pale yellow and light, 5 to 7 minutes. Add the oil and the molasses, and mix well. In a medium-size bowl, combine the hot water and the baking soda, and stir until dissolved. Beginning and ending with the dry ingredients, add the dry ingredients to the egg mixture alternating with the baking soda mixture, and mixing well after each addition.

3. Pour the batter into the prepared pans, and bake in the center of the oven until the cakes are puffed and spring back lightly when touched, 25 to 27 minutes. Remove the pans from the oven and let them cool on

wire racks for 15 minutes. Then turn the cakes out of the pans and let them cool on the racks. Carefully peel the parchment paper off the cooled cakes.

4. Prepare the filling: Melt the butter in a large heavy skillet over medium-low heat. Stir in the molasses and spices, then the apples, pears, and raisins. Cook, covered, until the fruit has softened, about 15 minutes. Remove the pan from the heat and set it aside.

5. Whip the cream with 1 tablespoon of the confectioners' sugar.

6. To assemble the dessert, slice each cake in half horizontally. Leaving the halves together, cut 6 rounds from each cake using a 4-inch cookie cutter or a glass. (Alternatively, cut out the rounds and then slice each in half horizontally.) Place the bottom rounds on dessert plates. Divide the filling among the rounds, mounding it on top. Place the top rounds over the filling. Dust the tops with the remaining confectioners' sugar, and garnish each with a dollop of whipped cream and 2 orange sections. Serve immediately.

12 SERVINGS

Buon Natale

ITALIAN CHRISTMAS CELEBRATIONS

When Italians gather for Christmas Eve dinner, seafood is always on the menu—an age-old tradition that began when the Catholic Church imposed *mangiare di magro*, or eating lean, on the eve of holidays. Italians have interpreted this to mean an absence of meat, but that doesn't mean the seafood dishes can't be sumptuous.

Christmas is an important family holiday for Italians, and they gather in a joyous frenzy of food and gift-giving. Guests usually head straight for the kitchen, some with covered dishes in hand, others with fresh ingredients to prepare.

At the DeLuca home in San Pedro, California, Christmas Eve is an important affair. Casual and familiar, it is rich with ritual and anticipation as everyone, from grandmother to granddaughter, prepares their favorite dishes. The DeLucas are the owners of State Fish, one of the largest seafood wholesalers in the state. In their home, seafood is not only important but also as good as it gets.

Vanessa DeLuca is surprised at the interest in her family's Christmas Eve feast. "You know, ethnic food is hip now, but we've always cooked like this," she said. "We're just doing simple, fresh cooking."

When she says fresh, she means live and wriggling. "When Italians eat a traditional Christmas Eve dinner, they've got live crabs, lobsters, eels, shrimp, clams, and oysters," she said. "Fresh" also refers to the vegetable accompaniments, such as broccoli rabe and Vanessa's famous escarole pie. "I always make it, and I have to tell you, it is really good," she said.

Traditionally, at least in this family, which hails from the island of Ischia off Naples, the seafood (except for the clams) is cooked all together in a tomato-based broth, cioppino style. When the seafood is cooked it is removed from the broth, and the broth is reduced to thicken. Pasta topped with the broth, rich with the flavor of all the seafood cooked in it, is served first. Then the table is heaped with dishes, from the fish to the greens to the signature stuffed clams, carefully prepared by Vanessa's grandmother, Filomena DiBernardo.

Her secret to the luscious clams is shucking them live. "She always makes a point of taking them out of the shell and chopping them," Vanessa said. "She says it makes a big difference."

ROSE CAIRO'S CHRISTMAS

There are twenty regions in Italy, each with its own cuisine, and Christmas Eve meals vary. For instance, Rose Cairo, whose maiden

name was Giardino ("My name means 'rose garden,'" she said with a giggle), hails from the small town of Ogliastro, south of Naples. Rose has lived in Providence, Rhode Island since she was ten years old, but she learned to cook Christmas Eve dinner in Italy, from her mother and grandmother. She still prepares it all for her three sons, their wives, and her four grandchildren.

Like many Italians, Rose serves seven kinds of fish, a rule she learned when she was younger. "I don't know why seven, but that's how it has always been," she said.

Each year she makes the same things, with minor variations based on her family's requests. Her meal begins with marinated vegetables called Insalada de Rinforzo. It has anchovies in it, which counts for one variety of fish.

She follows the first fish offering with an unsweetened dough that she fries into pastries called *crespelle*.

"They're supposed to be drizzled with honey, but I never get that far with them. In fact, they never make it out of the kitchen because as soon as I fry them, they get eaten," she said.

The dough is all-purpose, the same one she uses to make baccalao (salt cod) fritters. "If I make those, they don't make it out of the kitchen either," she said.

Stuffed squid in a light marinara sauce is the main dish, followed by conch salad and then a huge platter of fried fish sprinkled with pepperoncini.

"We make up the seven types of fish in the fried fish," she said. "And sometimes, I'll admit, there might be eight or nine kinds of fish."

REMEMBRANCE OF CHRISTMASES PAST

Sisters Heidi Loomis and Traci Maceroni have an Italian grandmother, Alice Castellucci, who came from the Emiglia Romagna region and who always created a memorable Christmas Eve dinner, with help from her sister Frances Fera. Several years ago Traci and Heidi took it over, and they re-create it religiously each year.

"I wish I could make you feel the warmth of those Christmas Eves when my grandmother and my great-aunt still made all the food," Traci said. "It was incredible. I'd stay at my grandmother's the night before and help her with all the cooking, and I just loved it. My mother used to talk about how when she was a child the table was so long it stretched through three rooms in the house, and they'd eat and eat and eat."

Traci's nostalgia for those meals and her love of cooking have positioned her to become head cook on Christmas Eve. Heidi helps, and her specialty is her grandmother's Conch Salad (see Index). "I make seven pounds every year, it takes four days to make, and it's the best thing I've ever eaten," Heidi said.

Following the rule of seven, Traci tries to limit herself to seven kinds of fish. "We rarely stick to it," Heidi said. "Traci seems to get out of control. She comes up with these new things, and they're so delicious we beg for them every year."

One of the favorites is her stuffed clams. Another is a variation on clams casino with piquant cilantro sauce. "We've got a friend who says she won't come to Christmas Eve if Traci doesn't make her green clams. And where do you think we are at 10 A.M. on Christmas morning? Heating up leftover 'stuffies' in the oven," Heidi said.

At least twenty people attend the Maceroni-Loomis Christmas Eve dinner. Traci has three children, Heidi has two, they have a cousin on the West Coast who tries to come home, their grandmother attends, and they always invite friends.

"Every year Traci invites someone who has never been to this kind of a meal, so they get a chance to see what it's like," Heidi said. "They beg to come back."

The meal always includes the conch salad, stuffed squid, shrimp cocktail, fried smelt—the tiniest they can find—linguine with red clam sauce, marinated eel, and sometimes baked baccalao.

Although their grandmother usually made zuppa inglese, a rich custardy dessert that resembles trifle, neither of the women makes a dessert. "We're not big on dessert in our family," Heidi said. "I remember when I was little and all the adults would sit at the table and eat biscotti and dried fruit and nuts and drink grappa. I didn't like any of it."

Nonetheless, she always has fruit, nuts, roasted chestnuts, and biscotti on hand. After all, it's traditional.

AN IRISH-ITALIAN MIX

Back on the West Coast, Angelina McElroy, a Californian whose mother came from near Naples, always prepares an Italian feast for Christmas Eve. "My kids are grown and gone," she said, "but they always come home for Christmas, and they always want the same food."

Mrs. McElroy, who is married to an Irishman, offers an eclectic meal that has grown to accommodate the tastes of her family. She has introduced meat in the form of seasoned hams and sausages, but the antipasti that covers her table revolves around seafood. There are lots of little dishes of things like sardines, shrimp with a spicy cocktail sauce, a variety of marinated vegetables, ratatouille, and squid marinara. "And we have to have anchovies," she said. "It wouldn't be right without anchovies."

Fourteen people sit down for Christmas Eve dinner at the McElroys. "I've outgrown my dining room table," Angelina said. First, they drink red wine through hollow fennel stems, a family tradition. "Fennel is important to the meal. So are chestnuts, nuts, and biscotti with a demitasse."

For Christmas Eve there are certain things all Italians agree upon, coast to coast. The rule is seven kinds of fish, eel is traditional, roast chestnuts must make an appearance, celery and/or fennel are important, clams are vital, a red sauce appears somewhere. More than that, however, they all agree that spending the evening with friends and family is the most important thing. As Heidi Loomis said, "We love it, we talk about it all year, and we can't wait to get together and do it again."

Rose's Christmas Salad Vegetables

An Italian Christmas Eve supper wouldn't be complete without an antipasto platter, and this is antipasto all rolled into one mixture. The vegetables are tender and full of flavor, the anchovies add a rich undercurrent, and the rosemary gives it a light freshness. Use the best-quality marinated artichoke hearts you can find, and be sure to salt the eggplant, to remove any bitterness from the flesh.

I like to have these vegetables on hand to serve as an hors d'oeuvre, to toss along with greens for a big salad, or to put on bread for a quick snack. They are also delicious stirred into vegetable or bean soup, or added to a simple cheese sandwich. Once you've tried those, you'll think of many more uses for them, so keep a supply in your refrigerator.

2 canned anchovy fillets
Milk, for soaking
1 large eggplant (20 ounces), peeled and cut into
  ½-inch cubes
1 tablespoon salt, plus additional to taste
½ cup plus 3 tablespoons extra-virgin olive oil
2 large green bell peppers
1 large red bell pepper
¼ cup freshly squeezed lemon juice
¼ teaspoon dried red pepper flakes, or to taste
Freshly ground black pepper to taste

1 heaping teaspoon fresh rosemary leaves, or a
  pinch of dried
¾ cup marinated artichoke hearts, drained and
  cut lengthwise into ¼-inch-thick slices
1 cup Italian or French black olives
4 ounces button mushrooms, brushed clean and
  thinly sliced
2 ribs celery, strings removed, cut into ⅛-inch-
  thick slices
2 large cloves garlic, minced

1. Soak the anchovies in milk to cover for 20 minutes. Drain, rinse quickly under running water, and pat dry. Mince the anchovies and set them aside.

2. Place the eggplant cubes in a colander, sprinkle them with 1 tablespoon salt, and toss so the pieces are evenly covered. Let drain for 30 minutes. Then rinse them quickly with cool water, and pat dry in a kitchen towel.

3. Heat 2 tablespoons of the olive oil in a nonstick skillet over medium-high heat. When it is hot, add the eggplant and cook, stirring frequently, until it is golden and soft, about 8 minutes. Remove from the heat and set aside.

4. Roast the bell peppers, speared on a long-handled fork, over the flame of a gas burner until their skins are completely charred. (If you don't have a gas stove, roast them under the broiler, placing them about 2 inches from the heat source.) Place the charred peppers in a brown paper bag to steam. When they are cool enough to handle, remove the skin, the core, and the seeds. Dice, and set aside.

5. Whisk the lemon juice and the remaining olive oil together in a large bowl. Whisk in the red pepper flakes, salt, and pepper. Mince the fresh rosemary leaves (or crush the dried leaves), and add them.

6. Whisk the anchovies into the dressing, and then add all the remaining ingredients, including the cooked eggplant. Toss until everything is thoroughly coated, and marinate, uncovered, for at least 2 hours at room temperature before serving. Covered and refrigerated, this will keep indefinitely.

4 CUPS; 8 APPETIZER SERVINGS

Castellucci Ricotta-Stuffed Squid in Wine

This is one of the favorite dishes at the Loomis-Maceroni home on Christmas Eve. Traci and Heidi's grandmother, Alice Castellucci, always served the stuffed squid in a marinara sauce. The two granddaughters decided they preferred it with the simpler white wine and garlic sauce, and this is how they make it now. It's wonderfully light and simple, with a decidedly parsley flavor underscored by a subtle hint of nutmeg. The addition of raisins at the last minute is Traci's inspired touch.

Buy fresh whole squid if you can, and clean them yourself. If you can't get fresh squid, buy frozen, which is generally very good quality although sometimes rather battered. (The mantles tend to have rips in them, which you must close with a toothpick to keep the filling inside.)

The amount of filling needed depends entirely on the size of the squid. The ideal mantle size to stuff is about 3 inches long. If those you have are varied, stuff the larger ones only half full so the stuffing will stretch to fill everything. If you have all large ones, increase the amount of stuffing accordingly, and bake the squid for an extra 5 minutes to cook the filling through.

Note that you will need two 13 × 10-inch baking dishes to prepare this dish.

3 pounds squid, cleaned (see Box, page 182)

STUFFING
About 12 cups (loosely packed) Italian (flat-leaf)
   parsley leaves
4 large eggs
2 pounds ricotta cheese
4 cloves garlic, minced
1 teaspoon freshly grated nutmeg
1 cup fresh bread crumbs
½ cup freshly grated Parmesan cheese
1 cup raisins

Salt and freshly ground black pepper

FOR COOKING THE SQUID
5 tablespoons olive oil
10 cloves garlic, minced
4 cups dry white wine
Salt and freshly ground
   black pepper

To Clean Squid

1. Pull the head with the tentacles from the mantle, which will also remove most of the viscera. Reach inside the mantle to remove any viscera that remain.

2. Inside the mantle is a long, transparent, flexible "pen," which is the "shell" of the squid. Pull it out and discard, then rinse the mantle thoroughly under cold water, and pat it dry.

3. Cut the tentacles from the head right in front of the eyes, then using your thumb and forefinger, gently squeeze out and discard the beak—a tiny piece of cartilage—from the center of the tentacles.

1. Rinse the mantles of the squid, and check them to be sure they are completely free of viscera. Separate the tentacles and the mantles. Pat the mantles dry. Refrigerate, covered, 6 ounces of whole tentacles for garnish, and finely chop the remaining tentacles.

2. Prepare the stuffing: Reserve 1 cup of the parsley leaves for garnish. Mince the remaining parsley.

3. Whisk the eggs together in a large bowl. Whisk in the ricotta, then stir in the minced parsley, garlic, nutmeg, bread crumbs, Parmesan cheese, and raisins. Mix until thoroughly blended, then season to taste with salt and pepper. Add the chopped tentacles and mix well. Set aside, uncovered, for about 30 minutes before stuffing the squid.

4. Check the mantles of the squid for any tears or cuts. If there are large openings other than at the top, close them with a toothpick. Stuff the mantles with the ricotta mixture, using a teaspoon or a pastry tube fitted with a #2 tip, until the squid is two thirds full. Gently press the stuffing down to the tip of the mantle, and close the mantle with a toothpick. Prick each stuffed mantle several times with a skewer to prevent it from popping during cooking.

5. Preheat the oven to 350°F.

6. Heat 2 tablespoons of the olive oil in a large nonstick skillet over medium-high heat. Add 2 teaspoons of the garlic and as many stuffed squid as will fit in the skillet with room between them. Cook until they are pale golden, which will take 2 to 3 minutes per side. Don't be

concerned if some of the stuffing seeps out and begins to brown on the bottom of the pan—it is impossible to avoid this and it actually contributes to the overall flavor and texture of the finished dish.

7. Transfer the browned squid to one of the baking dishes, arranging them in one layer.

8. Deglaze the skillet with ½ cup of the wine, allowing it to boil and scraping the brown bits from the bottom of the pan. Continue cooking and stirring until the skillet is clean and the wine has reduced by about one third, which will take just a few minutes. Pour the liquid over the squid.

9. Repeat Step 6 with the remaining squid, using 1 tablespoon of oil and 2 teaspoons of garlic for each batch.

10. After the last batch of stuffed squid is browned, remove them from the skillet, deglaze the pan with the remaining wine, and add the reserved tentacles, the raisins, and any remaining garlic to the pan. Cook, stirring and scraping constantly, until the tentacles are curled and tender-firm, about 5 minutes. Pour the contents of the skillet over the stuffed squid. Season to taste with salt and pepper.

11. Bake the squid on the center rack in the oven until they are white and firm and the sauce is bubbling, 25 to 30 minutes. (You may have to do one baking dish at a time.) Mince the reserved parsley, and sprinkle it over the squid after you remove them from the oven. Serve immediately.

8 SERVINGS

Traci's Baccalao

This is another of Alice Castellucci's Christmas Eve dishes. Made with salt cod that is rinsed of salt and plumped in fresh water, it is luscious, full of sweet and sour taste.

Because the cod remains somewhat salty no matter how long you soak it, I go very easy on salt in the other parts of the dish. In fact, the only other part I salt is the onions, and those get just a pinch.

This is delicious, beautiful, ultimately satisfying. Serve it on Christmas Eve—and whenever else you're in the mood for an aromatic seafood supper.

2 large fillets of salt cod (1½ pounds each)
1 cup unbleached all-purpose flour
Freshly ground black pepper to taste
2 large onions, thinly sliced
10 to 12 tablespoons olive oil
1 medium onion, coarsely chopped
2 large cloves garlic, minced
3 cans (28 ounces each) plum tomatoes with

their liquid, coarsely chopped
2 tablespoons fresh thyme, or 1 teaspoon dried
1 tablespoon fresh marjoram or oregano leaves or
  ½ teaspoon dried
Pinch of salt
2 tablespoons balsamic vinegar
2½ cups pitted prunes

1. Place the cod in a large container and add water to cover. Let it soak for 24 hours, changing the water at least three times to remove as much salt as possible. If the cod is still very salty after 24 hours, continue to soak it for another 8 hours or so.

2. Sift the flour and pepper together onto a piece of waxed paper.

3. Put the sliced onions and 2 tablespoons of the olive oil in a large heavy skillet over medium-high heat. When the onions begin to sizzle, stir them, reduce the heat to medium, and cover. Cook until they are translucent and soft, about 20 minutes. Remove the onions from the pan, and set them aside. Reserve the pan.

4. Cut the salt cod into serving-size pieces (about 4 ounces each), and dredge them in the flour.

5. Add 2 tablespoons of the olive oil to the same skillet you used for the onions, and place it over medium heat. When the oil is hot but before it smokes, add the fish and brown it on both sides, about 5 minutes per side. You will need to do the fish in batches, adding more oil for each batch, up to a total of 8 tablespoons of oil. Once browned, transfer the fish to a plate and cover to keep warm.

6. Preheat the oven to 350°F.

7. To make the sauce, place the chopped onion and 2 tablespoons of the oil in a skillet and cook over medium-high heat until nearly transparent, about 8 minutes. Stir in the garlic, then add the tomatoes and the herbs. Season with the pinch of salt and pepper to taste, and cook just until the tomato sauce has lost its edge and the flavors have begun to blend, about 10 minutes. Remove from the heat and stir in the balsamic vinegar.

8. To assemble the dish, place one fourth of the tomato sauce in each of two 8 × 14-inch baking dishes. Spread half the sliced onions in each, and then divide the cod between the

dishes. Follow with the remaining tomato sauce. Arrange a ring of prunes around the edge of the baking dishes, pressing them into the sauce. Bake on the center rack of the oven until the fish is hot and cooked through, about 25 minutes. Remove from the heat and serve immediately.

8 TO 10 SERVINGS

Holiday Conch Salad

Heidi Winkler Loomis makes this salad once a year: for Christmas Eve supper. She starts it at least three days ahead, tossing it and adding more marinade each day so the flavors stay bright and alive and completely permeate the conch, which absorbs a certain amount of the liquids. The result is a tangy, garlic-rich, crisp salad with an intriguing texture and flavor. The conch, which are very mild, add a sweet clamlike flavor of their own.

3½ pounds conch
4 ribs celery

DRESSING FOR THE FIRST DAY
2 cups best-quality red wine vinegar
⅔ cup freshly squeezed lemon juice
½ cup extra-virgin olive oil
½ teaspoon dried red pepper flakes
Salt and freshly ground black pepper to taste
*5 whole garlic cloves, smashed with the side of a
    chef's knife*
3 bay leaves

DRESSING FOR THE SECOND DAY
¼ cup freshly squeezed lemon juice
1 cup best-quality red wine vinegar
¼ cup extra-virgin olive oil
Salt and freshly ground black pepper to taste
Dried red pepper flakes to taste

DRESSING FOR THE THIRD DAY
¼ cup freshly squeezed lemon juice
½ cup extra-virgin olive oil
Salt and freshly ground black pepper to taste
Dried red pepper flakes to taste

1. Fit a food processor with the 2 mm slicing blade. Cut the conch so they fit in the hopper, and slice them. Discard any hard gristle that doesn't slice. (Alternatively, use a sharp

knife to cut the conch crosswise into paper-thin slices.) Slice the celery as well.

2. Combine the conch and the celery in a large bowl and toss with your hands. In a medium-size bowl, make the first-day dressing: Whisk together the vinegar and the lemon juice. Slowly drizzle in the olive oil, whisking constantly so the mixture emulsifies. Add the red pepper flakes and season with salt and pepper. Mix in the garlic cloves and the bay leaves, and pour the sauce over the conch and celery. Toss well, cover, and refrigerate. Toss the salad at least twice the first day.

3. On the second day, whisk the lemon juice, vinegar, and olive oil together in a small bowl. Pour this over the salad, toss, and adjust the seasoning with salt, black pepper, and red pepper flakes. Cover and refrigerate. Toss the salad at least twice on the second day.

4. On the third day, remove the salad from the refrigerator. In a small bowl, whisk together the lemon juice and olive oil. Pour it over the salad. Toss, and adjust the salt, pepper, and pepper flakes. Cover and refrigerate. Toss the salad at least twice the third day.

5. Either serve the salad on the fourth day, or continue to add olive oil, vinegar and/or lemon juice, and seasonings. The salad will keep well for at least 7 days.

10 TO 12 SERVINGS

Vanessa's Escarole Pie

*V*anessa DeLuca's family has been in the fish business in San Pedro for years, and she is now at the helm. She's a powerful leader, not only at the company but also in the fishing industry, where she is often called upon to lend her valued knowledge and opinions.

On Christmas Eve each year, twenty-five members of the DeLuca family assemble at Vanessa's parents' home for a traditional Italian meal. Vanessa's contribution is this escarole pie. "This is my favorite thing to

make all year round, and whenever I get asked to bring something, I always bring this pie," she said.

With its zesty combination of raisins, pine nuts, anchovies, and bitter greens, it reflects her Sicilian background. "Sicilians always serve bitter greens at Christmas—I'm not sure why," she says. "But I do know that everyone loves this pie." Serve this as a vegetable alongside the main dish.

6 *canned anchovy fillets*
Milk, for soaking
3 *heads escarole (about 12 ounces each), carefully rinsed and trimmed, leaves separated*
2 *tablespoons olive oil*
3 *large cloves garlic*
⅓ *cup pine nuts, toasted (see Note, page 223)*

½ *cup pimiento-stuffed olives, coarsely chopped*
½ *cup raisins*
1 *tablespoon drained capers*
Salt and freshly ground black pepper to taste
1 *egg*
2 *teaspoons water*
Double-Crust Pastry Dough (page 108)

1. Preheat the oven to 425°F. Place the anchovies in a shallow dish and cover them with the milk; allow them to soak for at least 30 minutes. Then drain the anchovies and finely chop them.

2. Fill the bottom of a vegetable steamer 3 inches deep with water, and bring to a boil. Place the escarole in the steamer basket, cover, and steam until the escarole has wilted and turned dark green, 3 to 5 minutes. Remove the steamer from the heat and drain the escarole thoroughly. Coarsely chop the escarole, and set it aside.

3. Place the oil and the garlic in a large heavy skillet over medium heat, and sauté the garlic until it softens and begins to turn golden, about 5 minutes. Add the anchovies, pine nuts, olives, raisins, and capers, and sauté until they are heated through, about 8 minutes. Then stir in the escarole and cook until it is heated through, about 10 minutes. Reduce the heat to medium and continue cooking until most, but not all, of the liquid has evaporated, an additional 2 to 3 minutes. Season with salt and pepper, and remove from the heat.

4. Whisk the egg and water together in a small bowl, and set aside.

5. On a lightly floured surface, roll out 1 of the pastry dough disks to fit a 10-inch pie plate or cast-iron skillet. Line the plate with the dough, letting the excess hang over the edges. Roll out the other half of the dough for the

dough top, and set it aside. Spoon the escarole mixture into the pie shell, patting it down evenly. Brush the edges of the dough with some of the egg wash, and place the dough top over the pie, pressing it gently onto the edges of the bottom dough. Trim and crimp the edges, brush the top with the egg wash, and make at least 8 small cuts in it to let the steam escape. Place the pie on a baking sheet, and bake in the center of the oven until the pastry is golden, about 55 to 60 minutes. Serve immediately.

8 SERVINGS

Zesty Lemon Broccoli

This is the only vegetable served at the Winkler-Maceroni table on Christmas Eve. Everything else is seafood. The twenty people who attend each year eat their way through everything, including this bright, simple salad, which is a refreshing counterpoint to the rest of the meal.

Serve this salad immediately after you make it, as the lemon juice causes the broccoli to turn a distressing olive green color if you let it sit.

3 *pounds broccoli*
2 *tablespoons minced garlic (about 5 cloves)*
⅔ *cup freshly squeezed*
    lemon juice

1. Trim off all the broccoli florets, and cut them into bite-size pieces. Peel the stems, and cut them into ½-inch-thick slices.

2. Fill the bottom of a vegetable steamer 2 inches deep with water and bring to a boil. Steam the broccoli just until it is beginning to become tender and has turned a bright green, about 4 minutes. Remove it from the steamer and transfer it to a large bowl. Toss with the garlic and the lemon juice, and serve immediately.

6 TO 8 SERVINGS

Almond Biscotti

These Italian cookies bake to a hard golden crunch. Deliciously infused with citrus, spices, and the toasty flavor of fresh almonds, they are quite sweet and perfect for serving after dinner for dipping in a cup of espresso, dark tea, or Sambuca. Biscotti like these are a favorite dessert after Christmas Eve supper.

2 cups unbleached all-purpose flour
1 teaspoon baking powder
1 teaspoon ground cinnamon
¼ teaspoon freshly grated nutmeg
Pinch of salt
7 tablespoons unsalted butter, at room temperature
1 cup (packed) light brown sugar
¾ cup granulated sugar
2 large eggs
1 teaspoon vanilla extract

Minced zest of 1 lemon
Minced zest of 1 orange
¾ cup blanched almonds, ground
2½ cups blanched almonds, lightly toasted (see Note) and coarsely chopped

EGG WASH
1 egg
Pinch of sugar
2 teaspoons water

1. Preheat the oven to 325°F. Line 2 baking sheets with parchment paper.

2. Sift the flour, baking powder, spices, and salt together onto a sheet of waxed paper.

3. In a large mixing bowl, cream the butter until it is pale yellow. Then add the sugars and mix until light, about 2 minutes. Add the eggs one at a time, mixing until fluffy. Then stir in the vanilla and the citrus zests.

4. Add the dry ingredients and mix quickly. Then add the ground almonds and mix well. Quickly stir in the chopped toasted almonds, making sure they are evenly distributed throughout the dough.

5. Divide the dough into fourths. On a lightly floured surface, roll one piece to form a 14 × 1½-inch log. Place it on one of the prepared baking sheets, and press on it gently to make a loaf about ½ inch high. Repeat with the remain-

ing dough, leaving at least 2 inches between the loaves. (The dough will almost double in bulk as it bakes.)

6. Whisk the egg wash ingredients together in a small bowl, and brush the egg wash over the top and sides of the loaves. Bake them in the center of the oven until they are golden and puffed, about 20 minutes. Remove the loaves from the oven and transfer them to wire racks to cool. Leave the oven on.

7. Cut each loaf into ½-inch-thick slices, return them to the baking sheets, placing them on their sides on the baking sheets. Bake until they are golden on one side, about 8 minutes. Then turn them over and bake until they are golden on the other, another 6 to 8 minutes. Check them to be sure they are not getting too brown.

8. Remove the biscotti from the oven and transfer them to wire racks to cool. Stored in an airtight tin, these biscotti will keep for a month.

ABOUT 72 COOKIES

Note: To lightly toast almonds, bake them in a 300°F oven until pale gold, about 12 minutes.

Chocolate Almond Cookies

Vicki Mastromarino, a neighbor of ours in Maine whose husband, Joe, comes from a rousing Italian family, makes dozens of cookies year-round, and these are the ones that always appear at Christmas. When she heard I was working on this book, she offered the recipe to me, and I found it too good to pass up. Vicki warned me that I might find the recipe a little strange—there is no butter or oil in it.

These are very intense cookies, filled with chunks of chocolate that stay slightly soft even as the cookies harden—and harden they will. They get so crisp they almost shatter, and so they are perfect for dipping in coffee.

These cookies, which are a slight variation of Vicki's, are delicious the day they are made, but they improve with age and will keep for several weeks in an airtight container. If you don't want to chop the chocolate, use very high quality chocolate chips.

4 cups unbleached all-purpose flour
½ cup unsweetened cocoa powder
1 tablespoon baking powder
1 tablespoon ground cloves
1 tablespoon ground cinnamon
Pinch of salt
16 ounces bittersweet chocolate, preferably Lindt
   or Tobler, or good-quality chocolate chips

2 large eggs
2 cups sugar
Minced zest of 1 orange
¾ cup very strong brewed coffee, cooled
2 teaspoons vanilla extract
1 pound whole blanched almonds, toasted
   (see Note, page 190)

1. Preheat the oven to 350°F. Line 4 baking sheets with parchment paper, or heavily butter them.

2. Sift the flour, cocoa, baking powder, cloves, cinnamon, and salt together onto a piece of waxed paper.

3. Chop the chocolate into chips the size of a pea. (The pieces will be uneven in size, but don't worry about it.)

4. In a large mixing bowl, combine the eggs and the sugar and whip until the mixture is pale yellow and light. Mix in the orange zest, ½ cup of the coffee, and the vanilla. Then add the dry ingredients and mix just until combined. If the mixture is very dry, add more of the coffee to make a sticky dough. Add the almonds and the chocolate chips, and mix until combined. The dough will be quite stiff and somewhat sticky, but it should be easy to handle.

5. Divide the dough into 4 pieces. Cover 3 of them with aluminum foil or a damp tea towel to prevent them from drying out, and set them aside. Roll the fourth piece on a floured work surface to form a log that measures 14 × 1½ inches. (Lightly flour your hands if the dough sticks to them.) Then take a rolling

pin and gently roll it over the log to flatten it. Using a chef's knife, cut the log diagonally into ½-inch-thick strips. Transfer the strips to one of the prepared baking sheets, placing them ½ inch apart. Repeat with the remaining dough.

6. Bake the cookies in the center of the oven until they are puffed and look dry, 15 to 20 minutes. (When they have baked for 15 minutes, the cookies will have a somewhat cakelike texture. During the last 5 minutes, they will harden like biscotti.) Remove them from the oven, and transfer them to wire racks to cool.

ABOUT 72 COOKIES

Sesame Seed Biscotti

*T*hese biscotti are very common in Italian bakeries but they are easy enough to make at home. Like other cookies of their ilk, they are perfect for dunking in coffee or Vino Santo, the Italian dessert wine, and make a wonderful sweet ending to any meal along with fresh or dried fruit. Serve these, with the Almond Biscotti and the Chocolate Almond Cookies, after an Italian Christmas Eve supper.

3 cups unbleached all-purpose flour
½ teaspoon baking powder
¼ teaspoon salt
¼ cup milk
2 teaspoons vanilla extract

8 tablespoons (1 stick) unsalted butter, at room temperature
¾ cup sugar
3 large eggs
1 cup sesame seeds

1. Sift the flour, baking powder, and salt together onto a piece of waxed paper. In a small bowl, combine the milk and the vanilla extract.

2. In a large bowl, cream the butter until it is pale yellow. Add the sugar, and mix until light, about 2 minutes. Then add the eggs one at a time, mixing well after each addition.

3. Alternating with the milk and vanilla, add the dry ingredients to the egg mixture, beginning and ending with dry ingredients. Mix

until well blended, then wrap the dough in waxed paper and aluminum foil and refrigerate for at least 1 hour, or as long as overnight.

4. Preheat the oven to 350°F. Line 2 baking sheets with parchment paper, or lightly oil them.

5. Place the sesame seeds in a shallow bowl or on a rimmed plate.

6. Pinch off teaspoon-size balls of dough and roll them into small log shapes. Roll them in the sesame seeds so they are completely covered, and place them on the lined baking sheets, leaving ½ inch between them.

7. Bake in the center of the oven until the cookies are pale golden, 20 minutes. Remove them from the oven and transfer them to wire racks to cool.

ABOUT 48 COOKIES

Winter Solstice Fishing Celebration

December 21 (or thereabouts) marks the winter solstice, the shortest day of the year, the farthest spot on the sun's journey south. One year I was invited to join a celebration in Camden, Maine, where Shebang!, a street theater company whose philosophy involves "revolution through magic," would enact their own winter solstice ritual.

It was bitter cold and in Harbor Park, which overlooks Camden Harbor, it was colder still. A crowd assembled and candles lit the night. I didn't know what to expect from this celebration, and before I realized it I was caught up in its magic and mystery.

Eerie wailing by several performers floated over the park, its pitch rising and falling on the wind. Just steps from the lights and shoppers of Main Street, a circle of haunting figures in layers of ragged clothing sat around a gnarled stump. Their eyes were piercing, their voices still. Some beat slowly on drums. Other performers, hidden behind masks and dressed in black and yellow, wove lightly through the crowd, waving smoking smudge sticks. Still others peered deeply into the crowd, beckoning.

Flickering in the darkness, candles, in bags marked with the phases of the moon, surrounded the entire performance area.

A hush fell. A flute sung out, and the seated figures rose and danced slowly, bringing onlookers into a circle of movement around and around the stump. Drums began to beat again, performers moaned and cried. The crowd moved away and many took up the chill moan while the figures tore at themselves and their clothing. They shuddered, they huddled in sadness and horror, they filled the clear night with a palpable, terrible sadness.

FISHING FOR LIGHT

Absorbed in mourning, they couldn't see that beyond the park a procession was arriving. The processional figures were jaunty, brightly dressed fishermen possessed with life and purpose, rolling an enormous wheel with crazy spokes of string, their symbol of a fishing net. They danced ahead with it, around the base of the hill and out of sight.

Suddenly the figures on the hill burst from their melancholy and moved to the crest of the slope, followed by the curious crowd. There, at the water's edge, the joyous fishermen, who had come in search of the sun, were snaring it with their artful net.

A cheer arose as they got him, a hollow, luminous, papier maché, yellow orb with fat cheeks and a smile. They balanced the sun in the center of the net and lifted it to carry him up the hill, helped by the figures whose cries had changed to shouts of joy.

As the sun came closer the drumbeats quickened, hands clapped, and the crowd burst into a dancing frenzy. Everyone, from the tiniest tots up, spun, jumped, and clapped in delight. A quirky bird figure passed out candles, another figure lit them, and all were placed along the roots of the stump in a blaze of fire and light. The sun was set in the center of the stump and the fiery roots became its hot rays.

Another bird came with bread, to nourish the spirit of the winter solstice. Gone are the darkest, shortest days, it motioned soundlessly as it offered bread and pranced through the crowd. To come is only the light.

When this beautifully enacted fishing celebration was over, it occurred to me that celebrations like this one, which glorify the seasons, the light, the coming and catching of food, are the foundation of all celebration. Since humans have inhabited the earth and lived within its seasons, they have celebrated.

They have rejoiced to see the days lengthen and the light return, relieved that the sun has not permanently slipped away. Those who live by the sea have equally rejoiced each year at the return of the fish.

In Camden on that cold winter night, She-bang! welcomed not only the light, but the recommencement of the warm seasons and the fish they bring. They welcomed the first shrimp, the smelt, the lobsters, the scallops, and all that would come after them.

Northwest Surf 'n Turf

FROM MAUNY KASEBURG—
"THE RADIO GOURMET"

Slurps greeted me as I entered a small, elegant room at Ray's Boathouse, overlooking Elliott Bay in Seattle. It was full of well-dressed people eating oysters on the half shell, slipping them down their throats with unabashed enjoyment.

Mauny Kaseburg had spent days planning for this gathering. Convinced that Seattle needed a midwinter event, she decided on a paean to the oyster. Along with Wayne Ludvigsen, chef at Ray's, she set up an oyster bar piled with ice, dozens of her favorite local oysters, and bottles of champagne, and invited friends from around the city.

This wasn't just a meeting of friends but an event with purpose, a chance to welcome local media and other influentials to Ray's and to impress them. Mauny is a public relations consultant who knows how to get favorable press for her clients, how to keep their name in lights. She gets right in the kitchen as she pokes, prods, and urges chefs to get out of the way of the ingredients. She nudges them to buy from local farmers and fishermen and does all she can to help them highlight local ingredients. She encourages them to celebrate, to plan events around local foods as they come into season, to make sure they're in tune with whatever is available. Ray's is one of her longstanding customers, and their association has been fruitful.

One of Mauny's talents is her ability to make a large group feel comfortably intimate, an effect she creates with a gentle challenge. Here, the challenge was oysters on the half shell. Even in the Northwest, land of abundant oysters, many people are uncomfortable at the thought of sliding a live bivalve down their throats. Mauny not only gets people to eat oysters, she gets them to dress up to do it, have fun in the process, and go home and talk or write about how wonderful it was.

A native Northwesterner, Mauny generates a cosmopolitan air with her intimate knowledge of world cuisines. She has cachet as Seattle's "radio gourmet," a role she plays each week as she regales listeners with tales of local bounty and the people who harvest, cook, or serve it. When it comes to meals, parties, and entertaining, she's a wealth of ideas.

ON USELESS BAY

One of Mauny's favorite meals is something she calls Northwest Surf 'n Turf, a luscious regional take on the traditional: butterflied marinated leg of lamb served with clams tossed in linguine.

"Washington produces some of the best lamb in the country, and you can't find clams that taste as good as these anywhere else," she says with unabashed chauvinism. She's right.

The idea came about when Mauny was planning a friend's fortieth birthday party. "It reminded me of being a kid, when we used to dig clams and things," Mauny said. "We all went out to Useless Bay on Whidby Island, where my friend grew up, and dug clams on this clam flat—which will remain nameless because we don't want to tell anyone where it is. I've never seen so many clams. At least five in every shovelful."

Mauny was referring to Manila clams, which are about the size of a quarter and as sweet as any clam in the world. Digging them is no simple matter. As the tide goes out the clam flat is exposed, so diggers must rush to intercept the clams before they burrow too deep into the sand. Armed with a "clam gun," which is a narrow shovel, the good clam digger spots an airhole in the sand and digs frantically. Depending on the abundance of mollusks, it can take either an hour or a day to fill a five-gallon bucket. "It took us—and there were a lot of us—about an hour," Mauny said.

Digging clams is wet, sandy fun, an essential part of such a Northwest meal.

Seagulls squawk overhead, the air is briny, fir-scented, and soft, and the scene is a riot of people bent over digging, running, stooping, crying, "I've got 'em! Bring the bucket!"

Because the clams must sit in saltwater for twenty-four hours to rid them of sand and the lamb must marinate overnight, appetites veered elsewhere after digging. It wasn't until the next day that preparations began in earnest.

Then Mauny was in her element as she carried on a conversation while effortlessly assembling the meal, from appetizer to dessert. She built a big fire in a barbecue grill with pure wood charcoal, and let it burn until the coals were fiery red. Meantime, the bread for the bruschetta was baking and she detailed a friend to mix up the tomato topping. Others were chopping, mixing, rolling and stirring.

Finally the lamb went on the grill. Everyone staked out a chair on the porch overlooking Useless Bay, enjoyed a glass of champagne, and waited for the feast.

The meal was a symphony of local foods, enjoyed at a large candle-lit table overlooking the clam flats, which were bathed in moonlight. It fit the drama of the occasion, and of the person who planned it all.

Bruschetta

Bruschetta is a traditional Italian appetizer—fresh crusty bread usually just rubbed with garlic and topped with fresh tomatoes. Mauny Kaseburg puts her own stamp on this version, mixing ripe tomatoes with herbs, vinegar, and fruity virgin olive oil. She likes to serve this as a prelude to her Northwest Surf 'n Turf. It's fresh and delightful, but it has a fatal flaw: It's so appealing that people tend to fill up on it, so space your courses accordingly! Or serve it as a special bread on the side.

It is worth making this simple rustic bread because it has the crisp, thick crust and moist interior you need for bruschetta. I like to make two loaves and use one for the bruschetta, the other for supper.

BREAD
2 cups lukewarm water
1½ teaspoons active dry yeast
3½ cups unbleached all-purpose flour
1 tablespoon kosher (coarse) salt
1½ cups whole wheat flour

TOPPING
2 large cloves garlic
1 pound fresh tomatoes, cut into ¼-inch dice
¼ cup extra-virgin olive oil
1 tablespoon balsamic vinegar
½ cup (loosely packed) fresh basil leaves
Salt and freshly ground black pepper to taste

1. Make the bread dough: Combine the lukewarm water and the yeast in a large bowl and mix well. Add 1 cup of the white flour and the salt, and mix well. Then add the whole wheat flour and mix well. Add enough of the remaining 2½ cups of white flour to make a smooth, somewhat sticky dough. Turn the dough out on a well-floured surface and knead it, adding just enough white flour so it doesn't stick uncontrollably to the work surface. It should remain moist and soft, but it shouldn't stick to your hands. Place the dough in a bowl, cover it with a kitchen towel, and let it rise in a warm place (68° to 70°F) until doubled in bulk, about 1½ hours.

2. Punch down the dough. Divide it in half and shape the halves into two long (about 14-inch) French-style loaves. Place each one on

a flour-dusted baking sheet and let them rise, loosely covered, for 30 minutes.

3. Preheat the oven to 425°F. Slash the tops of the loaves diagonally with a sharp knife, and bake them in the center of the oven until they are crisp on the outside and sound hollow when you tap them, about 30 minutes.

4. While the bread is baking, prepare the topping: Mince one of the garlic cloves. Place the tomatoes in a large bowl and add the olive oil, vinegar, and minced garlic. Tear the basil leaves into small pieces, and add them to the tomato mixture. Season with salt and pepper, toss well, and set aside.

5. Remove the bread from the oven and transfer the loaves to wire racks to cool.

6. Preheat the broiler.

7. When the bread is cool enough to touch, cut one loaf into 3/4-inch-thick slices (save the other loaf for another meal). Toast the slices on both sides under the broiler. Rub one side of the slices with the remaining clove of garlic.

8. Arrange the slices of toasted bread on a large serving platter, spoon the tomato mixture over the slices, making sure you include all the liquid, and serve immediately.

8 SERVINGS

Lamb 'n Clams

This is Mauny Kaseburg's *pièce de résistance.* Using lamb raised on the grasses of eastern Washington and Manila clams from coastal waters, Mauny creates her version of surf 'n turf.

Summer is the ideal time to make this dish, when you can sit near the grill with a glass of cool champagne. However, clams are available in winter, too, and there is nothing quite like a grilled dinner to bring back the scents, the tastes, the warmth—the very feel—of summertime.

Mauny likes to grill an assortment of vegetables alongside the lamb. I suggest parboiled Yellow Finn or Yukon Gold potatoes, bell peppers, eggplant, and quartered onions. Serve the clam linguine as a first course, or place it on the platter alongside the lamb. What sounds like an incongruous combination is wonderful, and deliciously appropriate, when you actually taste the various flavors together.

Mauny suggests using dried linguine because its more substantial texture stands up to the clams and the sauce.

LAMB
1 leg of lamb (7 pounds), butterflied
2 tablespoons olive oil
3 cloves garlic, cut lengthwise into thin slices
1 cup (loosely packed) fresh rosemary leaves, or
    2 tablespoons dried
2 lemons
6 tablespoons soy sauce

CLAMS
2 pounds clams, in the shell, scrubbed and purged
    (see Note)
Freshly ground black pepper to taste
Fish stock (page 119, through Step 2) or chicken
    stock or clam broth, if needed

2 tablespoons olive oil
2 large (10 ounces each) onions, coarsely
    chopped
¼ cup fresh thyme leaves, or ½ to ¾ teaspoon
    dried
2 cloves garlic, minced
¼ teaspoon dried red pepper flakes
¾ cup dry white wine
2 pounds dried linguine
¼ cup Italian (flat-leaf) parsley leaves
¼ cup freshly grated Parmesan cheese
Extra rosemary branches and Italian (flat-leaf)
    parsley sprigs, for garnish

1. Rinse the lamb and pat it dry. Trim off any excess fat, and rub the meat all over with the olive oil.

2. Smash the garlic slices with the side of a large knife. Coarsely chop the rosemary leaves.

3. Slice 1 lemon into thin rounds; cut the other into quarters, lengthwise. Lay half the lemon slices in the bottom of a noncorrosible baking dish. Place the lamb over the lemon slices.

4. In a small bowl, combine the soy sauce, rosemary, and garlic and pour the mixture over the lamb. Squeeze 2 of the lemon quarters over the lamb, then turn the lamb to coat it with the marinade. Make sure the lemon slices stay in the bottom of the dish. Lay the remaining lemon slices on top of the lamb, squeeze the remaining lemon quarters over it, and add the squeezed lemon to the dish with the lamb. Marinate at room temperature for 8 hours. You may marinate the lamb for up to 2 days, covered and refrigerated.

5. Prepare a good-size fire in a barbecue.

6. To prepare the clams, place them and 2 tablespoons water in a large saucepan over medium-high heat. Season generously with pepper, cover, and bring to a boil. Cook until the clams open, about 7 minutes, shaking the pan occasionally. Check the clams as they cook, removing any that are open, so they don't overcook. Discard any clams that haven't opened after 7 minutes. Shell all but 10 clams, reserving the shelled and unshelled clams separately. Strain the cooking liquid, and reserve. You should have 2 cups of reserved liquid. If you don't, make up the difference with fish or chicken stock or clam broth.

7. Heat the olive oil in a large heavy saucepan over medium heat. Add the onions, reduce the heat to medium-low and cook, covered, until they turn pale golden and soft, 20 minutes. Check the onions occasionally and stir, to be sure they aren't sticking. Add the thyme, garlic, and pepper flakes, and continue cooking, covered, until the garlic softens, 10 minutes.

8. Add the wine to the onions, increase the heat to medium-high, and bring the mixture to a boil. Add the reserved clam cooking liquid, and cook until the mixture reduces by one-third, 5 minutes. The mixture should remain soupy. Remove from the heat and keep warm.

9. Thoroughly oil a grill rack, using paper towels dipped in vegetable oil. When the coals are glowing red with some small flames still licking at them, place the rack 3 inches above the coals, and lay the lamb on the grill. Cover, being sure to leave the vents on the barbecue open, and cook until the meat is to your liking. For rare meat, it should take 10 to 15 minutes per side. Cook for additional time, depending on how well done you like your meat. Remove the meat from the grill and let sit for at least 10 minutes before slicing.

10. Meanwhile, cook the linguine in a large kettle of boiling salted water (about 1 tablespoon salt to 1 gallon water) until al dente (tender but still firm to the bite). Drain thoroughly.

11. Heat the onion mixture over medium heat. When hot, add the shelled clams and the parsley to the onions just to warm them. Place the linguine in a large serving bowl. When the clams are hot, pour the sauce over the linguine and toss. Garnish with the Parmesan cheese, and the reserved clams in their shells.

12. Place the lamb on a platter, garnish with parsley and fresh rosemary branches, and serve the lamb and clams immediately.

10 TO 12 SERVINGS

Note: To purge the clams: Place the clams in a large bowl or bucket of salted water (about 3 tablespoons sea salt to 1 gallon water); and stir in the cornmeal. Leave the clams in a cool place for at least 2 hours. Then drain the clams and rinse them.

Mauny's Filbert Shortcake

Another ode to the Northwest, this shortcake recipe takes full advantage of filberts (which the rest of the world calls hazelnuts), and plump fresh berries. Mauny uses whatever berries are ripe, from the first strawberries of spring to the panoply of blackberries, marionberries, raspberries, and loganberries that ripen throughout the northwestern summer.

BERRIES
8 cups ripe berries
2 tablespoons sugar

SHORTCAKE
1 cup unbleached all-purpose flour
¾ cup plus 2 tablespoons cake flour
½ teaspoon salt
2½ teaspoons baking powder
5 tablespoons sugar

Minced zest of 1 lemon
½ cup toasted hazelnuts (see Note), finely chopped
6 tablespoons (¾ stick) unsalted butter, chilled
1 cup heavy (or whipping) cream, chilled

WHIPPED CREAM
1 cup heavy (or whipping) cream, chilled
1 teaspoon vanilla extract
1 tablespoon confectioners' sugar

1. Preheat the oven to 425°F. Line a baking sheet with parchment paper. Chill a medium-size bowl and a whisk, or the whisk attachment of an electric mixer (for whipping the cream).

2. Place the berries in a large bowl. Toss them with the 2 tablespoons sugar and set aside.

3. In a large bowl or in a food processor, combine both flours with the salt, baking powder, 4 tablespoons of the sugar, the lemon zest, and the hazelnuts. Stir well, or process once or twice, to mix. Add the butter and process, or cut it in with a pastry blender or two knives, until it ranges from the size of a pea to the size of coarse cornmeal.

4. Add the 1 cup cream all at once, and lightly mix until the dough gathers together but does not completely adhere. Be very careful not to overmix. If you are using a food processor, pulse just two or three times.

5. Turn the dough out onto a well-floured surface, dust it lightly with flour, and press it down with a rolling pin until it is somewhat rectangular in shape and about ½ inch thick. Fold it in thirds like a business letter, and turn it one quarter-turn (90 degrees). Lightly flour the dough and gently press it out again until it is an even rectangle about ½ inch thick, fold it in thirds, and turn it another quarter-turn.

6. Lightly flour the dough again, if necessary, to keep it from sticking to the rolling pin, and roll it out to form a very even rectangle measuring about 6 × 12 inches; straighten the edges by pushing the rolling pin up against them. Cut it in half from upper left corner to lower right corner, then from upper right corner to lower left. Then cut each piece in half horizontally and vertically so that you have eight triangular pieces. Transfer them to the prepared baking sheet, leaving about ¼ inch between them. Sprinkle the pieces with the remaining 1 tablespoon sugar. Bake in the center of the oven until the shortcakes are golden and puffed, about 12 minutes. Slide the parchment paper off the baking sheet and onto a wire rack to cool.

7. Using the chilled whisk or mixer attachment and bowl, whip the cream with the vanilla and the confectioners' sugar until it holds soft peaks.

8. Place a shortcake in the center of each dessert plate, and top it with berries and a dollop of whipped cream. Serve immediately.

8 SERVINGS

Note: To toast hazelnuts, preheat the oven to 350°F. Place the nuts in a baking pan large enough to hold them in a single layer, and bake, stirring once, until they give off a toasted aroma, about 10 minutes. Wrap the nuts in a kitchen towel and rub them between your hands to remove the skins.

Shad Planking in Virginia

A MEETING OF
FOOD AND POLITICS

If you're gettin' on the stump in Virginia, you go to the shad planking," said Dean Wagenbach, manager of Chowan-Beattie Milling Company in Como. A member of the Ruritan Club of Wakefield, which sponsors a shad planking every year in the spring, Dean was referring to the social importance that the group's shad planking has assumed over the years.

It began modestly in the 1930s when a group of friends assembled to cook the succulent fish outdoors. They'd catch the shad, skin and bone it, nail the fillets to oak planks, and bake them over an open fire until they were cooked through and smoky.

It was such a successful gathering that the group continued each year, taking a hiatus only during World War II.

Each year the group invited more friends and relatives, until the event took on a regional importance. That's when politicians, eager to press the flesh of the local citizenry, made it a stop on the campaign trail. "We never intended to use the shad planking as a political forum," said co-chair William "Buddy" Savedge. "We wanted it to be an event of community goodwill and fellowship."

Nonetheless politicians are now invited as featured speakers, and others come to eat shad, shake hands, and leave knowing they've made a mark.

Times have changed in other ways, too. In the early days, the shad planking was reserved for men only. In recent more enlightened years women joined the celebration. The event has grown so much in importance that tickets are sold and more than 4,000 people attend.

HOW TO COOK A PORCUPINE

It takes months of planning and a small army of volunteers to prepare. The day before the planking, 1½ tons of shad are delivered to the Wakefield Sportsman's Club grounds, a cleared area surrounded by woods. There the men scale the fish and split them down the back, removing the backbone. Anyone who knows shad, which were dubbed "porcupine fish" by Native Americans because of the numerous tiny bones floating in their meat, understands that removing all the bones from 3,000 pounds is an unthinkable proposition.

After the shad are iced down for the night, a big supper of shad roe follows, to appease the hungry workers.

By dawn the following morning a long, narrow fire is built on the grounds. The "Nailing Committee" arrives, hammers in hand, to nail the fish—which are spread

open like butterflies—to planks, each of which holds two fish.

The planks are balanced at an outward slant—so the fish doesn't cook too fast—right near the fire, and the embers are fed regularly for the eight to ten hours it takes to cook the fish. During that time the numerous bones become soft enough to eat, and many of them actually dissolve.

As they cook, the shad are brushed dozens of times with a special sauce, the same sauce that has been used since the first shad planking. It accentuates the smoky tenderness of the meat.

NECESSARY ACCOMPANIMENTS

While the fish cooks, tubs of coleslaw are brought in, and mounds of hush puppies are fried.

Bill Gallaway, owner of the Virginia Diner in Wakefield, supplies the coleslaw each year. Pat Hill, head cook at the diner, is fussy about how it is made. "The cabbage has to be sliced in thin strips, and the soupiness of the slaw depends on the firmness of the cabbage," she says. "If it's really soupy we just drain it before we serve it."

Pete Ramsey has made the hush puppies for most of the shad planking's history, and his recipe is still the only one the group uses. They're mixed up in gallons and fried in big batches, and they vie with the shad as the most popular dish at the planking.

Is there any dessert? "No, just boobin' and beauh [bourbon and beer]," says Dean. "We don't go in for dessert—we don't need it heah."

Planked Shad

Cooking fish over a slow fire in the grill is the closest method to planking that you can do at home, short of building a fire on the lawn and setting some planked fish around it. The result here is subtle—the sauce has a depth of flavor that nonetheless allows the flavor of the shad to come through.

If shad is unavailable, use salmon or Arctic char as a substitute. Don't be alarmed at the amount of salt in the sauce—the result is not overly salty.

3 pounds skinless shad fillets, boned
1/3 cup Worcestershire sauce
1 tablespoon unsalted butter
1 tablespoon freshly squeezed lemon juice

Heaping 1/2 teaspoon freshly ground
   black pepper
1/8 teaspoon cayenne pepper, or to taste
1 tablespoon salt

1. Rinse the fish with cold water, and pat it dry. Refrigerate loosely covered in waxed paper until ready to cook.

2. Build a medium-size fire in a barbecue grill. When the coals are red and nearly covered with ash, place the rack on the grill. Crimp the edges of a large piece of heavy-duty aluminum foil to create a rim, and arrange the fish on the foil.

3. Combine all the remaining ingredients in a small saucepan, and bring to a boil over medium-high heat. Cook, whisking occasionally, until the sauce has thickened somewhat and most of the salt is dissolved, about 5 minutes.

4. Generously brush the fish with the sauce, and place it with the foil on the grill. Cover the grill, leaving vents just slightly open, and cook until the fish is opaque through, 20 to 30 minutes, depending on the heat of the fire. Baste generously every 5 minutes. Remove from the heat and serve immediately.

8 SERVINGS

Wakefield Coleslaw

Sweet and crisp, this slaw has a time-honored tang to it. The folks at the Virginia Diner like it soupy, but I always drain it, reserving the juice. Then if there is any left-over coleslaw, I just put it back into the juice to keep.

The vegetables are shredded for this coleslaw, which means sliced paper-thin. The cabbage can be shredded on the thin slicing blade of a food processor, and the other vegetables can be shredded on a regular shredder blade. The other option, of course, is to hand-grate everything.

This coleslaw keeps well for about two days.

1½ cups best-quality mayonnaise
½ cup distilled white vinegar
1 cup sugar
½ teaspoon salt
1 cabbage (2 pounds), cored and shredded

1 large carrot, grated
1 medium green bell pepper, cored, seeded, and grated
1 rib celery, strings removed, grated

In a large bowl, whisk together the mayonnaise and vinegar until smooth. Add the sugar and salt, and whisk until thoroughly blended. Then add the shredded vegetables. Mix well, cover, and refrigerate for at least 1 hour before serving. Adjust the seasoning and serve.

8 SERVINGS

Hush Puppies

Thelma Ramsey gave me this recipe, along with some advice: "We use oil so that they swim, and we turn them with a strainer, and shake them good and put them on paper towels to soak the grease when they are nice and brown."

When Thelma says nice and brown, she means nice and brown. These take about seven minutes to cook, which ensures a dark golden exterior and a moist, flavorful interior. They are delicious (though hot!) when they first come out of the oil, and more than edible even if you wait to serve them for at least an hour afterward.

2 quarts mild cooking oil, such as safflower
1 cup unbleached all-purpose flour
3 teaspoons baking powder
$1\frac{1}{2}$ teaspoons salt
2 cups white cornmeal

1 tablespoon sugar
$2\frac{3}{4}$ to 3 cups buttermilk
2 small cloves garlic, minced
1 small onion, minced

1. Heat the oil in a heavy pan, deep-fat fryer, or Dutch oven to 350°F.

2. While the oil is heating, mix up the hush puppies: Sift the flour, baking powder, and salt together into a large bowl. Mix in the cornmeal and the sugar. Then stir in $2\frac{3}{4}$ cups of the buttermilk. Quickly stir in the garlic and the onion so that they are evenly distributed throughout. The batter should resemble a thick cake batter, but it should fall from a spoon. If it is too thick, add the remaining $\frac{1}{4}$ cup buttermilk.

3. Using a tablespoon measure and holding the spoon very close to the surface of the oil, tip 5 to 6 individual spoonfuls of batter into the hot fat. Fry them, turning them occasionally, until the hush puppies are deep golden brown, 7 to 8 minutes. Transfer them to paper towels or baking sheets lined with unprinted brown paper bags to drain, and repeat with the remaining batter. Serve immediately.

ABOUT 45 HUSH PUPPIES

Port Washington Smelt Fry

A FESTIVAL OF GOODWILL
AND SMELT RITES

Sleepy Scharnow ambles up to the bar at American Legion Van Ells–Schanen Post 82, puts down a dollar and a half, and walks away with two schooners of beer, one of which he hands to me. "Here, have a drink and get the feel fer what's goin' on here," he says.

It's a rainy, blustery Thursday evening in Port Washington, Wisconsin, the day before the forty-second annual smelt fry put on by the Legionnaires. They've been planning the event since January, and the countdown has begun.

The Legionnaires fry more than a ton of smelt once a year to raise money for local scholarships. But the real reason for the months of planning, days of organizing, and hours of backbreaking soaking, breading, and frying goes much deeper than mere altruism. The Legionnaires are mostly native sons of this tidy, picturesque little fishing town, and genetic makeup causes their blood to quicken when the spring smelt begin to run in Lake Michigan.

Smelt, or schmelt as they are called in this German-rooted town (the *ch* is referred to as the "Luxembourg hyphen"), are considered a delicacy, and fishing for them is a male rite of passage. Visit Port Washington in the spring, and you'll find that every able-bodied male resident, from age ten to sixty or more, is out on the breakwater or in

The Big Day, The Big Meal

Saturday dawned gray, cold, and rainy, as is apparently usual for the smelt fry. When our bus rolled up at mid-afternoon, a line of hungry smelt fans already snaked around under the big tent outside, packets of tartar sauce clutched in many hands.

For almost a hundred of us, the day had begun long before we arrived. I, along with my friend Craig Hudson, was on a bus sponsored by Shaw's Crab House of Chicago, and we'd assembled at the restaurant early in the morning.

We piled into the bus at 11 A.M. Steve Lahaie, general partner of the restaurant and the one who spawned this trip into being, nervously attended to details. It was the third annual trip, but a record-breaking crowd.

Steve and his crew had plenty planned to keep everyone busy, from an elegant box lunch and cases of wine, beer, and soda, to a Great Lakes trivia quiz and a visit to a small winery. The quiz was tough and everyone attended to it with great seriousness.

After our answers were turned in, the mood lightened. We sang rousing choruses of smelt songs, looked at the bucolic scenery passing by, and prepared ourselves for a feast.

Despite the gloomy weather in Port Washington, a circus feeling pervaded the air. The Legionnaires never mentioned coming in costume, yet fish jewelry, fish-patterned clothing, and hats festooned with fishing flies were everywhere.

Inside, the frenzy was well under way. Smelt issued from the kitchen in a constant hot, crisp stream, and was served from a buffet table along with coleslaw and rye bread.

Eaters concentrated, elbows at their sides, as they munched their smelts. If a Legionnaire spied a pile of crisp tails on a plate, the call went out—"Eat dem tails!"—as they pointed their fingers at the guilty party.

It was a festival, a smelt jamboree, as everyone went back for seconds, thirds, as much as they could eat.

a boat dipping with nets for smelt. The men fish into the wee hours, take the fish home, and the next day the women of the family fry them up.

While the fishing goes on at the lake, two blocks away the Legionnaires and their families and friends ready the Legion Hall for the big event. Dozens of long tables are set up inside, and a big tent is going up out front. The kitchen behind the bar is stacked with boxes of cracker meal for breading the smelt, and four gas-powered deep-fat fryers are set up in the drafty garage.

DRY RUN

The Thursday night before the smelt fry is a significant moment, when the cooks "season the oil" for the year and loosen up their rusty frying skills. The nerve center is the kitchen, which opens into the garage. Only Legionnaires are allowed to prepare and cook, and three aproned men are rinsing, dipping, and breading in a precise choreography learned through years of experience. Each man is responsible for a particular part of the fry. Paul Tutas, fry chairman, mixes up the batter, someone else runs the fish through the crumbs, and a revolving crew stands over the fryers.

The Legionnaires claim the batter is the secret to their fry, and they won't part with the recipe. "Don't ask me how ya make it because I already forgot," claimed Mike Schmitz, longtime Legionnaire.

There isn't any secret to the method, however. The fish are rinsed three times in clear water, put in the batter to soak, then drained so that much of the batter has dripped off before they're coated inside and out with cracker crumbs. When the oil hits 450°F, the smelt go in with a sputter.

TOO MANY COOKS

"They've gotta be all golden brown and crisp," Sleepy said.

"There are always plenty of old eyes watchin'," Mike Schmitz added. "But we don't do any of the fryin' anymore. After so many years ya get promoted. Ya just yell at 'em all a lot."

"Yeh," said Sleepy. "If the smelt comes out too soft it's 'Ya jerk.' "

The cooks turn a mound of golden-brown fish out onto a baking sheet, and the circle of watching men dives in at once. They eat the whole fish—skin, bones, tail, and all.

"Ya gotta eat dem tails," Sleepy says. "During the smelt fry we watch everybody and make sure they eat the tails. If they don't, we start yelling 'Eat dem tails!' at 'em. The tails are the best part."

There is serious discussion as the men munch. "They could be a little more brown," Sleepy says. "They need salt," another one chimed in. "No they don't," the group cried in unison.

The cooks take the criticism stoically and put another batch in the oil. All twenty pounds of smelt are fried and eaten, everything is put away, and an excited crew goes home to get some rest before the big opening day of the forty-second annual smelt fry.

Real Fried Smelt

There are strict secrets involved in the preparation of the Van Ells-Schanen Post 82 smelts, and not one was divulged by the tight-lipped Legionnaires. However, they did allow me to poke around in the kitchen and witness the frying up close, and they ended up giving me just enough information, dispensed with sly grins and not-so-discreet whispering, that I was able to create a reasonable facsimile at home.

The men were proud to let a few details loose. They fry only in peanut oil, which they change every eight batches. They use only fresh smelt, never frozen, and they prefer the two- to three-inch-long fish from Lake Michigan. "Any bigger and they taste awful," according to Mike Schmitz, long-time smelt fryer.

Clean smelts are good smelts, and the men rinse the cleaned fish three times before they embark on the cooking process. The next step is to soak them in the secret batter, "just to moisten 'em up," Mike said.

Then they're ready for rolling, by hand, in cracker meal. "You've got to do it by hand so they get a good even coating inside and out," Mike explained.

The Legionnaires' favorite way to eat the smelts, once they've downed a handful or two just plain, is to make a smelt-and-coleslaw sandwich with rye bread. If you like tartar sauce with your smelt, see the Index.

No matter how you choose to eat the crisp, hot fish, always keep in mind, and be sure to follow, the orders of the Legionnaires, and "Eat dem tails!"

---

2 quarts peanut oil
½ cup plus 2 tablespoons unbleached all-purpose flour
2½ cups water

2 cups cracker crumbs
    (50 unsalted saltines)
5 pounds smelt, heads removed, cleaned, well rinsed, and patted dry

---

1. In an 8-quart heavy flameproof casserole or deep-fat fryer, heat the oil to 375°F.

2. Whisk the flour and the water together in a large bowl.

3. Place the cracker crumbs in a large dish with a rim, such as a baking dish.

4. Place about 6 smelts in the flour and water mixture and let them soak there for about 5 minutes, stirring them from time to time as the flour settles to the bottom of the dish.

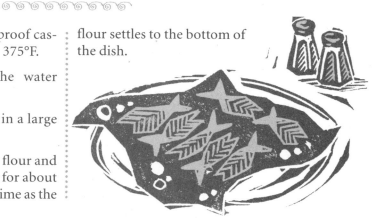

5. Set a strainer over a bowl, and transfer the soaked smelts to the strainer to drain. Then, using your fingers, toss them gently in the cracker crumbs, patting the crumbs on to make sure they are coated inside and out.

6. Check the temperature to be sure the oil is at 375°F. Then plunge the smelts into the oil and fry them until they are golden and cooked through, no longer than 4 minutes. Using a slotted spoon, remove them from the oil and drain on unprinted brown paper bags. Repeat with the remaining fish. Serve immediately.

8 TO 10 SERVINGS

The Legion's Coleslaw

The men in charge of mixing up the huge vats of chopped cabbage in the chilly garage behind the American Legion hall wouldn't divulge their recipe, but they allowed me to snoop around as they minced and mixed. They jokingly tried to shield their work, but one man, whose name remains withheld, took pity and secretly gave me a couple of valuable pointers. Those, and tasting the huge mound on my plate, helped me come up with this recipe, which takes me right back to the smelt fry.

This coleslaw has a specific role that goes well beyond providing something green on the plate. Smelt-fry etiquette calls for taking two pieces of light rye bread, heaping one with cloeslaw, balancing as many smelt as will fit on top, then covering it with the other piece of bread. It's a smelt-and-slaw sandwich, and at least 80 percent of those who come to the smelt fry eat their smelt in that fashion.

I must admit that I prefer mine separate, so I can savor the crunchiness of the salad and the crispness of the smelt.

This coleslaw is pretty, light, and flavorful, and the key to its success is mincing the vegetables. When they're all tossed together they give a satisfying, toothsome crunch.

Though the salad is best the day it's made, it keeps well for a day or so. I reserve the dressing once I've drained the salad, and pour it back over any leftovers before I refrigerate them.

¾ cup distilled white vinegar
½ cup mild vegetable oil, such as safflower
¼ cup sugar
¼ cup water
1 medium green cabbage (2 pounds), cored and
    finely chopped

2 large carrots, minced
1 small onion, minced
Salt and freshly ground black
    pepper to taste

1. In a large bowl, combine the vinegar, oil, sugar, and water, and mix well.

2. Half an hour before serving, add the cabbage, carrots, and onion to the dressing, and mix well. Let the salad sit at room temperature or in the refrigerator, as you prefer. Just before serving, drain the coleslaw, season it, transfer it to a large serving bowl, and serve.

8 TO 10 SERVINGS

Smelt Sandwich Rye Bread

The secret to a good smelt sandwich is delicious rye bread. But even if you don't like your fried smelt on a sandwich, you'll want to make this bread because it goes uncommonly well alongside most seafood. The combination of orange and caraway makes it light and sprightly, and it is quick and easy to make. If you like, prepare the dough through the second rising, punch it down, and refrigerate it overnight; then shape and bake it the next day.

2½ cups warm water
1 package (2½ teaspoons) active dry yeast
1 tablespoon sugar
3 cups rye flour

1 tablespoon salt
1 tablespoon caraway seeds
Grated zest of 1 orange
3 cups unbleached all-purpose flour

1. Place the warm water in a large mixing bowl, and stir in the yeast and the sugar. Then add the rye flour 1 cup at a time, mixing well after each addition. Stir in the salt, then the caraway seeds and orange zest, and mix well. Add the white flour, 1 cup at a time, until the mixture becomes too stiff to stir.

2. Transfer the dough to a well-floured work surface, and knead it, working in the remaining flour. Knead the dough until it becomes very smooth, about 10 minutes. It will be firm, yet easy to work, and somewhat sticky when you pinch it. You don't want it to be too stiff or dry, so be cautious if you are tempted to add extra flour.

3. Place the dough in a bowl, cover it with a moistened towel, and let it sit in a warm spot (65° to 68°F) to rise. When the dough has doubled in bulk, after about 2 hours, punch it down and let it rise again until nearly doubled in bulk, 1½ hours more.

4. Lightly oil two 8½ × 4-inch loaf pans.

5. Punch down the dough, and divide it in half. Shape each half into a loaf. Place the loaves in the prepared pans, cover them loosely with a towel, and let them rise until they have nearly doubled in bulk, about 30 minutes.

6. Meanwhile, preheat the oven to 350°F.

7. Slash the tops of the loaves crosswise with a sharp knife, and bake them in the center of the oven until they are golden and sound hollow when tapped, about 40 minutes. Remove the bread from the pans and let cool on a wire rack.

2 LOAVES

The Squid Marinara Show

STAR ATTRACTION AT
MONTEREY FESTIVAL

The squid marinara that keeps fans returning year after year to the Monterey Squid Festival also keeps Mark Staggs, the originator of the recipe, busy. "People always want me to cater weddings and parties—and to serve it," he says.

Mark lived in Monterey until recently. Now working in Portland, Oregon, he nonetheless continues his tradition of squid marinara, at the festival and beyond. When he caters parties in Portland, he carts along his propane burners and larger-than-life cast-iron skillet. There is no denying the gastronomic draw of his squid marinara, which he insists on making with the highest-quality fresh squid. But his performance counts, too.

Like the star of a vaudeville act, Mark turns the flame up high, wraps his girth in an apron, and with a steady patter of conversation moistened with swigs of beer, dramatically tosses ingredients into the skillet. The more they sizzle the faster he moves, simultaneously working the crowd and cooking the marinara. He squeezes lemon juice into the sauce, then tosses the lemon in after it, and an "Aaaah" rises from the crowd.

He adds oregano and a huge spoonful of pesto, followed by a shower of salt and pepper. He thrusts in his finger to taste, turns off the flame, and pronounces it done.

The crowd lines up for plates full of

the spicy red sauce and tender squid, and as they walk away they're already plunging their forks right into it. The flavors are as fresh and exciting as the preparation.

Squid Marinara

I love to make this for a crowd because it has universal appeal. It's different from most squid marinara because the lemon adds an intense citrus undertone. Whenever I make it I remember Mark's advice: "Be sure to have a great old time."

¼ cup olive oil

2 pounds cleaned squid (page 182), mantles cut into ½-inch-thick rings, tentacles left whole

2 cloves garlic, minced

4 cups Mark's Marinara Sauce (recipe follows)

¼ to ½ teaspoon dried red pepper flakes

½ lemon, seeds removed

⅓ cup fresh oregano leaves, or ½ to 1 teaspoon dried

¼ cup Peg's Pesto (page 223)

Salt and freshly ground black pepper to taste

1 small handful Italian (flat-leaf) parsley leaves, for garnish

1. Heat the olive oil in a large skillet over high heat. Add the squid and the garlic, and sauté just until the squid begins to turn white but is still translucent in the center, 3 to 5 minutes.

2. Stir in the marinara sauce and the red pepper flakes. Squeeze the juice of the lemon half into the sauce, and then add the squeezed half. Mince (or crush) the oregano and add it to the sauce. Cook until the mixture bubbles vigorously, about 8 minutes. Add the pesto, and cook until it is hot through, 3 to 5 minutes. Taste the squid to be sure it is tender, and season the sauce to taste with salt and pepper.

3. Mince the parsley.

4. Transfer the squid marinara to a warmed platter, garnish with the parsley, and serve.

6 SERVINGS

Mark's Marinara Sauce

The term *marinara* refers to sailors and fishermen, who cooked with ingredients that were readily available to them. Traditionally a marinara sauce is simply tomatoes added to garlic and olive oil, though over time it has come to include a variety of other ingredients. An essential element of Squid Marinara, this sauce, which bears Mark's personal stamp, can also be used as a topping for pizza, a dip for fresh bread, or even at room temperature as a dip for fresh vegetables.

¼ cup extra-virgin olive oil

2 large onions, thinly sliced lengthwise

12 ounces button mushrooms, brushed clean and thinly sliced

2 large ribs celery, strings removed and thinly sliced

1 can (15 ounces) tomato sauce

½ cup tomato paste

½ cup hearty red wine

½ teaspoon dried red pepper flakes

½ cup Peg's Pesto (recipe follows)

Salt and freshly ground black pepper to taste

1. Heat the olive oil in a large skillet over medium-high heat. Add the onions and sauté until they begin to turn translucent, about 8 minutes. Then add the mushrooms and the celery. Cook, stirring, until the mushrooms soften and begin to release liquid, 3 minutes.

2. Add the tomato sauce, tomato paste, red wine, and red pepper flakes. Stir and bring to a boil. Reduce the heat to medium, and cook until the sauce has thickened and mellowed, about 20 minutes.

3. Stir in the pesto, season with salt and pepper, and remove from the heat.

$4\frac{1}{2}$ CUPS

Monterey Squid Festival

Every year around Memorial Day, the Monterey Kiwanis Club hosts the Monterey Squid Festival, which celebrates the town's squid fishery and raises money to help children on the Monterey Peninsula. Twenty-eight thousand people come to learn about squid, everything from where they live to how they are prepared. Chefs from all over the region prepare squid dishes, and Mark Staggs' Squid Marinara has been a specialty at the festival since it began.

Mark used to live in Monterey, which is how he got involved in the festival. Now he lives outside Portland, Oregon, with his wife and three children, but every year the whole family gets in a van and drives down to the festival. Mark makes the squid marinara for the crowds, Peg Staggs helps, and the kids all serve. It's a family affair at a family affair.

For more information about the Squid Festival, call or write: The Great Monterey Squid Festival, 2600 Garden Road, Suite 208, Monterey, CA 93940; (408) 649-6547.

Peg's Pesto

*T*his pesto is perfect in the marinara sauce that Mark Staggs makes by the gallon each year at the Monterey Squid Festival, and for the many backyard parties and celebrations he caters in Portland. It adds a fresh herb flavor to the already flavorful sauce, and the parsley gives it a green pungency. Mark's wife, Peg, actually makes the pesto. She doesn't consider herself a cook but this is her specialty, and she's very precise about making it.

In the summertime I make quite a lot of this pesto to have on hand for serving as a dipping sauce for fresh vegetables or freshly baked bread. It's easy and keeps for several days, covered, in the refrigerator.

I like to use a fruity extra-virgin olive oil in this pesto because its flavor enhances those of the other ingredients.

2 cups (loosely packed) fresh basil leaves
2 cups Italian (flat-leaf) parsley leaves
1 cup extra-virgin olive oil
½ cup pine nuts, toasted (see Note)

6 cloves garlic, coarsely chopped
1 cup freshly grated Parmesan cheese
Salt

1. Place the basil, parsley, olive oil, pine nuts, and garlic in a food processor, and process to a fine purée.

2. Scrape the mixture into a medium-size bowl, and stir in the cheese. Season with salt to taste.

2 CUPS

Note: To toast pine nuts, bake them in a preheated 350°F oven, stirring them once or twice, until they turn pale gold, 10 to 12 minutes.

Blackberry Ice Cream

At the Staggs' home outside Portland, the meal was hardly over when two of the guests went to pick wild blackberries and the rest dispersed to collect the other ingredients for blackberry ice cream. It is the ideal finale to a full-flavored dish like Squid Marinara, and nothing could be better in mid to late summer, when the berries are so ripe they practically fall off the bush into your hand.

This ice cream is a gorgeous pale violet color, with a subtle but intense berry flavor. Use the best berries you can find. In a pinch, try frozen berries—if they are good quality, they will give good flavor.

6 *cups blackberries*
3 *cups milk*
½ *cup heavy (or whipping) cream*
4 *large egg yolks*
⅔ *cup sugar*

1. Purée 5 cups of the blackberries in a food processor. Then press the purée through a fine sieve to remove the seeds.

2. Combine the milk and the cream in a heavy saucepan, and heat to scalding over medium-high heat.

3. In a large bowl, whisk the egg yolks and sugar until the mixture is thickened and pale yellow.

4. Add the scalded milk-cream mixture to the egg yolks, whisking constantly as you pour it in. Return this mixture to the saucepan and cook, stirring constantly, over low heat until the custard has thickened enough to coat the back of a spoon, at least 5 minutes. Be careful not to overcook or the custard will curdle.

5. Immediately pour the custard into a large bowl. Let it cool to room temperature. Then add the puréed berries and refrigerate, covered, until chilled. The ice cream can be made up to this point several hours ahead or the night before.

6. Freeze the ice cream in an ice cream maker according to the manufacturer's instructions.

7. To serve, scoop the ice cream into serving bowls, and garnish with the remaining blackberries.

1 QUART; **6** SERVINGS

John ("J") Mayer, Master of the Fish Boil

COOKING WITH HOOPLA

Until I met John ("J") Mayer, president of J & H Heating in Port Washington, Wisconsin, I had no idea there were any variations on a traditional Door County Fish Boil (see page 228), a meal I learned to love several years ago while doing research on *The Great American Seafood Cookbook*. A simple meal prepared outdoors, a Door County Fish Boil consists of freshly caught local fish, usually Lake Superior whitefish or salmon, boiled in a cauldron along with onions and potatoes.

There is much fanfare to the preparation. The water is heated over a huge wood fire, and restaurant guests are invited to watch. Large baskets full of vegetables are lowered into the cauldron to cook, and then fish is added, so it all finishes cooking at the same time. Right before serving, whoever is tending the fire throws kerosene on it and flames shoot high into the sky. The cauldron is tilted slightly and the water boils up and over the edge, taking all impurities away with it. The food is taken inside and the spellbound crowd follows, to eat their fill, all of it drowned in plenty of melted butter.

Though Door County claims the fish boil as its own, it is a meal enjoyed all around Lake Superior. Fish is plentiful, people love to celebrate, and there is hardly a better way than by staging a fish boil.

A Certain Style

That's what "J" thinks, and once I met him I realized that no recipe, no matter how traditional, could ever remain the same after it passed through his hands. He's always on the lookout for a newer, better, tastier way to prepare the tried-and-true dishes of this lush, lake-filled region.

In Port Washington, "J" is considered the master of the fish boil because he organizes several large public affairs each year, usually as fund-raisers for local groups. At these, "J" cooks for up to 200 people. He also does a fish boil for friends and family.

He loves the job and he gets as many people involved as possible, taking time from his business to get them organized. He marshals the energies of his wife and his friends to make salads, bread, and a dessert, and ensures that it all runs smoothly.

"J" supervises the procurement of the fish boil ingredients and the cooking, infusing it with his own personal style. While the Door County Fish Boil relies on the fresh, clean taste of the ingredients, the fish boils "J" prepares have kick and color to them. He adds untraditional carrots, for one thing. But the real difference is a handful of pickling spices, which give the fish and vegetables subtle and aromatic flavor.

"J" loves officiating at a fish boil, grandly adding ingredients to the pot and cooking them *just* until they're done and not a second more.

Door County Fish Boil

In Door County, Wisconsin, the fish boil is an institution re-created daily in just about every local restaurant. Its origins are simple. Great Lakes fishermen had potbellied stoves aboard their boats to keep them warm, and when hunger struck they would fill a pot with lake water, stick it on the stove, and add potatoes and onions. They'd throw some fish in and boil it all up together, eating what they wanted and throwing the rest overboard.

In the 1940s and '50s the fish boil became a community supper dish, and cooks prepared them for parties at lumber camps and for church suppers. By the '60s, restaurants had taken them up, and they still prepare them outside in traditional fashion.

The affair is done with much fanfare, in a big stainless-steel pot over a hot wood fire. Steam flies from the pot, which looks like an ancient cauldron, as the ingredients are added in order of cooking time. Right before the fish is cooked and the dish is done, the boil master douses the fire with kerosene, the flames shoot up, and the slightly tilted caldron boils over. The crowd gathered round oohs and aaahs, then quickly files inside to partake of the succulent boil.

"I cheat a little," he said with no hint of remorse. "I use a gas burner instead of the fire they build in Door County, 'cause I figure those fires are just for show."

He does have the water boil over, though, as they do in Door County, because he says it removes any oil that collects on top.

"It's a dog and pony show, too, you understand," he added with a chuckle. "The show is as much a part of it as anything."

Accompaniments are important to a "J" Mayer fish boil. He serves fried fish and tartar sauce first as an hors d'oeuvre, then rye bread and a spinach salad with hot bacon dressing with the fish boil, and finally strawberry-filled Schaum Torte for dessert. It's a festive affair, and no one goes home hungry.

At-Home Fish Boil

ere's a fish boil you can do at home, on the stove. If you can't find whitefish, use salmon or steelhead trout. And you don't really have to trim the potatoes; they are prepared that way in Door County because in former times, trimming them was a way of policing the potato washers, to make sure they washed each one. It also isn't necessary to have the pot boil over. Just remove and drain the ingredients, and enjoy. This is an easy dish to make for a crowd—multiply the ingredients by the number of people you intend to feed. Serve plenty of melted butter alongside.

1½ pounds new potatoes, scrubbed
8 small (3-ounce) onions, peeled, stem end intact
2 tablespoons kosher (coarse) salt
4 whitefish steaks, 8 ounces each

Handful of Italian (flat-leaf) parsley leaves (optional)
Freshly ground black pepper
4 tablespoons (½ stick) unsalted butter, melted

1. Trim the ends from each potato, and cut an X in the stem end of each onion to prevent the center from popping out during cooking.

2. Place the onions and the potatoes in a large (12-quart) kettle, and add enough water to cover them by 2 inches. Add the kosher salt, stir, and bring to a boil over high heat. Cook, partially covered, until the potatoes are nearly tender through, about 15 minutes.

3. Carefully add the fish steaks, placing them on top of the vegetables in an even layer. Don't be concerned if they aren't covered with water. Partially cover the kettle, and continue cooking until the fish is opaque through, about 10 minutes.

4. Mince the parsley, if using.

5. Using a slotted spoon, carefully remove the fish steaks and set them on the edge of a warmed serving platter. Remove the potatoes and onions, and mound them in the center of the platter; then carefully arrange the fish steaks atop the vegetables. Sprinkle with a generous amount of pepper, and the minced parsley if desired, and serve immediately. Pass the melted butter alongside.

4 SERVINGS

"J" Mayer's Traditional Fish Boil

The traditional fish for a fish boil is whitefish, but "J" uses whatever is freshest, whether it be salmon, whitefish, or steelhead. It's tough to get whitefish outside the Midwest, and I think salmon works really well anyway.

Doing a fish boil in a kitchen may lack the panache of one outside, where the flame blazes up and the water boils over, but it tastes as good. You'll be surprised, in fact, at how good this simple mixture of boiled ingredients is. The secret is, of course, fresher-than-fresh fish, top-quality vegetables, and a good pickling spice mixture. I add a couple of hot peppers to mine because I like a little bite. You can play with the flavor, adjusting it to your taste.

If you can't find large fish steaks, use smaller ones and adjust the time. Keep an eye on the fish; when it is opaque through, it is cooked. This recipe is written for four people—a small celebration. If you want to feed more, just multiply the amount of ingredients.

8 small (3-ounce) onions, peeled, stem end intact
½ cup pickling spice mixture
8 whole cloves
4 teaspoons dill seed
1 tablespoon kosher (coarse) salt
14 cups (3½ quarts) water
1½ pounds new potatoes, scrubbed

4 carrots, peeled and cut into 1½-inch-long pieces
4 whitefish or salmon steaks, 8 ounces each
Handful of Italian (flat-leaf) parsley
    (optional)
Freshly ground black pepper to taste
4 tablespoons (½ stick) unsalted butter, melted

1. Cut an X in the stem end of each onion to prevent the center from popping out during cooking.

2. Place the pickling spices, cloves, and dill seed in a square of cheesecloth, and tie the ends to create a bag. Place the spices and the kosher salt in a large (12-quart) kettle, and add the water. Cover, bring to a boil over high heat, and boil for 10 minutes. Then add the onions, potatoes, and carrots, and return to a boil. Cook, partially covered, until the potatoes are nearly tender through, about 15 minutes.

3. Carefully add the fish steaks, placing them on top of the vegetables in an even layer. Don't be concerned if they aren't covered with water. Partially cover the kettle, and continue cooking until the fish is opaque through, about 10 minutes.

4. Mince the parsley, if using.

5. Using a slotted spoon, carefully remove the fish steaks and set them on the edge of a warmed serving platter. Remove the potatoes, onions, and carrots from the kettle, and mound them in the center of the platter. Then carefully arrange the fish steaks atop the vegetables. Sprinkle with a generous amount of pepper, and the minced parsley if desired, and serve immediately. Pass the melted butter alongside.

4 SERVINGS

Port Washington Spinach Salad

"J" likes to serve spinach salad with his fish boil, and his is a simple, delicious version. Highly flavored with bacon and balsamic vinegar, it's a great accompaniment.

If one egg per serving seems too much, use half the number of eggs. After arranging the tossed salad on plates, place two egg quarters on each.

10 ounces fresh spinach, trimmed
½ small (5-ounce) red onion, cut crosswise into paper-thin slices
½ pound slab bacon, rind removed

1 small clove garlic, minced
¼ cup balsamic vinegar
Salt and freshly ground black pepper to taste
4 eggs, hard-cooked and cut into quarters

1. Rinse the spinach well and pat it dry. Tear the leaves into bite-size pieces and place them in a large bowl. Separate the rings of the onion, and add them to the spinach. Toss so they are combined.

2. Cut the bacon into 1 × ¼ × ¼-inch pieces.

3. In a large heavy skillet, cook the bacon over medium-high heat until it is crisp and golden, about 6 minutes. Add the garlic, stir, and cook until it turns golden, about 1 minute.

Then, leaving the bacon and its fat in the pan, add the vinegar and deglaze the pan, stirring constantly and scraping up any bits on the bottom. There will be a lot of steam, so stand back.

4. Pour the hot dressing over the spinach and onions, tossing thoroughly so it coats the spinach. Season the salad to taste, toss it, and divide it among eight plates. Garnish each plate with four egg quarters, and serve immediately.

4 SERVINGS

Schaum Torte

Schaum Torte reminds me of a ballerina—it's light and sweet, beautiful and graceful. A simple meringue flavored with vanilla and filled with ice cream and strawberries, it is a trademark of Wisconsin, particularly Milwaukee, where, come Memorial Day weekend and strawberry season, everyone eats Schaum Torte loaded with fresh berries.

"J" Mayer likes to serve Schaum Torte after his spiced fish boil, and what follows is an old-time recipe that comes directly from a Midwest native, Rose Anne Tochstein. Her aunt Rose made it regularly for their family, and it is as authentic as they come. I love to make it because it is a fitting end to a rousing seafood celebration, and guests are always astonished when it comes to the table. No one could fail to feel part of something spectacular when they are presented with a plate upon which rests this sweet, crisp billow.

The meringue can be made the morning of the day you plan to serve it, or even the night before. It should be soft inside but not gummy. To check while it is baking, carefully remove a meringue from the baking sheet, turn it over, and gently tap on it. If it sounds hollow, it is cooked.

At Karl Ratzch's, the Milwaukee restaurant that is the city's most famous purveyor of Schaum Torte, they hollow out the meringue before it is baked to make a sort of nest, so it will bake thoroughly. I like the billowy look, so I trade that for a somewhat softer interior.

This is a very sweet dessert, and I don't really like to add sugar to berries, but it does help them exude juice, and juice is an essential part of a Schaum Torte. So I add a tablespoon and leave it at that.

The traditional topping is strawberries, of course, but I actually prefer raspberries. At Karl Ratzch's they fill the meringue with everything from berries to chocolate sauce. So, at the risk of offending traditionalists, use your imagination. And if it's December and nothing but Schaum Torte will do, use quality frozen, thawed berries.

MERINGUE:
1½ tablespoons vanilla extract
1 teaspoon best-quality white wine vinegar
4 large egg whites
Pinch of salt
1 cup sugar

TOPPING:
4 cups strawberries, rinsed and hulled, or the
fruit of your choice
1½ teaspoons sugar
¾ cup heavy (or whipping) cream
1 pint best-quality vanilla ice cream

1. Preheat the oven to 200°F. Line a baking sheet with parchment paper.

2. Make the meringue: Combine the vanilla and the vinegar in a small bowl, and set it aside.

3. In a large bowl, beat the egg whites with the pinch of salt until they are stiff and dry, beginning slowly and increasing the speed as the egg whites begin to break up and become foamy.

4. When the egg whites are stiff and dry, slowly pour in the sugar, beating just until it is incorporated. Then beat in the vanilla-vinegar mixture just until incorporated.

5. Using a half-cup measure, arrange 6 dollops of meringue on the prepared baking

sheet, placing them about 1 inch apart. Bake in the center of the oven until the meringues are crisp and a very pale gold color, about 1¾ hours.

6. Remove the baking sheet from the oven and carefully transfer the meringues to wire racks to cool. If you are preparing the meringues the night before, store them in a dry airtight container.

7. About 2 hours before you plan to fill the meringues, cut the strawberries into thin slices, mix them with the sugar, and set them aside at room temperature.

8. Whip the cream until it forms soft peaks. Refrigerate until ready to use.

9. Slice the top quarter from each meringue, using a sharp knife. Don't be concerned if they chip a bit, though you do want to avoid breaking them. Place each meringue on a dessert plate. Divide the ice cream among the meringues, gently fitting it inside. Spoon the berries over the ice cream, drizzling the juices around the edge of the meringue. Top the berries with the whipped cream, and set the meringue caps onto the whipped cream. Serve immediately.

6 SERVINGS

Index